Mass Media, Politics and Democracy

John Street

palgrave

First published in 2001 by
PALGRAVE
Houndmills, Basingstoke, Hampshire, RG21 6XS and
175 Fifth Avenue, New York, N.Y. 10010
Companies and representatives throughout the world

PALGRAVE is the new global academic imprint of St. Martin's Press LLC Scholarly and Reference Division and
Palgrave Publishers Ltd (formerly Macmillan Press Ltd).

ISBN 0–333–69304–3 hardback
ISBN 0–333–69305–1 paperback

This book is printed on paper suitable for recycling and made from fully managed and sustained forest sources.

A catalogue record for this book is available from the British Library.

Library of Congress Cataloging-in-Publication Data
Street, John, 1952-
    Mass Media, politics, and democracy/John Street.
        p. cm.
    Includes bibliographical references and index.
    ISBN 0-333-69304-3 – ISBN 0-333-69305-1 (pbk.)
    1. Mass media–Political aspects. 2. Democracy 1. Title.

P95.8 .S77 2001
302.23–dc21   2001021274

10   9   8   7
10   09   08   07   06   05   04

Copy-edited and typeset by Povey–Edmondson,
Tavistock and Rochdale, England

Printed in China

To Marian, Alex, Jack and Tom

Contents

Acknowledgements

My thanks to a variety of people who have, sometimes unwittingly, contributed to this book: Sigrid Baringhorst, Michael Billig, Marian Brandon, John Corner, Ian Forbes, Marion Forsyth, Steve Foster, Simon Frith, Peter Golding, Andy Grantham, John Greenaway, Brian Loader, Lee Marsden, Anne Martin, Carla Moore, Kate Nash, Keith Negus, Pippa Norris, Keith Povey, Alex Rousso, Roberta Sassatelli, Alan Scott, David Sinclair, Steve Smith, Mike Stephens, Hazel Taylor, Liesbet Van Zoonen, Frank Webster, several anonymous reviewers and many generations of students at the University of East Anglia. I owe a particular debt to my publisher Steven Kennedy who has been unfailingly helpful and encouraging, and who has showed a degree of patience that I have done little to deserve. I hope the wait has been worthwhile. My family – Marian, Alex, Jack and Tom – have also had to live with this book for a long time. It is dedicated to them.

JOHN STREET

This book draws in places on some earlier articles by the author: 'In Praise of Packaging', *Harvard International Journal of Press/Politics*, 1(2), 1996, 43–55; 'Remote Control? Politics, Technology and "Electronic Democracy" ', *European Journal of Communication*, 12(1), 1997, 27–42; 'Prime Time Politics: Popular Culture and Politicians in the UK', *The Public/Javnost*, 7(2), 2000, 75–90; and (with Alan Scott) 'From Media Politics to e-protest: The Use of Popular Culture and New Media in Parties and Social Movements', *Information, Communication and Society*, 3(2), 2000, 215–40.

Introduction

During the US presidential campaign in 2000, the *Washington Post* revealed that George W. Bush, then challenging for the Republican nomination, liked to listen to Van Morrison, while his rival John McCain preferred Frank Sinatra's *Songs for Swingin' Lovers*. Their Democratic opponent, Al Gore, chose to play 'Rock this Country' by Shania Twain at his rallies. Why were valuable column inches in major newspapers being filled with these revelations? Why did politicians think it necessary to discuss their musical tastes (and can we be sure that they thought carefully about their selection)? These men were competing for the most powerful political office in the Western world, and we were being encouraged to judge them, not by their record, but by their record collection.

Later in the presidential campaign, further newsprint was expended on which movie star was backing whose campaign, on which candidates told the best jokes, and on how they were preparing for their televised debates (as if they were athletes training for Olympic gold). On the stage at the Democratic Convention, Al Gore kissed his wife passionately. The picture of this moment appeared everywhere. Maybe the couple were overcome suddenly by the desire to express their affection for each other – right then and there, on the rostrum, in front of all the TV cameras and photographers. Just as maybe Bill Clinton, when he was running for office, felt the urge to play saxophone on the *Arsenio Hall Show*, or just as Prime Minister Tony Blair felt that it would be nice to invite Noel Gallagher of Oasis and a few other showbiz stars around to drinks at Number 10 Downing Street. Or maybe, just maybe, Gore and his advisers had decided that they needed to give the impression that the vice-president was not the dry, uptight man that he sometimes appeared; maybe Clinton and Blair hoped that their gestures would make them look 'popular' or 'in touch' or even 'cool'. This is the stuff of modern political campaigning: getting the right image, making the right (celebrity) connections, ensuring that both appear on the nightly news or the next day's front page. Such practices are not confined to the USA and UK – Nelson Mandela greeted the Spice Girls, Boris Yeltsin sang on Russian television.

Intimately connected to this style of campaigning is the increasing focus on the individual politician, and the politician not as a representative of an ideology or a party, but rather as a 'personality'. Revealing your taste in music, kissing your spouse in public, these are acts designed to tell the people something about you as a person, about who you 'really' are: that you are like us, that you can be trusted. This is why politicians are as keen to appear on chat shows as they are to appear on news shows.

This kind of behaviour has led people to talk of the 'dumbing down' of politics. Serious debate and discussion, it is argued, has been replaced by cynically crafted sound bites and photo-opportunities; politics has been trivialized and democracy has been damaged. If this is right, it is an important and worrying charge; but if things are to be changed for the better we need to do more than to bemoan the latest stunt or gimmick of this or that politician. We need to ask why it is happening. This question cannot be directed just to the politicians, with their entourage of media consultants, advertising executives and spin doctors. It needs also to be addressed to the media which print the spin and broadcast the images. After all, the media could (and in some countries they do) ignore all the razzamatazz. If we want to understand the character of political communications, obviously we need to look at the changing incentives and practices of the modern politician, but equally obviously we need to note changes in the contemporary media corporation. The two are linked.

Politicians are adapting to the medium upon which they have come to rely. They design their campaigns and their approach to fit the media. Their schedules are timed to coincide with journalists' deadlines; their public performances are intended to look good on the screen. They are in the 'popularity' business and they seek out the populism that the world of entertainment offers. Politics is moulded to fit the medium. But the medium is not just an instrument of the politicians' will. It creates the rules and sets the agendas for the coverage of politics. And as politicians embrace the world of celebrity politics, they also pay the price it demands. Flaws in their personality become flaws in their political standing, as President Bill Clinton found when his relationship with White House intern Monica Lewinsky became national news. Suddenly the president's sex life was not only a matter of legitimate media concern, it was also a matter of constitutional importance. This did not just happen because of what Clinton did – other presidents, it would seem, have behaved little better. It happened because of what now counted as news and how politics was to be covered. These were linked to the way politicians were campaigning, but they were also connected to increasing media concern with 'human interest' stories, with gossip and celebrities, rather than with traditional political news. It is as important to explain the incentives at work in the media – increasing competition for audiences and advertisers – as it is to explain those acting on politicians.

One implication of the transformation of both media and politics is that the traditional boundaries marking where politics ends and entertainment begins no longer hold. This is not just because politicians now communicate through the world of entertainment, telling us about their favourite records or their family, but because politics has, in part, to be understood as 'entertainment': its language and conventions are those drawn from the pop video, the advert and the chat show host. But what the political use of such things reminds us is that entertainment is itself 'political'. When politicians choose their items of popular culture, this is not an innocent exercise. They are deliberately selecting the images and associations of those films and stars. 'Entertainment' is often looked down on or ignored in the study of mass media. As James Curran notes (2000: 139), entertainment is not thought to involve 'rational exchange' and therefore 'not [to] belong to the political arena'. But entertainment is intimately linked to politics through the values it articulates and the passions it generates: think of the films of Oliver Stone or of the urban anger of hip-hop; think of the way every state censors and regulates access to popular culture. Understanding politics' relationship to the media cannot be confined to analysis only of news and current affairs; it has to take account of entertainment too. Game shows, situation comedies, films and music, all of these are bearers of meaning, making sense of our world and our responses to it – structuring our feelings, as Raymond Williams (1981) suggested. Media output, whether in the form of news or of soaps, acts upon our emotions and our reason.

This raises the important question of what kinds of meanings and understandings we derive from the media we consume. What are people being told about the 'world' in their papers and programmes? What story is being conveyed in reports of natural disasters and election results, in gossip columns and soap stories? One way of giving an answer is to talk in terms of the 'truthfulness' or 'fairness' of the picture. Media content is to be described and judged by the accuracy of its account, and one of the key ideas in this analysis is that of 'bias'. It is common to hear politicians and political activists complaining that their case and their claims have been misrepresented, or that there is a systematic bias against their view of the world. These complaints come from the left and the right, from Russian and American presidential candidates. They refer to a bias in favour of one point of view over another, or of one group over another; they refer to the way women or gays or ethnic groups are portrayed; they refer to the fact that some parts of the globe are ignored and others receive favoured treatment.

So one way in which political content can be analysed is in terms of its 'bias', by the way one perspective is given preference over another. But 'bias' is just one possible criterion for analysing media content. Another is not to ask about the balance or truthfulness in the report, but rather to focus on the narrative; to be less concerned with the events and details, and more with the way they are linked to tell a story. Stories create a causal chain: this happened because she did that, he responded by doing this. They identify notions of responsibility and blame; they make sense of the chaos of events 'out there', and in doing so steer the audience's response towards one view of the world rather than another.

However media texts are understood, their content matters because it is assumed that we believe what we see or read and that, in believing it, we change the way we think and act. Sometimes study of the relationship between politics and the media is left here, with the focus on media content and its effects. But this omits other, equally pressing concerns: most obviously, why the content takes one form rather than another; who or what decides the coverage and character of the media?

The relationship between politics and the media is a power one, and there are two dimensions to this: there is the power *over* the media – what gets shown or reported – and there is power *of* the media – what gets changed by the media. In respect of the first dimension, if the media does not simply mirror or distil reality, if it imposes particular biases or stories upon the world, we need to ask who is to blame for the result. One obvious response is to look to those with a direct interest in the outcome, those with most to gain: the governments, parties and politicians. This is the assumption behind the interest in the use of spin doctors, sound bites and photo-opportunities, all intended to produce the images and ideas that keep these politicians in power. It is the spin doctor whose job it is to pre-empt unfavourable bias, or to introduce a favourable one, enabling the politically powerful to manipulate and distort the democratic process. Such claims deserve careful analysis because they go to the heart of media's relationship with politics, but the focus on political devices – on spin doctors and sound bites – can obscure the other interests involved in this relationship. These include the journalists who produce the copy and the programmes, and the corporations who employ them. In understanding media content, we need to understand the politics of journalistic practice: why *this* story, why *that* image? And perhaps more importantly, we need to understand corporate politics, and the interests and influences that circulate within the global multimedia empires. To what extent is the 'news' and its coverage a product of the ambitions and designs of the companies that produce the papers and programmes? Figures like Rupert Murdoch and organizations like his News Corporation, with its newspapers, television stations, film studios and book publishers, are sometimes portrayed as using their media outlets to advance their own political cause; this is why the coverage takes the form it does. No attempt to make sense of the relationship between politics and mass media can afford to ignore such possibilities.

But equally, if not more, important is what impact the media have on the world they report. This is the second dimension of media power: the media's power over people and events. Politicians' desperation to appear on television (and to create the right image) is matched by the capacity of the media to make or break political careers. It sometimes seems that 'politics' *is* what appears on TV or in the press, that appearance is everything in political life: those who control the image control the reality; we no longer have real politics, we have virtual politics. This idea is taken to its logical extreme by the Hollywood film *The Matrix*. 'Perception: the everyday world is real,' reads the blurb on the posters for the movie, 'Reality: The world is a hoax, an elaborate deception spun by all-powerful machines of artificial intelligence that control us.' The film plays with the proposition that our 'reality' is the product of someone else's will, exercised through their power over the means of communication. *The Matrix* may occupy the dystopian end of views about political manipulation, but it taps into a conventional wisdom about the power of the media and those who wield it; this is why the media matter: they determine who wins and loses, what we think and say. But do they?

Claims about media power need to be examined carefully. Take one example. A senior official in the United States' Securities and Exchange Commission was alleged to have beaten his wife. This accusation emerged in his divorce proceedings in the early 1980s. Nearly two years after the divorce hearing, the *Wall Street Journal* reported the accusation as front page news. The government official was forced to resign. At first glance this seemed to be another case of a public figure being removed from office by the power of the press. The *Wall Street Journal* did, after all, agonize long and hard over whether to publish the revelation (Thompson, 1998). But the story could be told differently: the man lost his job because of the way he treated his wife, not because of what the papers said. In other words, it was not the editorial decision to publish the item that was important; it was the husband's behaviour that mattered (and the media were simply conveying an established fact). The appearance of media power can be deceptive. Nonetheless, there are still pressing reasons for looking closely at the media's capacity to order the world.

Power is rarely exercised directly through the use of brute force. Typically, people obey rules and regulations, not because the authorities stand over them waving a baton or pointing a gun (though, of course, this does happen), but because they already recognise the right of those authorities to direct their actions. Insofar as coercion is involved, the threat of it is usually enough, and threats depend on words and impressions as well as actual deeds. Power relies on our 'common sense' view of how the world is and how it works; threats and authority depend on how we *perceive* those who make those threats or claim that authority. These thoughts, the unexamined assumptions of our routines, help us to know our place and our identity. And they are daily disseminated through news and current affairs, situation comedies and blockbuster movies.

It is no surprise that, when political coups take place, the rebels head first for the radio and television stations in order to secure their victory. It is also obvious that one device for subsequently maintaining control is to manage strictly the flow of information. Secrecy is a key weapon of the powerful; they hold the information that is denied to the rest. When NATO bombers began attacking his country in 1998, President Milosevic of Yugoslavia responded by removing the head of Belgrade's independent radio station B92. And when Milosevic was deposed in 2000, demonstrators set fire to the state television station and attacked its director. The writer Gabriel Garcia Marquez reports how, in Venezuela, a shift in political power turned on the skill with which rival leaders made use of the country's television studios (*The Guardian*, 2 September 2000).

Just as media can serve authority, they can also subvert it. Challenges to 'common sense' can find expression in the same media that reinforce it. The power of the media is not just measured by the way citizens may be controlled. That power can be used to unsettle and even unseat the powerful. The media have humbled many politicians, whether American presidents (Richard Nixon) or British cabinet ministers (David Mellor). Those politicians suffered because their *reputation*, as John Thompson (1997) points out, is their key political resource, and it is one that is, to a large extent, supplied by and through mass media. In destroying political careers (or at least, in being the catalyst for their destruction), the mass media often style themselves as the 'voice of the people'. It is this role that entitles them to interrogate public figures and to scrutinize the actions of public institutions. Indeed, there are commentators, such as Andrew Marr (1996), now the BBC's political editor, who claim that the media are more effective at ensuring democratic accountability than the arrangements formally designated for this purpose.

In Western liberal democracies, the mass media have claimed the right to represent the people and to uphold democracy, and the consumers of newspapers and television have come to treat these media sources as the basis on which to think and act in the world. We need only to recall public behaviour during scares about fuel shortages or about genetically modified food to see how media seem to influence thought and action. But things are, of course, not this simple. Not every piece of news has the same effect. Not only do people discriminate between the origin of news and the credibility they attach to it, but in different parts of the world television and newspapers perform quite different functions to those fulfilled in the West. The media are not automatically and inevitably treated as sources of information which is blindly acted upon. Endless reports have appeared on the dangers of smoking, but people continue to buy cigarettes. The argument still rages about the consequences of media portrayals of violence or pornography. One side contends that media content actually alters the levels of violence in society or that it changes for the worse the relations between men and women. Others argue that such claims are entirely unproven, and that media content is, at most, a reflection (rather than a cause) of social attitudes.

Similar arguments emerge in discussion of political behaviour. There is the familiar debate between those who see biased media coverage as winning elections for one side or the other. There are others who worry about the divide between those who are information rich and those who are information poor, because the first has the power which the other lacks. For some, the cause of this social chasm is television itself (Putnam, 1995). Others note the uneven distribution of people's capacity to control, or be controlled by, the media they consume. Interpreting media is a skill, a skill that is dependent upon social and educational background (Bourdieu, 1986).

Whatever side you take, the argument about mass media's power – whether as the power over media or the power of media – cannot be resolved easily. This is hardly surprising. As Nicholas Garnham (2000: 5) has recently pointed out, studying media means engaging with issues that have troubled social scientists for a very long while: 'it can be argued that the central question underlying all debates about the media and how we study them concerns the way in which and the extent to which humans learn and thus how through time identities are formed and actions motivated'. When and where do people act freely, as the authors of their own fate; when and where do they act at the behest of others? These persistent questions pervade the study of the media–politics relationship, and derive from the desire to know how the world is organized. But accompanying them is another set of related questions. As well as wanting to know how things *are*, we are also concerned about how they *ought* to be. What sort of control over media is acceptable or necessary in a democracy?

This question tends to divide people along political lines, between those, on the one hand, who advocate public regulation, either provided by the terms of media ownership or by the rules which apply to journalists and editors, and those, on the other, who advocate complete deregulation, leaving the market to arbitrate. This crude divide is, of course, more complex than it appears here. It is more complex because there are many competing notions of 'democracy' in circulation; it is also made more complex by the rapidly changing context in which the argument takes place. The emergence of the internet and digital television transforms the means of communication as well as the balance of power. Any useful discussion of the place of mass media in a democracy must address both the different conceptions of democracy and the emerging new technologies. Only then can we make sense of the debate about the political significance of the internet; only then can we compare the attempts of those, like China and Singapore, who aim to control net use, with those on the other side who see the 'information superhighway' as the last truly free political forum, and who use it to advance an alternative democratic order. This debate is about how modern media should function in a democracy. It is an argument which extends from questions about what is meant by a 'free press' to ones about whether the internet can create an electronic democracy that recalls the glories of Ancient Greece. It is assumed that mass media contribute in some way to the political life of citizens, furnishing them with a means of representing themselves and their interests, and allowing them the space – a 'public sphere' – within which they can reflect on the conditions of their lives and how these might be changed for the better (Habermas, 1989;1996). But can such an ideal coexist with commercialized media directed at consumers rather than citizens?

It should be evident by now that there are a large number of issues and areas that come together in the relationship between politics and mass media. This book is an attempt to bring some order to them and yet still reflect their complexity and interconnectedness. Making sense of the relationship between mass media and politics requires us to think about its ever-changing character and its cultural peculiarities. To take one obvious example: what is meant by 'political coverage' has varied over time and between places, as we can see by the way in which politicians have been treated, from the vicious satire directed at the politicians of the eighteenth century, to the deference of the mid-twentieth, to the cynicism of the twenty-first century; from the protection their privacy receives in France to the intrusive glare that they encounter in the USA and UK. Seeing the relationship historically and comparatively allows us to identify the forces which shape its current form, to realize that it has not always been like this and that it is unlikely to remain this way.

Equally, the relationship between politics and mass media has to be understood in terms of the institutions which manage the flow of power: the systems of regulation and patterns of control that organize the media. The history of the relationship between politics and mass media has to be understood as the product of particular institutional forms which shape the media. Comparison of national broadcasting systems reveals considerable variations in the role assigned to the state and the type of regulation to which media organizations are subject, whether measured in terms of control of content, opportunities for access to the airwaves or the strictures of libel legislation.

This book is concerned to reflect the constantly changing nature of the relationship between politics and mass media, and to draw attention to the institutional interests that shape the change. The discussion is divided into three parts. The first considers the ways in which politics is represented in the mass media and the debate about how this content affects thought and action. Part Two deals with the institutional interests – whether those of the state or the commercial sector – which organize mass media and impose their politics upon them. If the first two parts are about how things are, then the final part is primarily about how they might be. This is partly an opportunity to reflect upon the future form of mass media's relationship to politics, but it is also a chance to debate the normative question of how that relationship ought to be organized.

Within these parts, individual chapters deal with specific issues and arguments. Chapter 1 begins the discussion of media content by looking at the idea of 'political bias', in particular at what sorts of biases are said to be contained in the press and television, and at how such bias is to be detected. Moving on from discussion of 'bias', the chapter introduces an alternative approach which stresses the 'framing' of politics, the way political stories are told. This provides the basis for the next chapter, which analyses the ways in which 'politics' is represented in mass media: the political institutions and actors that are included and excluded, the motives that are recognized and those that are marginalized. Chapter 3 continues the concern with the representation of politics, but moves the attention away from news and current affairs to look at the politics of entertainment, including satire, movies, soap operas and sport. Part One ends with a critical review of the debate about media influence, and the ways in which it is claimed that media content shapes thought and action.

Part Two begins with a chapter on the ways in which the state, through its legislative power and other resources, is able to shape the content of mass media. Chapter 6 turns attention to the equivalent power of the new multimedia conglomerates; Rupert Murdoch's empire is used as a case study of claims about corporate control of media. One of the arguments against placing too much emphasis on the power of people like Murdoch is that journalists and editors enjoy some relative autonomy, and that any explanation of the particular character of media content must acknowledge their role. Looking in particular at the fate of investigative journalism, Chapter 7 examines the power of journalists by comparing different models of their behaviour, from those that see journalism as an independent activity to those that see it as a controlled process. Chapter 8, which concludes Part Two, considers the impact of globalization on the state, media corporations and journalism, to see how the emerging global political economy affects the ways in which media and politics are related.

In contemplating this emerging world, the final part of the book begins with a detailed discussion of the debate about the 'packaging of politics'. It is this that is seen to symbolize the 'dumbing down' of political communication. In analysing the argument, Chapter 9 looks at the possible reasons for 'packaging' – the use of sound bites, photo-opportunities and celebrities – having become prevalent. It argues that the fears of those who talk of 'dumbing down' are exaggerated. In a similar vein, Chapter 10 considers the thought that the internet is providing the basis for a new 'electronic democracy'. It contends that such predictions or ambitions are misguided, and that political uses of new media are not inscribed in the technology itself, but in the interplay with the political order into which they are introduced. The last two chapters tackle the themes that lie at the core of the book, and are constant features throughout it: power and democracy. Chapter 11 looks at competing claims, deriving from different ideological standpoints, about the power of mass media, and their implications for some of the key concerns in this book: political bias, media influence and public regulation. Chapter 12 reviews the arguments for changing the organization of media in the name of democracy, and at the implications of these for the practice of journalism, public access and media ownership.

In summary, *Mass Media, Politics and Democracy* connects the many issues and arguments that are raised by any attempt to make sense of the relationship between politics and mass media. The book links the different aspects of that relationship: how the political use and content of mass media is shaped by the commercial and political incentives that drive the state and media conglomerates, how claims of media power are linked to media effects, how the 'packaging of politics' and new media technologies are linked to the notion of democracy and how the use of popular culture is implicated in the 'personalization' of politics and media corporate interests. Without understanding such things, we cannot hope to understand either the nature of modern media or modern politics.

PART ONE

REPRESENTING POLITICS

1
Political Bias

In March 2000, South Africa's human rights commissioners demanded that 30 journalists appear before them. These journalists were to face charges of racial bias in their papers. The accusations against them were contained in a 200-page report which identified what it saw as 'media racism' in the use of language and imagery. The report became the focus of an intense political debate between those who derided its methods and conclusions and those who saw its accusations as accurately describing media coverage of South Africa. If anyone needed proof that it matters how the media cover politics, then here it was. Failure to appear before the commissioners could incur a six month prison sentence. The report, and the reaction to it, illustrate the importance that attaches to the content of mass media, but they also raise the question of how this content is to be analysed and judged. In South Africa, the key term was 'bias': the extent to which media content was systematically favourable to a particular set of interests. But can such bias be proved and does it provide the best way to make sense of the politics of media content? This chapter is devoted to answering these questions.

Political bias seems sometimes to be the only important issue in the relationship between politics and mass media. It is the one topic which is guaranteed to ignite the anger of politicians and their media advisers. They all expend considerable effort in firing off complaints about their treatment by interviewers and journalists. During the Russian presidential elections in 1996, Boris Yeltsin's rivals complained, with some justice, that they were being denied the favourable coverage that he received (Mickiewicz and Richter, 1996: 120–1). In Britain, the Conservative Party became convinced that the BBC's morning radio show *Today* dealt more harshly with Tory politicians than with their Labour opponents (a feeling that was reciprocated by Labour politicians who felt that they were treated unfairly compared to their Conservative opponents). In the

USA, the same sense of injustice is echoed in arguments between liberals and the right, both of whom feel under- or mis-represented. The Australian Broadcasting Corporation has had its funding cut by successive governments – of different political persuasions – each of whom regarded the corporation's coverage as 'biased' (Schultz, 1998: 5–6). The political attention given to bias has been reflected in academic discussion of the media, most famously perhaps in the work of Edward Herman and Noam Chomsky in America and the Glasgow University Media Group (GUMG) in the UK, two examples to which we return later.

Why does 'bias' occupy so much space? The answer lies in the way in which bias is tied to fundamental assumptions about 'power' and 'democracy'. It is assumed that, in a democracy, no one group or set of interests is systematically preferred over another and that the information available to citizens is accurate and impartial. Under these conditions, the principles of political equality and accountability can operate. What makes 'bias' a problem is the thought that the media can, if they distort the representation of the world, skew and thwart the democratic process. If the media systematically promote some interests and misinform the citizenry, the democratic process itself will not operate effectively. In identifying biases, critics of the media are voicing a fear that misrepresentation or partiality has important consequences for the way people regard themselves, how they are regarded by others, the outcome of political processes and the practice of democracy.

Implicit in these complaints is a view about the power and effect of the media. Put another way, 'bias' will seem much less of a problem (a) if you adopt a different account of democracy and (b) if you do not think that representations of the world actually shape thoughts and practices within it. These are not arguments to be considered here; they are dealt with later. In this context, they serve merely to remind us that the extent to which 'bias' matters is a consequence of a set of underlying political assumptions. This chapter concentrates first on what 'bias' means, what sort of distortions it refers to; secondly, it looks at the way bias can be detected, at how it can be shown to exist.

The claim that the media are biased begins with the idea that the practices of journalists and editors result in articles and programmes which favour one view of the world over another, providing sustenance for one set of interests while undermining an alternative. These interests may be those of the particular corporations for which they work or they may be those of a particular ideology. The notion of bias is not confined to the battle between political parties. It applies equally to competing value systems, to the representation of women and men, to the portrayal of ethnic groups and to the priority accorded to whole countries and their peoples. 'Bias' refers to any systematic favouring of one position, but it has further implications. It entails a critical judgement. To call someone or some account 'biased' is to challenge its validity and to see it as failing to be 'truthful', 'impartial', 'objective' or 'balanced', terms which appeal to slightly different ideals. These implicit contrasts hint at the complexity of 'bias', and hence the need to look more closely at what it means.

Defining Bias

If being biased is to prefer one side in a dispute, or to favour one interpretation or to sympathize with one cause, it does not follow automatically that this is wrong. There are many occasions when we take up such a position in our relations with our friends and family, and in political arguments in informal settings. In these situations, bias is viewed as natural or reasonable. It is only on particular occasions in particular roles that such behaviour is liable to be criticized. Teachers, for example, are not expected to award high marks for essays just because they echo their own political prejudices. It is because journalists and broadcasters present themselves as unbiased, or are required to appear to be unbiased, that bias becomes a matter of political concern. A journalist can argue for any political cause in private, but if she were to do the same in reporting a story, this would be regarded as a dereliction of her responsibility as a reporter. This view is itself the product of a larger set of assumptions about the character of 'news'. Sometimes these assumptions form part of the rules governing broadcasting (that is, regulations laid down by such bodies as the Federal Communications Commission (FCC) in the USA or the Independent Television Commission (ITC) in the UK); sometimes they are part of the law (libel legislation, for example); and sometimes they are a part of professional codes.

Whatever their source, these arrangements establish mechanisms by which 'journalism' is defined. Contained within this definition is the distinction between 'opinion' and 'fact', a distinction that is formally reproduced in the layout of papers or the format of programmes. Opinion is seen as the expression of a personal view; it is biased and its bias is openly acknowledged. News reporting aspires to objectivity, to stating the facts; or it aspires to balance and impartiality in recording competing interpretations of an event, without favouring one view over another. These practices are enshrined in codes of conduct or in training manuals.

The fact that such rules exist does not mean, of course, that they are always followed, or indeed that they *can* be followed. The very terms themselves hide their contradictions and complications. It might be assumed that 'neutrality' is a simple enough idea. To be neutral you must just report the facts: 'The election was won by Bill Clinton'; 'Gianni Versace was shot at point-blank range as he unlocked his front door'; 'The IRA announced a cease-fire.' As Ken Newton (1989: 131) notes, the ideal of neutrality can be stated easily: 'A neutral media will present a full and fair account of the facts.' It is, though, impossible to get even close to this notion of neutrality. Newton offers two reasons for this. Firstly, the practicalities of the media's daily routines mitigate against giving a 'full' account. The media are constituted as businesses who have to serve a market (audiences, advertisers), and this means tailoring the reporting to the needs of that market. Long, factual accounts may drive viewers or readers away; besides, there are deadlines to meet.

Beyond the practical and commercial pressures that compromise a complete, factual account, there is a second set of problems. These might be classed as the theoretical problems of neutrality. The first of them is that reporters cannot record *all* the facts. Any event contains an infinity of facts. The name of every individual who voted for Clinton is a 'fact' involved in his election, as is the name of all those who did not vote for him. Facts have to be selected on some criterion of relevance: is it important for people to know what Versace was wearing when he was shot, or that he was gay, or how much his house cost? Secondly, the selected facts have to become part of a 'story' with a narrative that links them together. These processes of selection and interpretation obviously cause reporting to deviate from the ideal of recounting the facts.

The theoretical ambiguities identified by Newton are also part of journalistic practice. As Holli Semetko (1996) notes, 'objectivity' and 'balance' actually demand contradictory practices. To be objective is to let *news values* determine the coverage an event receives. News values are the working assumptions of journalists about the extent to which an event matters and what is significant about it. To be balanced, by contrast, is to give *equal coverage* to all the parties to an event, irrespective of the news value of their contributions. A reporter who is being objective may judge that it is appropriate to ignore certain views because they are marginal or inconsequential to the main story. A reporter who wants to provide balance may feel compelled to represent the full range of views. This sort of tension (and there are many others involved in the reporting of news) is resolved or managed through the routine practices of journalists, the codes and rules which evolve to make journalism possible. Together they form what Semetko labels 'journalistic culture'. This is not a fixed entity, but varies with time and place. The way it operates can be illustrated by the way in which elections are covered on television. Essentially there are two dominant cultures. The first places the emphasis on balance, and tries to allocate equal time, as measured by a stopwatch, to all the leading contenders. The second places the emphasis on news values. Election coverage is determined by journalists' judgements about the importance of what each party is saying or doing. In the USA and in Germany, the news value approach dominates. For British broadcasters the tendency is to use the stopwatch to measure balance. It was noticeable, though, that when one news broadcaster (ITN) ceased using the stopwatch, their coverage became more 'evaluative', while their rival (the BBC), using the stopwatch, produced 'descriptive' reports (Semetko, 1996). Nonetheless, whatever strategy was adopted, these news organizations shared the same purpose: to establish a journalistic code of conduct that was defensible as 'unbiased' in the face of conflicting demands.

But if 'neutrality' cannot exist, if balance and objectivity are incompatible, the notion of bias needs to be qualified. It cannot simply be treated as any 'deviation from reality'. It is not that bias is a meaningless term, it is just that a distinction has to be made between what is acceptable or reasonable and what is unacceptable and unreasonable. How these boundaries are drawn varies with forms and systems of communication. In Britain, terrestrial broadcasting is constrained to be balanced in ways that newspapers are not. In Italy, broadcasting institutions are explicitly and deliberately assigned to different political interests. What bias is and what significance attaches to it will, therefore, vary. There is always a distinction drawn between where it is acceptable and where it should be condemned. This is not an argument for discounting bias as a viable concept in analysing media content. The fact that it is definitionally complex and institutionally mediated does not reduce it to an empty category. Quite the contrary, its continued usage in discussion of media, and its place in the idea of a legitimate political order, underline the need to give it attention.

Types of Bias

Bias appears in a variety of (dis)guises. Denis McQuail (1992) identifies four types of bias. They are to be distinguished by their place in a two-dimensional matrix. The first dimension concerns the 'explicitness' of the bias – whether it is open or hidden; the second dimension concerns the intention behind it – whether the bias is a result of some deliberate policy or a product of some ingrained, unconscious process. These two dimensions yield a useful set of categories for thinking about bias.

Partisan Bias

Here a cause is explicitly and deliberately promoted. Examples of this are editorial comments which recommend support for one political party or take sides in a policy controversy. This can take the form of explicit recommendations to vote for one party or another, or it can be identified in the blatant endorsement of a cause. There is little difficulty in detecting such examples.

Propaganda Bias

This is involved where a story is reported with the deliberate intention of making the case for a particular party or policy or point of view, without explicitly stating this. So stories about high-living students or social security fraud or asylum seekers are reported as news, but in such a way as to make a particular point (about welfare 'scrounging' or immigrants 'swamping' a country). The apparent purpose of the story is to report the details, but disguised within it are thinly veiled attacks upon students or the unemployed or refugees. Readers are encouraged to generalize from the particular case and to see students or others in an unfavourable light. Racial imagery in the reporting of crime can express propagandist value judgements about ethnic groups (Gilliam *et al.*, 1996). Propaganda can also be detected in the way that national media report the activities of other countries. There is a tendency to publish stories about corruption, scandal or disasters in other countries, thereby reinforcing negative perceptions of life in these 'foreign' places (Wallis and Baran, 1990).

Unwitting Bias

Newspapers have a finite number of pages; news broadcasts have limited time slots in the schedule. Hard choices have to be made about what to include and what to exclude. These decisions are about the 'importance' to be given to a story, and they are reflected in the item's place in the running order or its place in the paper or on the page. Inevitably these decisions involve a judgement about the issue and/or the people involved. The convention of journalism is that what appears on the front page is the most important of the day's news. The same implication is carried by the ordering of broadcast news: the main stories are dealt with first and at length. These judgements constitute a form of bias: X matters more than Y. But though this bias is explicit (the decision to give a particular story one column inch on page 4), it is not conscious or deliberate. It is the product of ingrained routines about what is 'news' and a story's 'newsworthiness'; it is a product of journalistic culture. Detection of this type of bias involves looking at the standard operating procedures of papers and newsrooms, to see how these practices routinely create hierarchies of values.

Ideological Bias

In McQuail's final category, the bias is hidden and unintended, and it can be detected only in a close reading of the text, where the hidden assumptions and value judgements can be revealed. The attention is upon the 'norms' against which news is created.

Incorporated in all reporting is some version of the 'norm': of what 'usually happens' or how people 'usually behave'. These are based on the assumption that something is 'newsworthy'; that is, it is both out of the ordinary and also part of a general framework of expectations (that is, it is a 'typical' news story). These assumptions are grounded in ideologies which seek to explain the way the world works, and these are themselves 'biased'. Think of the way in which women are represented in papers (Herzog, 1998; Norris, 1997a). Firstly, their activities receive less coverage than do men's; secondly, descriptions of them refer to their appearance or to the men in their lives (they are not accorded an independent existence). Such representations articulate a particular ideological view about men and women.

To identify different types of bias is a necessary task, but it does no more than to establish what biases might exist. To give substance to McQuail's categories poses two obvious methodological problems. The first relates to the way we 'read' bias, how we discover meanings that are 'submerged' within the text, as distinct from those that seem to sit on the surface. This is linked to the second methodological issue: how do we know what is intended? Think of the difficulty of discerning whether something is said 'ironically': when the rap star Eminem gives vent to aggressive attitudes to women, is he parodying male attitudes or does he really mean it? It is clear that it is hard to 'prove' the existence of any particular bias, whether explicit or implicit, whether offered ironically or not. What one observer sees as unwitting bias another may see as propaganda and another as fair reporting. The problem stems, in part, from the difficulty in establishing agreed definitions of bias and agreed methods for identifying it. It is certainly not sufficient to rely on public perception, because readers and viewers make unreliable witnesses. Readers of newspapers tend to see them as reflecting their own prejudices, while they see television as being biased against their own views. Thus the same programme can be seen by left wingers as having a right-wing bias, and by right wingers as having a left-wing bias (Miller, 1991). Then again, there are people who appear to be oblivious to (or ignorant of) the bias in their papers. Such evidence tells us little about the fact of bias; it merely serves to illustrate that detecting it is less simple than might at first appear.

Looking for bias is not just a matter of 'reading' the news or transcripts; it is about establishing a method which, on the one hand, is able to capture what is being said implicitly as well as explicitly and on the other, to provide a technique that can be used by others (or can persuade others of particular findings). To illustrate the problem of discovering bias, consider the case of television coverage of the British general election of 1987. Under the laws and regulations governing coverage, television felt obliged to give *exactly equal time* to the three main parties (Labour, Conservative and Alliance). This commitment was honoured, and would seem to suggest a complete absence of partiality or bias; it would seem to meet, at the very least, the conditions of what Semetko (1996) defines as 'balance'. But, as William Miller and his colleagues reveal (Miller, 1991; Miller *et al.*, 1989), within this equal treatment there was considerable evidence of bias, if you look at the *character* of the coverage rather than the quantity alone. The researchers measured coverage in terms of time spent on camera and in terms of the message being conveyed. Close examination revealed that, although all three contending parties received equal screen time, the way that time was organized gave the impression that the contest was only between the Labour and Conservative parties. The Alliance was marginalized as an 'also ran'. This impression was created by covering the Alliance on their own, but covering the other two parties locked in controversy.

In order to demonstrate the existence of bias, Miller's team combined quantitative and qualitative research methods. Quantitative work employs a version of content analysis. This aims to provide a scientific method for recording the use of words and pictures. It focuses upon the frequency with which certain words are used to describe an event. It examines the space (in time or column length) devoted to different news items. It allows researchers to observe the frequency with which certain words are used and the way words are combined. Robert Entman (1996), for instance, shows how in the coverage of the environmental policy debate – to deregulate or not – the word 'extreme' is applied much more frequently to one side than the other, as are aggressive words like 'backlash', 'attack' and 'assault'. Qualitative work, by contrast, tends to draw on semiotics and the pioneering work of Roland Barthes (1967) and others. This approach is concerned with the way meaning is contained in what is not said as well as what is, in images and impressions as much as in words. John Thompson (1988) provides a neat summary of the different linguistic techniques that can be employed to favour one group, view or interest over others. He identifies four ways by which a bias can be communicated. A set of arrangements can be made *legitimate* by attributing popular support or expert authority to them. Secondly, the text may serve to *dissimulate*, to cover up the particular social relations, for example by attributing blame to identifiable individuals, rather than to underlying processes and systems. A third device is *fragmentation*: the media represent groups as opposed to each other, when in fact they may have a common cause (the treatment of refugees as an 'alien threat', for example). And finally, Thompson talks of *reification*, by which he means the ways in which the media present the world as naturally ordered and fixed, thereby marginalizing the claims of those who want to change that world. Together these devices, and many more besides, are seen as presenting a 'commonsense' view of the world which actually serves to preserve particular interests. Thompson's focus is on the way images and words interact to suggest a meaning that goes beyond any literal reading of the text. This approach builds upon the idea that words do not simply describe an object or event but evoke an entire edifice of ideas and impressions.

Each of these techniques has strengths and weaknesses. The richness of interpretation provided by semiotics is limited by the problem of comparability or replicability. Why should one reading of a text be preferred to another? Content analysis does at least allow for systematic comparison, but at the cost of reducing meaning to words. Most attempts to identify bias use both techniques (for example, Anderson and Weymouth, 1999; Entman, 1996). It is important, therefore, in judging these attempts, to be aware, first, that bias cannot simply be 'seen', and second, that in detecting it, there is unlikely to be universal agreement about the 'right' interpretation.

Given the many attempts to deal with these problems of proving bias (although fewer than the attention to the subject would suggest), we cannot do justice to them all here. Instead, we shall concentrate on two, one concerned with bias on television and the other with bias in the press. Each has assumed the status of a 'classic' or 'pathbreaking' study.

The Bad News Studies

In a series of very detailed, and much debated, studies of television reporting of news and current affairs, the Glasgow University Media Group has claimed to identify systematic ideological bias. The GUMG's central claim is that 'news is not a neutral and natural phenomenon; it is rather the manufactured production of ideology' (GUMG, 1980: xvii–xviii). Each study has taken a different topic – trade unions (*Bad News*), the economy (*More Bad News*) and war (*War and Peace News*) – and examined the way in which TV news has covered them, and in each case they have revealed systematic distortion and the propagation of an ideological slant. The Glasgow researchers argue that, although the news may report facts, it nonetheless produces a skewed account. This is because of the particular way that the facts are presented: ' "facts" are situated in dominant story themes . . . such themes build upon basic frames of reference – basic assumptions about society viewed in particular ways – which often hinder the full and proper coverage of the events in question' (GUMG, 1976: 9).

To validate its claims, the GUMG deploys a wide variety of research tools, borrowing from both semiotics and content analysis. Not only do the researchers observe practice in a working newsroom, they also examine in minute detail the subsequent reports. They analyse the words, the camera angles, the presentation format, and the range and setting of the people interviewed. As one of the Group's founding figures explained (Eldridge, 1993: 5), their research was concerned to reveal 'the verbal and visual grammar . . . the use of graphics and other symbolic expressions . . . the use of headlines . . . who is interviewed . . . in short, the way information is organized and the implicit and explicit explanations that are put before us'. The media's presentation of the news is then set against alternative explanations of the situation being portrayed.

Take one example of this technique: *More Bad News* (1980). In this book, the GUMG focuses upon the reporting of the economy and upon the explanations given for its performance. It is hard to exaggerate the importance of the economy to politics, especially given recent studies of electoral behaviour (Sanders, 1996) that have demonstrated an intimate connection between perceptions of the economy (and of the relative economic competence of political parties) and the outcome of national elections. Mass media can play an important role in forming those impressions.

More Bad News begins by recording the different possible academic and political interpretations of the British economy in the 1970s. It contrasts these with the single explanation that tends to dominate news coverage. The impression created by television, argues the GUMG, was that wage-led inflation was the root of the problem: 'Often the argument over whether inflation was in fact caused in this way was pre-empted by simply prefixing references to wage settlements with the word "inflationary"' (GUMG, 1980: 15). Attempts to promote an alternative explanation would be thwarted by the way interviewers set their questions or by the selection of those whom they interviewed (ibid.: 17–18). These conclusions were reached on the basis of examination of the words used in reports and in detailed analysis of the conduct of interviews. The GUMG sought to expose the assumptions that underlay the journalism.

Further evidence was acquired through examination of journalists' reliance upon official statistics and the presentation of those figures. Both served to reinforce a particular view of economic reality, a view which was challenged by other commentators and different statistical data (ibid.: 29–31). The GUMG (ibid.: 48–9) argued that the evidence was selected to fit the underlying ideology: 'An essential feature of the television news coverage is that the figures were used invariably to suggest that wages were ahead of prices . . . the predominant feature of this news coverage therefore was the manner in which official figures from which a number of conclusions could have been drawn were used consistently to emphasise only one interpretation.' In the same way, a study of television coverage of the 1984/5 coal dispute strike revealed journalists' reliance on statistics produced by the Coal Board (Philo, 1990). These figures recorded the 'drift back to work', and were designed to give the impression that the strike was crumbling. Other figures (about the numbers staying home or about gestures of support for the strike) were absent or marginalized.

In *More Bad News*, the GUMG identified four competing political interpretations of the economy, and then examined the attention received by each. Attention was measured by the number of references made to the various interpretations and to the manner of the reference: whether it was positive or negative (GUMG, 1980: 57). Frequency measures of this kind were also used to analyse the words deployed to describe certain events. The team found that, overwhelmingly, industrial action was identified by the word 'strike', thereby shifting responsibility to the unions and appealing to the pejorative judgements associated with the word: the 'disruptions' caused by strike action, for example (ibid.: 180). These tests of the frequency and manner of references revealed a general disposition (albeit an unconscious one) to favour one interpretation of economic performance and to marginalize the other. The preferred explanation – wage-led inflation – had clear implications for the attribution of blame to trade unions. The way in which wage negotiations were reported also emphasized this allocation of blame: trade unions were presented as making 'demands', while the behaviour of employers was largely overlooked or presented as reasonable and legitimate (ibid.: 91).

In summary, the GUMG described its project as an attempt 'to reveal and analyse the linguistic designs' (ibid.: 121) which constitute news bulletins, and to show that these designs favoured particular interests and the world views that legitimated them: 'All descriptions close off or foreclose on sets of alternatives' (ibid.: 123). In its detailed examination of the way in which industrial news is reported, the GUMG argued that the stories were 'heavily weighted against the trade union and labour point of view' (ibid.: 129). Similar conclusions were reached in the GUMG's parallel concern with the images used in news coverage. The Glasgow group painstakingly analysed the images on the screen, and the ways in which words and pictures were juxtaposed (ibid.: 193ff). Here too an ideological bias was found in that people's status, and the respect in which their position was held, was reflected in the way they were filmed (ibid.: 401). The authority and credibility of figures could even be conveyed in the choice of still photographs: one of the left-winger Tony Benn looking up to the camera was followed by another of Winston Churchill looking down (ibid.: 317–19).

Through their analysis of all aspects of news coverage, and armed with the assumptions the researchers make about the way meaning is conveyed, the GUMG concluded that television reporting of the economy contained a systematic bias. This bias was primarily, in McQuail's terms, ideological and unwitting; that is, it was not explicit, and it was deliberate only in the sense that it was informed by routinized journalistic practices. The GUMG (ibid.: 138) argued that biased news reporting was the result of habit and training, rather than conscious deliberation, a view that was reinforced through the observation of daily newsroom practices.

The GUMG studies represent one approach to the problem of demonstrating the existence of political bias in the media. Using a variety of research tools they produce evidence of distortion, misrepresentation and omission which, when taken together, constitute a systematic promotion of one reading of the world over another. What the GUMG found in television, others have claimed to find in the press.

Manufacturing Consent

Like the GUMG, Herman and Chomsky (1988) conclude that the media have a systematically biased world view. But in their case this conclusion is reached through an analysis of the content of the US press. Their hypothesis is that the US press acts to sustain the US government's foreign policy interests, themselves the product of a particular ideology and particular material interests. In one sense, Herman and Chomsky go further than the GUMG. They do not seek simply to reveal bias, they also want to explain it. Their explanation lies in the thought that the US media act as propagandists for dominant corporate interests in the USA. They write (ibid.: xii): 'Most biased choices in the media arise from the preselection of right-thinking people, internalized preconceptions, and the adaptation of personnel to the constraints of ownership, organization, market, and political power.' Herman and Chomsky also differ from the GUMG to the extent that they compare the output from a variety of media outlets, where the GUMG concentrates, at least in its formative work, on just one.

Herman and Chomsky examine the way in which the US media treated the same kind of event as it occurred in different contexts. One of their case studies involved the murder of religious leaders and other religious workers. They took the instance of Cardinal Popieluszko, who was murdered in Poland in 1984, and of religious workers killed in South America at various times. Two features of their analysis of these stories are worth noting here. The first is that the killing of the Polish priest received far more coverage – as measured by column inches and by position in the paper – than did the other murders. Secondly, in the reporting of these events, the

US press dwelt upon the perpetrators in Poland, tracing responsibility back to the communist regime, whereas in the second case very little is said about the murderers. Herman and Chomsky explain this disparity in terms of the USA's propaganda interests. Attributing blame to the authorities in Poland contributed to the USA's struggle with communism; close investigation of the Latin American case was likely to have revealed CIA involvement. Herman and Chomsky (ibid.: xv) argue: 'A constant focus on victims of communism helps convince the public of enemy evil and sets the stage for intervention, subversion . . . an endless arms race . . . The public does not notice the silence on victims in client states, which is as important in supporting state policy as the concentrated focus on enemy victims.'

Herman and Chomsky use similar techniques to those deployed by the GUMG. Their analysis of the murders, for instance, relies upon detailed documentation of the column inches allocated to various comparable cases, to the number of stories about each case, and to the prominence they were accorded in the paper or magazine (ibid.: 40–41). This is supplemented by an analysis of the words and narrative used to tell the various stories. The authors draw attention, for example, to the way in which sympathy is elicited or denied by the use of emotive or flat language, the first creating feelings of concern, the latter those of neutral indifference (ibid.: 43, 48, 63).

Manufacturing Consent also compares the treatment of national elections in El Salvador, Guatemala and Nicaragua. The authors argue that the treatment given to each varies, from being taken seriously as exercises in democracy to being dismissed as cynical gestures, and that this treatment is itself directly correlated to the relationship between the state concerned and the USA. Where relations were friendly, the election was seen as 'democratic'; where they were unfriendly, the coverage was less sympathetic. In short, Herman and Chomsky claim that journalists operated double standards. To demonstrate this bias, they again analyse the texts, in terms of the space allocated, the tone used, the expertise referred to, and so on (ibid.: 132–6). Other cases – treatment of Indochina, for instance – are added to their claim that the media act as a propaganda tool.

Although Herman and Chomsky do not command the range of techniques and the sophistication of the GUMG, their use of a

comparative approach provides a persuasive basis for their conclusions. Their main focus is on the language used and on the
space allocated. The US media act, they contend (ibid.: 298), 'to
inculcate and defend the economic, social, and political agenda of
privileged groups that dominate the domestic society and the state.
The media serve this purpose in many ways: through selection of
topics, distribution of concerns, framing of issues, filtering of
information, emphasis and tone, and by keeping debate within
the bounds of acceptable premises'. In short, the US press
demonstrates a systematic, political bias in its coverage of foreign
affairs. This claim is sustained by revelations about the attention
and language accorded to ostensibly similar events, and the
correlation between this differential treatment and the USA's
foreign policy interests.

Critiques of Bias Research

Both *Manufacturing Consent* and the *Bad News* studies appear to
provide evidence for the existence of systematic bias. Such bias is
seen as undermining the claims of the USA or the UK to enjoy the
benefits of a 'free press'. In the USA, the freedom is compromised
by the thought that the media act as instruments of propaganda; in
the UK, it is the impartiality of public service broadcasting that is
called into question. In other words, this evidence, if valid, has
profound political implications. It is not surprising, therefore, that
such studies have been the object of intense debate. Criticisms have
come from a number of different directions, from both the left and
the right, from journalists and from academics.

Martin Harrison's *TV News: Whose Bias?* (1985) has provided
the most detailed examination of the GUMG's research technique.
He argues that, despite the vast edifice of formal analysis, the
results owe something to the prior assumptions of the researchers
and do not make allowance for the conditions under which journalists work. The biases detected by the GUMG would not be seen as
such by other observers. In effect, the GUMG was selective in its
use of the data, picking out those features that served their general
argument. Harrison is not convinced that the GUMG had provided
the kind of 'scientific' method which would reveal the same results
whoever did the experiment. He noted, for example, that the

GUMG sees the word 'idle' as being used pejoratively, as a way of criticizing the (in)activity of the workers, but, Harrison claims, the word is actually used by the strikers themselves. The Harrison critique can, in this respect, be seen as an attack on a particular research method; but Harrison is also sceptical about the existence of the 'dominant ideology' to which the GUMG relates media coverage. Certainly, if there is no such pervasive ideology, which systematically promotes the values and interests of one group, then the particular biases of the media cannot be explained in terms of a 'dominant ideology'.

Criticisms of bias research also focus on the assumptions that underlie the notion of 'bias' itself. The complaint here is that 'bias' assumes the possibility of an objective reality, which, according to the critics, is a myth. Implicit in the study of bias is the thought that there is a 'truth' against which television or press reports can be judged. The GUMG often compares the claims made by broadcasters with an 'independent reality': 'viewers were given a *misleading* portrayal of industrial disputes in the UK when measured against *the independent reality*' (GUMG, 1980: xiii; emphasis added). Herman and Chomsky presume a proper or fair distribution of coverage and use of language. It is these general assumptions that trouble other critics of the bias studies (see Bennett, 1982a; Hall, 1982). For them, the idea of an independent reality is not plausible. All events, indeed the notion of an 'event' itself, are the product of an ideological framework which creates order out of an infinite number of possible observations or impressions. As Stuart Hall points out, 'the event must become a "story" before it can become a *communicative event*' (1980: 129, original emphasis). This line of criticism builds from a general assumption that there is no independent truth against which media representations can be judged. Instead the suggestion is that there are competing interpretations, some of which reinforce the status quo, while others diverge from it. Media reporting is engaged in an attempt to establish a truth and the criteria for the validation of something as 'true'. In the case of TV news, it is seeking to claim that 'seeing is believing'. The criterion for truthfulness is to be found in pictures and eye witnesses, and the reporting of expert or personal testimony. But, as all social scientists are aware, appearances are deceptive, personal testimony may be partial and witnesses may be mistaken. Hall is not claiming that there is a truth to be found through the use of the correct method; rather he is asserting that each interpretation is a product of a particular ideology.

Constructing Reality?

One attempt to provide an alternative approach to media content, which retains a notion of bias, but which tries to avoid the assumption of an independent reality, is found in the work of Douglas Kellner. Kellner writes about media culture generally – *Beavis and Butthead*, the Rambo movies – and not just news, and what makes him interesting is the way his analysis of news and popular culture uses the same approach. In his account of coverage of the 1991 Gulf War, Kellner treats the war as a 'media construct', by which he means its 'reality' was not located in the desert battlefields: 'In a sense, the 1990s war against Iraq was a cultural–political event as much as a military one' (Kellner, 1995: 198). Kellner is not prepared to take the extreme view attributed to Jean Baudrillard that the war existed only as a media spectacle, but he does suggest that the reporting of war entails a struggle to define its meaning and to chart its course. 'The war against Iraq,' he writes (ibid.: 199), 'can be read as a text produced by the Bush Administration, the Pentagon, and the media which utilized the images and discourse of the crisis and then the war to mobilize consent and support for the U.S. military intervention.' Kellner sees the media, not as covering the war, but as being used to create support for the US government's military strategy. News reports were not neutral observations of events on the battlefield but a product of a government public relations exercise.

The American government, argues Kellner, was able to control the images and information available to the press corps. The combined effect of government manipulation and journalistic practice (and prejudice) served to create conditions that legitimated the war and US policy. For Kellner, the media's version of the war and the crisis that preceded it are a product of US interests and can be understood in terms of these alone. But note that, in making these claims, he himself adopts an alternative perspective on the Gulf War, against which he sets the dominant version. In talking about the 'disinformation' spread by the government, he is acknowledging another account of events. He refers, for example, to US media reports of Saddam Hussein's 'intransigence', when subsequent evidence revealed that he was willing to negotiate (ibid.: 201–2). In short, Kellner argues that there is another story to be told.

Kellner's emphasis on the textual formation of reality is not an invitation to relativism. In moving away from the idea of 'bias', he is not embracing an indiscriminate pluralism. Rather he is inviting a different approach to the analysis of media content, in which the debate does not focus on the bias/reality issue, but rather on the *quality* of the story. Kellner believes that there are alternative versions which represent a 'better' account of events, and that not all coverage is to be viewed as equally valid or invalid. What this suggestion raises, of course, is the problem of judging between different accounts. The selection cannot be based on accuracy alone, even though it does clearly matter that details of fact be correct. It must also be based on the credibility attributed to different sources of information. Kellner, for instance, relies upon contrary accounts of events in order to challenge the media version. In doing so, he is assuming these to be more persuasive (if not more 'true'). He judges the minutes identifying Hussein's willingness to negotiate as more accurate or reliable than the briefings given to the press corps. This view is, though, a judgement of the relative veracity of accounts of events. So Kellner's understanding of the reportage is informed by his judgement of the possible interpretations. It also depends on who is telling the story: he places trust in stories by papers like *In These Times*; he mistrusts *The Washington Post*.

Kellner's approach moves us some way from the idea of 'bias' as it is traditionally conceived. Instead, he suggests that we confront competing truth claims, different interpretations of a putative reality. He is not offering a simple dichotomy of truth and lies, but rather a 'truth' that is constituted and conveyed within different genres and narratives. His approach to interpreting the news and political coverage draws heavily on the approach associated with cultural studies, in which interpretation emerges through an understanding of the generic conventions which order the text and the associations that are linked to it. The implications of this approach are explored in the next two chapters.

Conclusion

The Kellner approach argues that all political coverage is ideological and has to be understood and judged as such. The implication of this is not that all perceptions of bias are a result of personal prejudice and perspective, that bias is merely in 'the eye of the beholder' and, therefore, an empty and useless notion. Nor is the implication that, given the presence of an ideologically dominant group, bias is systematic and consistent. Such conclusions are too comforting (there is nothing to worry about) or too defeatist (there is nothing to be done). The picture is more complicated. As writers like John Corner (1995) and Andrew Goodwin (1990) argue, there is reason to retain some version of 'bias' in order to criticize and analyse competing accounts of the world. As Goodwin (1990: 57) writes: 'It is quite plausible to believe that the media images are constructed and still maintain that some constructions are more truthful than others. Surely there are competing explanations of social reality, and surely all factual statements are also statements of value. But none of this means that there are not real events in the actual world that do take place and unreal events in the minds of policemen, politicians and Coal Board officials that do not take place.' This is an argument for shifting the terrain on which the debate is conducted and the criteria which distinguish the relative merits of competing accounts of media representation; it is not one for rejecting critical judgements altogether.

From the point of view of public policy for a democratic media, this conclusion has important consequences. As Newton (1989: 132) notes, it suggests the need for 'airing all opinions, including those which are unpopular, eccentric, or supported only by small minorities'. This leads to a further injunction: 'the media should be broadly, not narrowly selective; judgements should be open, not doctrinaire or party political; the emphasis should be on inclusion rather than exclusion, and in presenting all sides they should take no side' (ibid.: 133). In a similar vein, Corner (1995: 64–5) writes, 'television news is inevitably the product of a "point of view" and . . . the best arrangement for television services is therefore to have a multiplicity of outlets (national and local) each of which is able to declare the broad political and social assumptions informing its news production'. We return to these policy issues at the end of this book. They are raised here because it is important to emphasize the possible implications of the debate about bias.

More immediately, the qualified notion of bias has important implications too for the way we analyse media content. It suggests, for instance, the need to be aware of the contradictory and complex content of a media text. News programmes do not tell one simple, consistent story, but reveal many different, conflicting dimensions to the way that politics is conveyed. From the point of view of analysis, this means introducing a more reflexive understanding of media representations of the world. Coverage of politics needs to be read not just in terms of 'bias', but as 'narratives', as stories about the world which call into play some actors (and marginalize others), which suppose some motivations and ignore others, and so on.

These stories, furthermore, are not flat reports, devoid of drama and sentiment, they are designed to capture the viewers' and the readers' attention and to engage their emotions. And just as we judge feature films and soap operas in terms of their 'authenticity' or 'truth', so we judge news reports. We do not 'know' whether a reporter is telling the truth; rather we judge the way they tell their story. How we respond to their words and pictures is not predetermined, but is a consequence of a complex set of factors, of which one is an aesthetic judgement. The criteria may not be identical when dealing with news and fiction, but the element of judgement is there in both cases. These judgements may not ever be settled, they may not be validated by 'hard data', but this does not make them any less important. For the analyst of media content, it follows that the texts under consideration should be studied not just as 'accurate' documents of real events, though this is clearly relevant, but also as works of imaginative reconstruction, as works intended to produce responses and feelings in viewers and readers.

2
Telling Tales: the Reporting of Politics

When television or the press report politics, they are recounting stories about the world. They are not just holding up a mirror to events or pointing a telescope at them. The mass media do not simply 'cover' observable events and report facts; they animate them by turning them into narratives with plots and actors. Just as they create 'the Gulf War', so they create the political process itself, the context in which the events take place. Movies use the artifice of cinema to tell a story, to create characters in a believable world; news does a similar job for the events that are its concern. News reporters tell stories too. They describe the pursuit of political ambition, the rivalries and pacts, the human frailties and strengths. Political careers sometimes assume epic form, ending in tragedy or triumph; more often they take the guise of soap opera. This is not a metaphor; this is how news is told. 'News' is, in this sense, an art form and news reporting an art, and political coverage is one particular genre of this art. This is the central theme of this chapter, which looks at the way the story of politics is narrated. A key device for analysing these narratives is provided by the notion of the 'frame'.

Frames versus Biases

The last chapter showed how the idea of bias was used to analyse media content, but it also revealed some of the dissatisfaction felt with this approach. In particular, there was the feeling that the focus on bias, with its emphasis on systematic misrepresentation, tended to obscure as much as it revealed. Instead of concentrating on ideological bias in order to understand media content, recent research has preferred to utilize the notion of the 'frame' and 'framing'. These ideas are deliberately intended to expose the ways in which news stories work *as stories*: the way they generate a narrative with protagonists, whose motives and actions assign causation and responsibility. 'News' is a distilled form of the multiple 'events' taking place in the world. The media not only selects particular events, it also has to make sense of them. It has to make them matter to the readers and viewers, and this entails setting them within a narrative, a story of social change.

This process of selection and narration is captured by the idea of framing. Robert Entman offers this definition: 'A *frame* operates to select and highlight some features of reality and obscure others in a way that tells a consistent story about problems, their causes, moral implications, and remedies' (1996: 77–8; original emphasis). The way the frame achieves its effects is through the use of a variety of techniques. William Gamson and Andre Modigliani (1989: 3) refer to metaphors, historical examples, catchphrases, depictions and visual images, all of which function as 'reasoning devices' that offer a view of the causes, effects and principles that animate the story. This means privileging one account of the world over another. Entman, for example, uses a framing analysis to show how the US media gave a particular slant to the debate, which took place in the mid-1990s, over affirmative action and its value in promoting equality between blacks and whites: 'The most prominent elements of the message – the headlines, the visuals, the highlighted quotes, and the journalists' narrative emphases – framed the policy dispute as a zero-sum conflict of interest between whites and blacks in which only one group could win and one must lose' (Entman, 1997: 40). The point is that the story did not have to be told like this; other frames could have produced a different outcome.

Although frames are devices for seeing the world in a particular way, they differ from the notion of bias in the sense that they do not presume a single ideological position. The frame 'implies a range of positions' and 'should not be confused with positions for or against some policy measure' (Gamson and Modigliani, 1989: 3–4). Where bias is associated with the *general* disposition of the newspaper or broadcaster, framing makes no such assumption, treating each case on its merits. Entman summarizes the position like this: 'A *bias* defines a tendency to frame different actors, events, and issues in the same way, to select and highlight the same sort of selective realities, thus crafting a similar tale across a range of potential news stories' (1996: 78; original emphasis). The point is not that the word 'frame' replaces the word 'bias'; rather it is that, firstly, framing does not assume that all biases point in the same direction, and secondly, not all biases are *ideological* biases. In coverage of environmental policy in the USA, Entman (1996) identifies a variety of different biases: a 'popularity' bias, by which the media favour the popular view; a class bias, by which journalists adopt positions on environmental issues that serve their class interests; and a cynicism bias, by which policy is presented as exclusively self-interested.

In focusing on ideological biases, argues Entman (ibid.: 78), media analysts are liable to overlook what he sees as the real biases: 'All of the concern with ideological bias has obscured the systematic, consistent biases that the media truly do impose on their narration of politics and policy. The real media biases favor simplicity over complexity, persons over institutional process, emotions over facts, and, most important, game over substance.' This version of the systematic biases, revealed through framing analysis, indicates a different approach to the study of media content. It suggests that we look at the way in which the media give life and form to the entire political process. It also suggests that we pay attention to the evaluative and rhetorical character of news. Entman (1997: 32) talks of 'emotion-arousing vocabulary'.

This chapter draws heavily on the framing approach in discussing the ways in which 'politics' and the political process are represented within the media.

Producing News

As Entman, Gamson and others suggest, reporting is a form of rhetoric, it is about *persuading* us – the readers, the viewers – that something happened. Very few people actually witness the political events that are reported. We are not present at Bill Clinton's inauguration; we do not peruse the medical reports on the state of Boris Yeltsin's heart; we do not witness Benazir Bhutto being deposed. And yet when we read or see news broadcasts about Clinton becoming president, or about Yeltsin's health or about

Bhutto's fall from favour, we do not just believe that they happened: we *know* they did. We are sure about these things even though we have no direct corroborative evidence.

This belief cannot be explained simply by the claim that 'I read it in the papers' or 'I saw it on the news'. The mere fact of reading something does not make it true. Novels are not accounts of true events, and although we are moved to tears or laughter by them, we are aware that we are reading stories that do not map directly onto a real world. This does not stop us saying that a film or novel is honest or truthful, but we mean something different than when we talk about accuracy in news. The point is, though, that in each case – in fiction or news – we are being *persuaded* of its truthfulness, and the difference between genres lies in the techniques they use to do this. The credibility of any story is undoubtedly enhanced by the fact that every other paper carries it too. But even if this is not the case, when the press boasts of an 'exclusive', we are still disposed to believe the story. It is, of course, the case that the level of credibility varies between sources: some papers or programmes are seen as more 'trustworthy' than others; and scandals about journalistic fabrication or faked documentaries do damage the trust people have in media sources. In 1985, a third of Americans felt their press was inaccurate; by 1997, the figure had risen to over a half. A similar, if not as dramatic, decline was detected in people's trust in US television networks (Kohut and Toth, 1998: 112–4). The key is that the decision to believe or to disbelieve rarely has anything to do with any direct knowledge of the events reported. It is a matter of being persuaded that the journalist has not just invented his or her story.

In the same way, seeing something on the TV – seeing pictures of refugees or peace negotiations – does not provide proof that the event occurred. On either side of these images are soap operas, situation comedies and movies. We see events taking place in these too, and yet we do not believe they are picturing real moments in real people's lives. Or rather, when viewers come to believe that the characters are 'real', this is seen as a symptom of some kind of failure on their part. Most viewers recognize that the characters in soaps are no more real than Homer, Bart and Marge Simpson. Whatever happens, we know that we will not end up living next door to them.

But what is important is that the 'reality' of the news, the 'real' events which it describes, are not formally any different from the soaps. They are part of the same medium that carries the soaps or prints the fiction. The difference between what is true and what is fiction is not something which can be 'seen'. It is something we learn and it is something which we are taught; making sense of media content requires skills and clues. To apply this skill we have to be given guidance or signals that allow us to recognize what is truth and what is fiction.

One way of thinking about this is to imagine the conditions under which we might be persuaded *not* to believe the news. Imagine that news reports were peppered with jokes, or were written in very florid language, and were delivered by the Hollywood actor Robin Williams adopting one of his funny voices. Imagine that the news broadcast began with the newsreader saying: 'It seems to me that the president is up shit creek without a paddle' and that this announcement was accompanied by the sound of a studio audience cheering or booing. Imagine that newscasters dressed in jeans and t-shirts, that the TV news used a song by the Spice Girls for its theme tune, or that reporters were sponsored like football or tennis professionals and wore their sponsor's logo on their clothes. If the news was like this, we would not believe it; we would not be able to take it seriously as 'reality'. This is despite the fact that we would have no more or less evidence for the reported facts than we do when we believe the news in its current format. In other words, the format, the *style* of the news, does a great deal of work in establishing the status and significance of its content.

News reports tend to be written in a dry, impersonal language. Newscasters dress soberly and their broadcasts are introduced by music that is portentous. News reporters use film and photos, experts, eye-witnesses and official sources to validate their report. News stories, while formally committed to reporting the unusual or the untypical, actually stay firmly within strict conventions. They report fluctuations in the exchange rate, not the price of bread in the local supermarket. A whole range of signals and conventions establish that something is 'news' and serious, that it is about the real world. In the same way, other codes and devices tell us that something is fictional.

These techniques are supplemented by the image of the professional journalist and the codes of conduct that attach to such an occupation. Their credibility has to be sustained by these and other means. Journalists found guilty of fabricating stories are sacked, as a way of protecting the credibility of their profession and their employers. But even without breaching professional codes, credibility can be damaged. The BBC newsreader Angela Rippon lost some of her authority after she appeared on the *Morecambe and Wise Show*, where she took part in a high-kicking dance routine. She continued to work as a newsreader, but ended up on *The Big Breakfast*, a fast-paced, jokey show that makes little pretence of journalistic seriousness.

These methods for persuading us of the truth of particular stories and programmes are themselves built upon a larger edifice. Firstly, there is the assumption that there exists something called 'news' which we need to know about and believe; and secondly, there is the idea that the mass media are legitimate providers of this news. We could, after all, manage with gossip exchanged in the street; the fact that people watch the news instead is a consequence of the operation of social conventions and the political interests underlying them. In other times and places, 'news' does not impose the same compulsive pressure. Nor is the pressure felt equally by all; the desire for news correlates with the socioeconomic position of the consumer: the poor feel less 'need' for news (Putnam, 1995). In other words, we have to be aware of the process both by which news is constituted and by which it comes to be important: how, that is, it becomes institutionalized.

'News' is, in one sense, a consequence of economics. It is a product of the need to trade. Where communities have no such need, where their actions do not depend on those of their neighbours, there is little reason or incentive to create news, save as a form of entertaining gossip. News is also a product of politics. In *The Structural Transformation of the Public Sphere*, Jürgen Habermas (1989) connects the rise of the press with the development of public political dialogue. This was itself a result of changes in the structure of power in industrializing countries, where a new political order was struggling into life, one in which the business class sought to control public policy. The emergent press provided a means of articulating these political views. What was to emerge, through the publication of journals and magazines, was what became known as 'public opinion', the construction of views which had legitimacy through the fact that they were held by the 'people'. This was, as it continues to be, a construct of the system of communication. The 'public' is the product of mass media and their relationship to authority. The press and broadcasters represent themselves as the voice of the people. Public opinion is called into existence through the rhetoric of public communication. Opinion and information are products, on the one hand, of the attempt to make political power accountable and, on the other, of the rise of systems of communication that give shape to that process of accountability.

For Habermas, the emergence of a public sphere, created through the circulation of a political press and facilitated by coffee house society, was a significant moment in the process of modernization and democratization. But it was a moment that was contingent upon many factors, and as those factors changed, so did the public sphere. Habermas himself, and those who have followed him (for example Nicholas Garnham, 1986), argue that the industrialized and commercialized media have effectively eliminated the public sphere. Nowadays, the citizen of the public sphere has been replaced by the consumer of the private sphere. The new order does not serve the need for public discourse about political goods; instead, it aims to link audiences and advertisers.

This shift has direct implications for news. Where news was used previously to constitute public opinion among active citizens, it has become increasingly geared to servicing the commercial market. In the USA, advertisers have begun to insist on control over the editorial content of magazines; editorial and advertising branches of newspapers have been amalgamated. This is captured in the concept of the 'total newspaper', described by Daniel Hallin (2000: 221) as 'the idea that circulation, sales and editorial efforts must be integrated, all directed towards the project of marketing news-information'. In the UK, News International titles have been accused of tailoring their coverage of China in order to accommodate their owner's commercial interests in that part of the world. The very notion of 'news' itself has changed under the influence of commercial pressure. The move towards 'human interest' stories can be seen to accord with the desire to produce a more consumer-friendly news. Hallin (ibid.) talks of the change in the content of American papers: 'They include shorter stories, colour and graphics, and a shift in the news agenda away from traditional "public affairs" and towards lifestyle features and "news you can use".' The same trend may explain, for instance, the obsession with President Clinton's affairs (with, among others, Monica Lewinsky) in 1997–8, even as the world appeared to edge closer to another war in the

Gulf. It might explain too why, in 1992, 37 per cent of front page stories in the *Sun* were about royalty or showbusiness, and only 7 per cent about politics. Newspapers do not, however, have to take this form. The press in Germany, for example, found space for lengthy and sophisticated debate of the war in Kosovo, with contributions by such academics as Ulrich Beck and Habermas (Scott, 1999). 'News' is a media product, and like all such products it is the result of a complex process and history.

So to summarize what has been said so far: in presenting a version of the world, news has first to persuade us of its veracity through the use of various techniques, and secondly the character and role of that news have to be seen as circumscribed by wider commercial and political processes. These general points have a considerable significance for the way we then think about how news represents politics. The logic of the argument is that news has to be understood as just another media product, like soap operas, chat shows, drama series, lifestyle magazines and so on. Each of these too has a particular history and are the result of a particular concatenation of interests. News is not an isolated example of media production, but just one among many such instances. What defines each of them is not simply, or even, their relationship to the truth, but rather the rules and conventions and interests with which they operate. The way to capture this is to say that 'news' is just a particular genre within the system of mass communications. And it is this aspect of it, as a genre, that has to be borne in mind as we consider the way it constitutes politics and the political realm.

Genres are defined by Steve Neale (1980: 19) 'as systems of orientations, expectations and conventions that circulate between industry, text and subject'. News reporting forms a genre of which 'political coverage' is a sub-genre. It is in working with these genres that journalists come to frame events. In this sense, the frames are the practical realization of the genre. As the journalist Sarah Benton (1997: 137) argues, political coverage is organized around pre-established story lines or frames. The plot is always the same: 'there are only old stories which we know already . . . We know it all already because information about politics only becomes the news when it can be fitted into a story that we know already.' Thus, for example, coverage of the British debate about Britain's relationship to the European Union was organized, in the 1990s, around two basic plots: the destruction of the Conservative Party or the end of national sovereignty (ibid.: 138). But the politics frame does not just work with particular plots, it also involves specific characters and predicaments. This is most obvious in the focus on leaders, and their representation as individuals motivated by the desire for power. The genre of political coverage creates the political process; its conventions define politics and its narratives organise the plot lines of political stories.

Genres and Political Coverage

A genre, like the frames it gives rise to, is not fixed or universal; it institutes general regularities, establishing practices that allow the production of any particular cultural form. But genres do not emerge out of nowhere, nor do their rules or conventions provide absolute and unbreakable rules. Genres change and have histories. So it is that the genre of political coverage is a constantly evolving form, and the paths taken by the press and by broadcasting are different, not only between countries but within them too. Genre conventions are specific to their context. News genres differ, for example, according to their dependence on advertising or according to their regulatory regime. Such factors help explain, for instance, the different ways in which general elections and political leaders are covered in different countries (Masters *et al.*, 1991; Negrine, 1996; Semetko, 1996).

In the same way, change in political coverage has to be understood in terms of the increasing competition for space between it and sports and lifestyle coverage, and the competition for readers and viewers with an ever-expanding range of media sources to choose from. Such processes lead to claims that news is being 'dumbed down', a charge that is supported by reference to the decline in column inches devoted to representative assemblies (Congress, Parliament) since the Second World War, and to the rise of the political sketchwriter, for whom politics is a source of amusement (Franklin, 1994; Negrine, 1996; Tutt, 1992). There has been a move away from direct reporting of representatives' business, and a rise in *commentary* upon that business. The job of the political commentator is more akin to that of the television critic than to that of the reporter. Political commentators review performances and amuse their readers by dwelling on the quirky aspects of the political representatives.

Such commentary can be seen as framing politics as soap opera or situation comedy. This is one political commentator, Mathew Parris, writing about the British Conservative Party leader, William Hague: 'We saw Big Chief Bald Eagle, the young warrior recently anointed leader of the Tory tribe, down on the reservation at Smith Square, spiritual homeland of his people' (*The Times*, 24 July 1997). In the Netherlands, politicians are framed within the conventions of gossip writing. Liesbet Van Zoonen (1998a: 57) documents the ways in which Dutch magazines write about the marriages of politicians as well as about their alleged corrupt activities: 'Now that Elco Brinkman is no longer minister, he can give more attention to wife Janneke and their children Eduard, Christine and Henriette'; 'SCANDAL! This is the way politicians fill their pockets with your tax money'. Such accounts invite ridicule and cynicism. The use of these styles of reporting politics shapes the way politics is seen, and marks the changing relationships between audiences, politics and their media. Readers are there to be amused rather than informed; they are expected to laugh and mock. These particular frames, together with their overarching genre, have a history.

Political coverage does not just change within a particular medium, but across media. Where the press began as a highly politicized form, broadcasting in Britain began as an apparently apolitical one. The Post Office's management of the then British Broadcasting Company in the early 1920s required that the company avoid controversy and comment. This constraint was reinforced by the BBC's competitors. Lord Reith, the BBC's first director-general, tried to develop a news service, but was frustrated by the press, who saw broadcasting as a dangerous rival. It was only in 1927 that the BBC was allowed to broadcast news during the daytime. Until then it could only report news after 7pm, and it still had to confine itself to copy supplied by the Reuters news agency. After 1927, it began to rely on its own sources. It remained tied by the rule that forbade it to editorialize, but gradually the bar on controversy was lifted. In 1944, the 'Fourteen Day Rule' was introduced, preventing the BBC from mentioning any issue that was due to be discussed in Parliament in the next two weeks. Elections also were not covered.

This cautious distance between politicians and broadcasters began to break down with the founding of commercial television. The Fourteen Day rule was scrapped and the 1959 general election was the first to be subject to direct coverage by the broadcasting media. Slowly, too, the deference which broadcasters accorded politicians was eroded, helped by the so-called 'satire boom' of the early 1960s. Nonetheless, representative politics still enjoyed a protected existence. The first election phone-ins did not take place until 1974; radio microphones were not installed in Parliament until two years later; and cameras were not introduced in the House of Commons until 1990.

In Australia, news and political coverage changed in response to technical development. With the laying of coaxial cables in the 1960s, it was no longer necessary to fly news film to the broad-caster; it could be sent instantaneously. Prior to this, coverage of the government in Canberra was largely ignored, with preference given to local (accessible) news. Full-time coverage of Parliament, therefore, did not occur until the 1970s. In the same way, satellite television gave an increased incentive to cover world politics. Political coverage changed for other reasons too. As in Britain, there was a gradual shift from deferential, descriptive reporting of politics to a more assertive, irreverential approach. This shift owed something to changes in broadcasting rules and to a growing professionalization of journalists (Tiffen, 1989: 25–8).

The point of these different histories is to establish the context within which the broadcast form of political coverage emerged. Coverage of politics was shaped by rules laid down by the political elite, and the treatment of politics reflected this balance of power. Where commercial interests are pre-eminent in forming the generic type, another set of rules will apply. Chapter 6 looks in more detail at the ways in which corporate considerations influence the shape of the genre. What needs to be discussed here is how existing genres represent or constitute the political realm. With this in mind, we look now at the frames that currently distinguish the way politics is presented to readers, viewers and listeners. It is not intended to offer a comprehensive picture, but rather to identify some of the most salient aspects. The question is straightforward: in the framing of politics, which aspects of the political process are organized into political coverage and which are organized out?

Telling Political Stories

Political coverage, like all news reporting, tells a story. Whether explicitly or implicitly there is a narrative which connects characters and events. How the story is told is determined by the frame, and different narrative frames are available. For example, a news story can tell how actors cause events (how Henry Kissinger and Richard Nixon covered up the bombing of Cambodia, how Western political leaders intervened in Yugoslavia). Equally, news stories can tell how those same political actors are driven by events. The way the story is told, the narrative devices used, will be the way the political process is created. To illustrate this, let us consider how elections are covered (Lichter and Smith, 1996). The political motives of all politicians are commonly understood in terms of their desire to win elections, and their actions are interpreted in relation to this dominant concern.

Elections are typically represented as the culmination of titanic struggles in which leaders battle for supremacy. The right to rule is secured by the power won as a result of a heroic victory, in which a leader puts his or her rivals to the sword. These rivals are not simply the leaders of other parties. They also inhabit the leader's own party. As Sarah Benton (1997: 146–7) caricatures it: 'Behind every leader there are dark forces; if the leader is weak, the dark forces are really in control . . . A great leader is hampered and surrounded by buffoons . . . Leaders are always beset by conspiracies . . . The job of the *young* leader is to wake the inert people from their long sleep.' These rivals exist first within their own party; they have to win the battle to lead the party. In the USA, the primaries and the party conventions provide the formal setting for the playing out of these rivalries, whereas in Britain leadership elections and annual party congresses provide the theatre. The successful leader is then engaged in a battle with his or her opponent, which is resolved in the head-to-head that is the national election.

One metaphor that is typically associated with the account of these electoral struggles is the horse race (Gitlin, 1991; Lichter and Smith, 1996; Zhao and Bleske, 1998). If representative assemblies are covered as if part of the world of light entertainment, elections are covered as if they are sporting encounters. Opinion pollsters act as bookies and election day is the winning post. Commentary on them is driven by poll data and by other estimates of the parties' chance of success; each day's campaigning is seen as an opportunity to comment upon the relative performances of the parties: who is ahead, who has just fallen, and so on. But the horse race is just one of the many metaphors deployed. Another is the idea of battle, with talk of battle zones and war rooms. Whatever the allusion, the story of the election is narrated through words and images, themselves the product of the frame, that construct a particular vision of the political process.The presence of this general narrative structure is evident in the way leaders dominate the coverage of politics. 'Parties' do not exist as a chorus of different voices, but as one: that of their designated leaders. The political position of the Social Democrat, the Republican, the Conservative parties is assumed to be contained in the speeches and pronouncements of their leaders. Or put another way, the story is told in terms of a leader who dominates his or her party and who is constantly fighting off rivals. Leaders tend to dominate election campaigns. Research (Billig *et al.*, 1993; Deacon *et al.*, 1998) into coverage of the 1992 and 1997 British general elections revealed that the party leaders were greatly in evidence. In 1992, where the Conservative leader (John Major) appeared 175 times, his chancellor, Norman Lamont, appeared a mere 62 times (indeed the grand total for appearances by other members of the party was 247). The corresponding leader/rest figures for Labour (162: 185) and the Liberal Democrats (152: 118) were similarly disproportionate. In 1997, the pattern was much the same. Tony Blair appeared 531 times, while his deputy, John Prescott, mustered only 56 appearances. However much this imbalance is the product of party management, the media conspire in this arrangement and thereby generate a picture of politics in which competition between leaders (and aspiring leaders) defines the game. This is not a peculiarity of British media coverage. Research into news coverage in France, the USA and Germany reveals that in these countries as well leaders occupy a great deal of the available screen time (Masters *et al.*, 1991).

This emphasis on leadership is underpinned by a (largely unarticulated) social theory which holds that collective action needs to be explained by the actions of leaders (hence the references to the existence of 'ringleaders' or 'militants' in discussion of unofficial or illegal activities). The media favour an explanation of political action that follows the formal contours of the bureaucratic/democratic hierarchy. There is a reluctance to attribute behaviour to spontaneity or to social forces or processes. Politics is framed as the product of the activity of key individuals; ordinary people are essentially passive followers (either portrayed positively as 'supporters' or negatively as 'sheep' or 'dupes'). In such a world view, there is no space for structural factors to shape the course of events.

Another feature of this coverage of leaders, according to Joshua Meyrowitz (1985), is the *way* leaders are viewed. According to Meyrowitz, television treats leaders as 'people like us'. This is as much a consequence of its technical character, its use of the intimate close-up, as of a choice on the part of programme makers. Leaders are portrayed (and judged) by their performance as human beings under pressure (the interview) or in conversation (the chat show), rather than as leaders in the traditional sense (Meyrowitz has in mind Churchill and Roosevelt). Under the glare of the studio lights, leaders are seen as personalities. This is a topic to which we return when considering new forms of political communication (Chapter 9). For the moment it is sufficient to note that, in thinking about the way politics is portrayed, we need to be mindful of style as well as content.

The concentration on individuals and events, on personalities and ambitions, inevitably marginalizes an alternative account of political change. Such an alternative might draw attention to the social forces or structures that drive change, and which make events the contingent result of these larger processes. To return to the case of the election: the extensive media treatment it receives reinforces the idea that the outcome is decided in this period. Much of the research on voting behaviour indicates, however, that this focus is misplaced (Curtice and Semetko, 1994). Sociological accounts, which place emphasis on class, see patterns of voting changing more gradually and over longer periods of time than is allowed by election campaigns. Even those theories that dwell upon the impact of political factors also see votes as being determined well in advance of, or independently from, the election campaign (Heath *et al.*, 1991).

Telling the story this way also plays down the part played by parties (as collective bodies). Other collectivities are also identified through their leaders: companies by the chief executive; the European Union by its president. Even where there is no formal organization, the media will still seek a leader. So it is that the media will expect 'community leaders' to talk on behalf of some putative 'community'.

In portraying leaders as the key actors and elections as the key political event, there then comes the question of the motivation: what is it that drives the actors engaged in the election? Cappella and Jamieson (1997) identify two competing sets of motives: one is marked by a devotion to some principle which determines what policy is to be offered or advocated, the other by a strategic calculation which produces policies according to their vote-winning potential. In ascribing these different motives to politicians, journalists are establishing different frames through which to view political action. The frame is constructed by the ways that language, phraseology and imagery are used to paint a picture of the political process as animated by particular kinds of politician with particular kinds of motivation.

The motives attributed to leading actors are not applied universally, or without concession to who they are. This is most apparent in foreign coverage, in the way the world is drawn and reported. The portrait of the world is marked by a process of inclusion and exclusion: certain countries share in the narrative, others do not. And those that are part of the story may themselves be narrated in a particular way – hence the emphasis on scandal and corruption (Wallis and Baran, 1990). Chris Paterson (1998: 91–2) gives this account of the problem of persuading Western news agencies to carry stories about Africa: 'All they want out of Africa is death, blood, famine, corruption, and all that. We've got plenty of that in Africa – there's no shortage of that. But we've also got a hell of a lot of other stuff in Africa which is much more important to the continent than just the various wars that go on.' Africa is framed as a site of struggle and dependence (where America is framed as a site of power and autonomy).

The conventions which demarcate the world also affect the people included within it. Pippa Norris (1997b), for example, has explored the narratives that frame accounts of women in politics. Her concern has been to examine the conventional wisdom that women leaders receive less attention than their male equivalents and that the coverage they receive is based on female stereotypes. Norris' research examined the treatment of 20 world leaders, of whom ten were women (for instance, Margaret Thatcher, Benazir Bhutto and Indira Gandhi). The coverage included both print and broadcast media, and was analysed both quantitatively and qualitatively. Over 130 000 stories were examined. The evidence revealed that men leaders (1600 stories per year) did indeed receive more coverage than women leaders (1400 stories per year). Perhaps extraordinarily, this meant that 'the gray John Major receives more daily news coverage than the remarkable Mrs Thatcher' (Norris, 1997b: 158). On the other hand, though there is some evidence of sex role stereotyping, it is less than might be expected. There are occasional references to appearances or other irrelevant personal details in coverage of women, but says Norris (ibid.: 159), these remarks are 'exceptional'. Men and women are described in broadly similar terms.

There is, however, evidence of the use of different framing devices for the reporting of men and women. These frames have both positive and negative effects. Norris reveals how women often appear within a 'breakthrough' frame: they are seen as the first of their sex to achieve a particular goal. A second frame treats them as 'outsiders', and in doing so denies them credit for their experience and qualifications. A final frame detected by Norris treats women as 'agents of change, most especially in sweeping away corruption' (ibid.: 163). The idea of the 'frame' then complements the idea of the genre. Both serve to draw attention to the ways in which coverage of politics gives prominence, firstly, to individual actors and, secondly, to the particular kinds of motives and expectations that guide their actions. But representations of politics are not couched only in terms of leaders. Indeed the activities of these leaders have to be understood through the generic convention which attaches them to some other representative body – a parliament, assembly or congress. The role accorded by the media to elected representative bodies is shaped by a number of factors. One of these is the formal constitutional reading of the role of the elected assembly. Where, as in the USA, the elected assembly is accorded distinct separate powers, it is able to claim more media space against the rival claims of the executive. Different constitutional arrangements produce different pictures. Roger Masters and his colleagues (1991: 386) note that the attention given to a leader tends to 'mirror [the] constitutional and political structure' of his or her country. A second factor shaping reportage is the means by which information is disseminated: codes of secrecy or rights to freedom of information, as well as other informal systems of news management, determine what appears in papers and in broadcasts. See, for example, the difference between the practices of the Washington lobby and the Westminster lobby. A third factor is the use of sources. In his study of the affirmative action debate, Entman (1997: 36) notes: 'Journalists, it seems, built their frame on claims by elite sources with an interest in promoting the impression of white arousal.' A similar lesson derives from Kellner's (1995) account of coverage of the Gulf War.

A fourth, related factor involves the way in which the sourcing of news is financed and the balance of power between journalists and their sources. David Miller (1993), for instance, argues that the reporting of Northern Ireland is a product of the control exercised by the Northern Ireland Office and the Northern Ireland Information Service. Using its considerable resources – 58 staff, £7 million (in 1991–2) – the NIIS produced thrice daily press releases, which, says Miller (ibid.: 76), 'present its view of the conflict as the legitimate and rational perspective in opposition to that of the paramilitaries and other "extremists".' A fifth factor shaping media portrayal of representative institutions is the standing of the relevant institution. In the mid 1980s, for example, Blumler and Gurevitch (1995: 89) talked of British press treatment of Parliament as 'sacerdotal', placing it just below the monarchy and the Church; today, the attitude is less respectful and this is reflected in the coverage and prominence accorded to Parliament (Franklin, 1992; Negrine, 1996). This, though, is not a simple fact of all political coverage, but of the peculiarities of a particular system. In other constitutional settings, with other party structures, leaders still feature, but the number of leaders and their actions will be framed differently.

What this teaches us is that, in looking at the coverage of politics, we need to focus upon who is viewed as the key political actor and what motives drive them. We have seen how there is a general tendency to focus on leaders, but the treatment of them varies between systems. Whatever the coverage accorded to leaders, such attention will tend to overlook the role played by 'ordinary' participants, or by participants outside the political mainstream, by principle or wider political forces. Indeed, this is a necessary result: making elected leaders the focus of attention also accords them legitimacy which is denied to others; making liberal democratic assumptions about the normal order of politics makes other kinds of political assumption 'extreme'. Insofar as politics is presented as an electoral game in which individual political ambition is the core motivating force, the media engage in a process of constituting and legitimating a version of the political process. In telling the story of politics this way, the media are also engaged in other important cultural processes. They are constructing a citizenry and a political realm, and distributing social and cultural capital – the ability to contribute to that society – in accordance with the picture they paint.

We the People

Contained in every news story is an implied audience or readership. Stories are written for a particular group, and the way they are written assumes a particular set of responses or values. There is an assumption about what 'we' are interested in, what we do, care about and know. Gamson and Modigliani (1989: 9) quote a newscaster reporting on the Chernobyl accident: 'Is there anyone out there not thinking about this nightmare of the nuclear age, talking about it, learning from it?' The everyday conversation of editorial offices is about whether 'our readers' or 'our audience' are interested in X or Y. The ex-BBC political editor, John Cole, recalls how his colleagues made assumptions about the political interests of their audiences: 'Editors, even on more spacious programmes than the news bulletins for which I used to work, judge that viewers' and listeners' attention span in political matters is very limited; that they cannot listen to an uninterrupted speech; that their tastes must be titillated by confrontational studio discussion' (*The Guardian*, 4 March 1996). A measure of a paper's success is its ability to deliver a product that is appreciated by its target audience. Different papers and programmes work in different markets. This process is not simply a matter of responding to economic forces; the market is being created in the commercial process.

Readers and viewers are themselves constructed through the stories they see or read or hear; their concerns and worries are shaped and constituted by the way they are addressed by their papers and programmes. Journalists and editors may think of themselves as reflecting their audience, but actually they are imagining and constituting them. Fear of genetically modified foods did not spring spontaneously from the public. Concern was orchestrated by the interaction of journalists, lobbyists, scientists, and so on. Journalists have very limited access to the public, and what access they have is often mediated by other media and other interests. This means that they have, in a sense, to invent or create their audience. News values, what counts as an important issue, are attempts to establish a particular kind of audience/readership. They are ways of saying 'this is what matters to you'. Brian McNair (1995: 69) writes of the British press: 'The *Sun* claims to "speak" for the conservative working class, making it frequently racist, sexist and anti-socialist, while at the same time irreverential and critical of the establishment, whether it be in the form of Royal "scroungers", gay judges, or two-timing Tory politicians.'

What is involved in this process is the creation of 'them' and 'us'. The magazine *Index on Censorship* (2000) devoted a special issue to the creation of 'them'. It was entitled *Manufacturing Monsters*, and described how 'they' are created in different media for different audiences, as 'refugees' or 'Arabs' or 'gypsies'. Franklin Gilliam and his colleagues (1996) show how in the USA the media create the fear of crime: of 'them' attacking 'us', and the way 'they' are configured as 'black'. These constructions of an audience, a particular 'we', is achieved through a series of contrasts and oppositions, through the implicit and explicit orchestration of 'us' and 'them'. National borders are drawn and redrawn this way, as are norms of sexuality and of political behaviour. At a trivial level, this can be discerned in sports commentary for international competitions where it is assumed that the audience is on one side or another; at a more serious level, it is involved in the construction of an enemy in the prelude to, and conduct of, war (Carruthers, 2000).

Interviews are conducted with a similar ethos in mind. Interviewers legitimate themselves by reference to their audience. Their claim is that they ask the questions that the public want answered; they are part of some democratic process. This understanding is reinforced by the way in which the interview is presented. Typically, only the interviewer addresses the camera directly; the politician addresses the interviewer. The audience only has access to the interviewee via the interviewer. The style of the interview also affects the relationship to the audience. It can be aggressively combative or informally gossipy. These conventions are wittily exposed by the comedian Ali G who satirizes his guests' pomposity by feigning a naive innocence. The formal rules and expectations of interviews are revealed as they are mocked.

More subtly, if more pervasively, 'the people' are also constructed through other aspects of the media, from a mode of address, or a tone of voice, to the setting of a schedule. Radio stations, like papers and programmes, are concerned with creating specific audiences. They do this through the style of programme and choice of presenter. When the BBC began broadcasting, there was only one channel, and it sought to create the conditions for a particular general public, that of a family gathered round the hearth (Frith, 1988). By contrast, the early days of American radio saw the emergence of stations which created regional, taste-specific audiences. With the proliferation of channels, the audiences have become ever more variegated, but the same principle holds. All forms of communication involve creating audiences and making certain assumptions. The 'people' are constituted in the process, and their existence is confirmed through the artifice of public opinion polls and market research. Individual answers to pollsters' questions are aggregated into 'public opinion'. The creation of this phenomenon then becomes a tool for legitimating partisan opinion or media agendas. The media's definition of the people (through the use of news values, editorials and interviews) and representation of them (through opinion polls and phone-ins) construct a particular version of the people. Opinion polls represent the aggregation of individual opinions expressed at particular times in particular settings. Using other techniques, or asking different questions, could create a different picture. Roberta Sassatelli (1998: 111) describes how an Italian corruption case was televised in such a way as to turn the viewing public into a participant in the trial.

Consider the techniques which can be used to create other images of the people. Editorials could work from different assumptions; interviews could be staged in different ways. Current news values work with an assumption that what matters is our immediate well-being (itself defined by the assumption that 'we' are nuclear family house owners). Imagine, though, a newspaper, not written from the perspective of families in a single country, but from the point of view of the world's population of poor and destitute. Would the 'news' be the same? Would fluctuations in the mortgage rate matter? Would not market speculation on the price of grain count for a great deal more? The point of this argument is not to suggest that there is, in fact, a single 'people', or that one account of who 'we' are is necessarily more accurate than any other, but that different forms of address create different versions of the people. In creating one version, the media marginalize another.

In constituting the people (or, in fact, many different peoples), the media also constitute politics. First, and most obviously, this is achieved by the contrast between the 'us' who are reading and watching, and the 'they' who perform the political acts. This simple move constitutes 'politics' as a distinct realm. But there is more to this process. Borders are also drawn round the realm in which politics takes place. Politics is defined as the activities of public agencies (parliaments, public utilities and so on), of politicians and political parties, and of pressure groups. The activities of all of these are treated as being directed to the exercise of power and as being legitimated by a set of constitutional rules. 'Politics' is the topic of news pages or current affairs programmes; it does not appear on sports pages, nor is it typically part of entertainment programmes. There are, of course, exceptions in each case: political dramas, protest songs and satire.

If media representations organize themselves around the picture of politics described so far, what is left out? What stories are not told, what forms of politics are marginalized or overlooked? Apart from the way a focus on leaders omits the ordinary members, and the focus on parties and Parliament omits the administrative structures of the state, the account of politics offered by the media also tends to exclude the pervasive influence of commercial interests. 'Business' is treated as separate from politics; it occupies its own part of the paper, it has its own programmes. The financial markets are seen as autonomous and strangely unpredictable creatures that rise and fall on whim, and are reported in terms similar to those accorded the weather forecast: rises in the Dow-Jones index are spoken of as if they resembled the movement of high pressure zones.

It is not just business and the financial markets that may be missing from politics. It is everything that appears under a different heading in newspapers or in broadcasting that is excluded: entertainment, lifestyle, travel, sport. These are not – apparently – part of 'politics'. But there is another level to what is excluded. Definitions of politics are primarily about the 'public' realm, the world of political debate and policy. This is not to say, of course, that the private realm is ignored. The media devoted huge effort to reporting allegations about President Clinton's sex life. The media's interest in these matters is, however, primarily occasioned by the view that these private matters are of direct relevance to the performance of the protagonists' public duties. Political coverage is not interested in sexual relations or family decisions *as politics*, but only as they relate to conventional understandings of politics. Such matters are, of course, the dominant concern of much else in the media, and the politics of soaps (and the polity they construct) should not be overlooked.

Explaining Political Stories

It should be clear by now that the reasons for the stories of politics presented by mass media do not lie simply in the values and perceptions of individual journalists and editors, though these no doubt play a part. Rather, they lie in the processes which organize the daily practices of these individuals, the way genres and frames are produced by commercial, professional and political pressures. This is a theme which is developed later in this book, but it is worth just illustrating briefly the kind of factors that shape (and misshape) the portrayal of politics. Sreberny-Mohammadi (1990) argues that the West failed to anticipate the demise of the shah of Iran and the rise to power of Ayatollah Khomeni because of *systemic* features of media organization. The revolution of 1979 was largely unantici-pated by the Western press, who saw the shah's position as unassailable and the Ayatollah as a religious extremist of no great consequence. The popular forces behind the Ayatollah were ig-nored. As Sreberny-Mohammadi observes (ibid.: 300): 'Almost no attention was paid to the living conditions of ordinary rural people, the bulk of Iran's population . . . Almost no attention was paid to the fast and ungainly growth of Tehran, its traffic, pollution, and inflation . . . Almost no attention was paid to human rights abuses.'

The media not only failed to report these things, they also failed to note the disaffection that was being organized around each of these issues, and the predictions of those who thought that a revolution was possible. Instead, the press reported on the stability of the shah's regime. Little serious credibility or legitimacy was given to the Shi'ite opposition, which was seen as 'fanatical' (ibid.: 302). As a result the Western media failed to account for the processes that led to the revolution in 1979, just as ten years later it failed to anticipate the collapse of the Soviet communist bloc. And when the media did try to make sense of the process, they tended to resort to vague and unhelpful metaphors drawn from nature, such as the idea of 'winds of change'.

A similar failure to appreciate the nature of the opposition to the dominant authority is claimed for the way terrorism in Northern Ireland has been reported. Philip Schlesinger and others (1983: 37) argued: 'The coverage of Northern Irish affairs in the British media has tended to simplify violent incidents, to avoid historical background, to concentrate on human-interest stories.' The effect, says Carruthers (2000: 192), is that terrorism then appears as nothing more than 'psychotic behaviour'. Enemies of the state tend to be demonized in ways that reinforce their illegitimacy and deny rationality to their actions. So it was that Saddam Hussein was portrayed as a modern 'Hitler' (ibid.: 42; Said, 2000). These gaps in the media's account of political change and political action are further examples of the way in which generic convention shapes news coverage and organizes a particular perspective on politics.

Conclusion

Media coverage of politics differs between countries and political systems. This simple observation contains some important lessons. The first is the assumption that, however this coverage differs, it is about the same thing: creating a narrative of the political process, bound by the genre conventions, and moulded by the frames, which journalism deploys. Secondly, the picture produced is not a mirror image of the political system, but a creation shaped by political and media processes. It may be true that the mass media are obsessively interested in the minutiae of campaign tactics, or in the private lives of political leaders, but this is not some sort of universal media fact. It is the product of a system of news reporting, itself shaped by commercial, political, professional and other factors.

Why reporters tend to ignore processes and favour personalities is not to be explained by the prejudices of journalists and their editors. The phenomenon is too pervasive to be reduced to the personal foibles of lone actors. Rather, the answer lies in the structure and organization of the media, in the need to deal with events in a limited space and under the demands of tight deadlines. But these constraints are themselves the product of the larger pressures and interests to which the media have to respond. They have to sell their product, and lengthy explorations of the background to events (or refusal to make much of news events) may be very unattractive to readers or viewers.

Covering politics means creating a believable story about actors and agencies deemed to be important. Firstly, it entails convincing those who read, listen or hear news reports that they are getting the truth. Secondly, it involves identifying a particular terrain as 'politics'. As we have seen, these ends are achieved in a variety of ways. Reportage is made credible through the use of various rhetorical devices and, in the process, the media create a mode of address that, in turn, establishes an audience. What is 'covered' by these techniques is itself defined as politics. As a result, certain aspects of the story and other audiences are excluded. Other techniques would result in different coverage. The representing of politics is itself part of a political process.

One feature of that politics, as we have noted, is the way in which the boundaries of the political realm are themselves drawn. The media's coverage of politics is confined to particular pages and programmes, to particular practices and places, but this does not mean that politics itself remains confined within these borders. The next chapter explores the way politics is constituted elsewhere in the media, away from the news pages and the current affairs programmes, in the world of entertainment.

3

It's Just for Fun: Politics and Entertainment

In a candid description of his company, News Corporation, Rupert Murdoch once remarked: 'We are in the entertainment business' (quoted in Shawcross, 1992: 261). With this aside, Murdoch called into question an assumption that lurks in much analysis of the politics of the media, that any such discussion should be confined to news and current affairs. Television schedules and newspaper layouts draw seemingly neat boundaries around what is 'politics' and what is 'entertainment'. These boundaries are marked in a variety of ways: by a tone of voice and a style of writing, by format and layout. As viewers and readers, we are given these clues as to how to respond to what is before us, whether we should take it seriously as information or political debate, or whether we should be amused by it. In thinking about the representation of politics in mass media, there is a strong temptation to reproduce this distinction; to concentrate exclusively upon those areas of mass media which deal with what is formally designated 'politics' (that is, news, documentaries and current affairs). But this formal distinction between what counts as 'politics' and what does not is not as clear as it sometimes seems. Some people watch news as 'entertainment': they admire the clothes of the newsreaders, they mock the pomposity of politicians (Taylor and Mullan, 1986). Equally, they may treat Hollywood movies or television soap operas as serious matters. Think of the earnest concerns of the music fans who populate Nick Hornby's book *High Fidelity* (and its film version); think too of the way in which America's experience of the Vietnam War has been charted in Hollywood movies like *The Green Berets*, *Platoon*, *Apocalypse Now*, *The Deer Hunter* and *First Blood* (Carruthers, 2000: 252–8). Whatever the response of audiences, it is evident that politics does not disappear from the television as the newscaster bids us 'goodnight'. From sports matches to satires, from conspiracy films to chat shows, political values and views are being produced and reproduced, just as they are in news coverage and current affairs.

This idea, that politics is contained and constituted within non-political arenas like entertainment, is, of course, a familiar one. In his study of the world of the American slave, Eugene Genovese (1976) tells how the oppressed workers used songs to articulate their defiance, just as E.P. Thompson (1968) recounts how the emergent industrial working class of eighteenth-century England challenged their masters in song and poetry. In generalizing from such examples, James Scott (1990) talks of the way the 'hidden transcripts' of the poor and the downtrodden have been inscribed within their culture. Seeing popular culture as 'political' remains a feature of the modern world. From the birth of rock'n'roll in the 1950s, through flower power in the 1960s and punk in the 1970s, on into rap and dance culture in the 1980s and 1990s, pop music has been both a vehicle for radical sentiments and the object of conservative anger. Political identities and arguments feature constantly in popular culture.

This chapter is devoted to drawing out more fully the politics contained within these forms of mass entertainment. This is a particularly important task as the boundary between the two realms, between conventional politics and popular culture, becomes ever more porous. Increasingly politicians are drawing upon the language, icons and expertise of popular culture (see Chapter 9), just as news producers appear to rely ever more heavily upon the repertoire of gestures and styles traditionally associated with entertainment.

This latter trend began some time ago. In the early 1990s, James Curran and Colin Sparks (1991: 215) noted that 'less than 20% of the editorial content of the popular national press is devoted to news and comment about political, social and economic affairs'. The rest was given over to human interest stories, celebrity gossip and the like. The same thought is made rather more graphically by Kelvin McKenzie, who as editor of the *Sun* was reported to have said to the paper's political editor: 'Forget all this crap about politicians – who's interested, eh? . . . the readers don't give a fuck about politicians . . . why don't you get a story for them, eh? One with people they've heard of for a change?' (quoted in Marr, 1996: 135). Such thinking lies behind the attention that the press devotes to the activities of film, television, sports and pop stars (and, especially in the UK, to royalty). It also lies behind the tendency to report on the private misdemeanours and sexual adventures of politicians rather than on their public, political deeds. More generally, it is the logic that accounts for the spread of lifestyle and culture sections in newspapers. These topics resurface later (see Chapter 6); here our concern is with the politics contained within the entertainment, because, as Curran and Sparks (1991: 216) observe, 'press entertainment has an important ideological dimension'. Such claims have far-reaching implications. If we want to understand how politics is represented in the mass media, we need to look at the full range of media, and at the full range of broadcasting and newspaper coverage.

Curran and Sparks (ibid.: 228–9) take two stories, each apparently devoid of political content. The first tells how an Irish international footballer punched a taxi driver; the second is about a 39 year-old woman who leaves the family home and has an affair with a 19 year-old man. These are just two of a multitude of different stories which jostle for our attention in our daily papers. These stories do not just tell us anecdotes about our world, they are not just gossip; they are reinforcing wider norms. 'Entertainment features,' write Curran and Sparks (ibid.: 231), 'promote social integration within a "model" of society in which the existence of fundamental differences of interest is tacitly denied and a commonality of interest and identity is regularly affirmed.' The news items may not appear to be about politics, but they each tell a political story, and they serve to reinforce the status quo. Curran and Sparks (ibid.: 231–2) conclude: 'the popular press foregrounds stories that do not pose a challenge or problem to the social order. Its perspective on the world – with its focus on individuals, its "commonsense" frameworks of explanation, its moral rather than its political solutions – also provides tacit support for existing power relations.'

In this chapter, the idea that politics is not confined to the explicitly political is developed by looking at the way in which forms of entertainment construct an account of politics and power relations. We begin by examining forms of entertainment which make the world of politics an explicit object of their amusement, most obviously in the guise of 'satire'. Attention then turns to the portrayal of politics as a source of drama, especially within the genre of conspiracy movies, and after this the discussion moves on to consider the deliberate use of popular culture for political ends, whether for the promotion of a political ideology or for that of a political identity. The argument is not that the politics of entertainment lies only with forms of popular culture that deal explicitly with the political, but that it is embedded in all forms of entertainment.

Political Satire: Politics as Deluded and Corrupt

It is a notable fact, if a not altogether surprising one, that, despite the blurring of the boundaries, politics is treated with considerable reverence in news and current affairs television and in broadsheet papers. Politicians are viewed as legitimate and influential political actors whose views are to be canvassed, cross-examined and recorded. Politicians may complain that they are given insufficient time, or that they are treated unfairly, but these complaints do not undermine the shared assumption that they *should* be accorded respect. This deference is not, however, evident in the treatment accorded to politics in the world of entertainment. There we find cynicism and disdain in roughly equal measure. Politicians are ridiculed for their vanity and pomposity, for their craven pursuit of self-advancement, for their lack of integrity and intelligence. Two obvious examples from television are the deluded mayor in *Spin City* and the slow-witted Jim Hacker of *Yes, Prime Minister*. Satire – the mockery of politics and politicians – is perhaps the most obvious way in which political life becomes part of entertainment.

Satire is defined as the use of art – traditionally, prose and poetry – to make a moral point and 'to attack vice and folly'. Using 'wit and ridicule,' writes Dustin Griffin (1994: 1), satire 'seeks to persuade an audience that something or someone is reprehensible or ridiculous'. The classic period for satire is that occupied by Pope and Swift, the era between 1660 and 1800. What was it that allowed satire to arise then, and what accounts for its subsequent appearance? Why, for example, did both the USA and the UK see a satire 'boom' in the late 1950s and early 1960s?

Satire, Griffin argues, can only work under certain specific conditions. These conditions are not simply produced by a rise in political corruption or venality; nor does satire take its cue from the state of public morality (whether that be one of conservatism or of confusion). In other words, there is no straightforward correlation between public behaviour and political satire. Indeed Griffin suggests that the rise of satire may have had more to do with movements in *literary* trends than in political or social ones. Satire supplies a genre in which literary power or authority can be usurped, a kind of revenge of the children on their parents. The thought is that the origins and character of satire should be looked for in the satirists and their social location as much as in the general features of their political times. Griffin (ibid.: 143) writes that 'the satirist was not a professional writer but a talented gentleman – usually without independent income'. It is notable that many latter-day British satirists, though not their US counterparts, came from a similar background (Carpenter, 2000).

An important related condition is the existence of an audience for satire. Griffin argues that the audience must display a familiarity with the genre, that it must understand the assumptions and tolerate the barbs that constitute satire (just as audiences must understand the generic conventions of news). Typically this means that it will be a 'fairly small, compact and homogenous reading audience . . . located in the cultural and political capital' (Griffin, 1994: 137). Such an audience knows the protagonists and appreciates the in-jokes: without this knowledge and understanding there can be no satire. One final condition that helps explain the rise of satire in the seventeenth and eighteenth centuries was the persistent threat of censorship and the prospect of official disapproval.

Set against this background, it is possible to see parallel conditions foreshadowing the rise of satire in the 1960s, the period known as the 'satire boom'. In Britain, this era saw the birth of the magazine, *Private Eye* and the television show *That Was the Week that Was (TW3)*. In the USA, it saw the rise to prominence of performers like Mort Sahl, Tom Lehrer, Bob Newhart and Lenny Bruce. It is important to understand the conditions and circumstances that produced the politics of satire. We will concentrate first on the British case, before turning to the American example.

In the postwar decades in Britain, censorship was still a feature of both the theatre and the publishing business. The satirists themselves, people like Alan Bennett, John Bird, Peter Cook, John Fortune, Jonathan Miller, Dudley Moore and Richard Ingrams, were gifted gentleman amateurs – products of public (that is, private) school and Oxford and Cambridge Universities – with limited resources. Eleanor Bron and Millicent Martin were among the few women who featured in this generation of satirists. Their targets were largely metropolitan and depended upon inside knowledge of what were later to be called 'the chattering classes'. Modern mass media may have changed the reach and immediacy of satire, but they did not affect its metropolitan smugness.

Satire emerged slowly from cautious and constrained broadcasting institutions. Jokes about politics only gradually became acceptable (Wagg, 1992: 256). A parallel policy could be found among film censors who were equally reluctant to pass films that dealt explicitly with politics (or indeed anything controversial) (Mathews, 1994). In Britain, the idea that politicians were funny, that they deserved mockery rather than deference, emerged in the 1950s with *The Goon Show* (whose main characters were played by Spike Milligan, Peter Sellers and Harry Secombe). The Goons' surreal humour was used to make fun of stuff-shirted aristocrats and bureaucrats. And, as Wagg suggests (1992: 257), *The Goon Show* was to inspire the more overtly political satire of the Cambridge Footlights revues, and of the Oxbridge humour of Cook, Bennett, Miller and Moore in their 1960 hit show, *Beyond the Fringe*. Politics featured prominently as the object of their mocking humour. It was not, however, inspired by any clear ideological position; it was a generalized attack on authority and those who styled themselves as leaders. This spirit animated the television show that represents the highpoint of the 1960s 'satire boom', *That Was the Week that Was*. As one of *TW3*'s team commented: 'We had no campaigning motives, no political beliefs' (quoted in Carpenter, 2000: 240). The idea for the show, according to Andrew Crissell (1991: 149–50), came from the then director general of the BBC, Sir Hugh Greene, but its genesis depended on the intimate links between the BBC and the elite universities who furnished the talent upon which broadcasting relied. Humphrey Carpenter (2000: 26) writes: 'Universities are natural breeding grounds for satire.' *TW3*'s success depended on this talent finding an audience, and, according to Crissell, this was supplied in part by the reforms instituted by the 1944 Education Act. By extending access to education, the Act produced an audience that was politically aware and critical of the old order.

In Robert Hewison's view (1988: 29), there was little in *TW3* that was 'threateningly subversive', but it did succeed in annoying Mary Whitehouse, who has devoted her career to 'cleaning up' television. *TW3*, she said, 'was the epitome of what was wrong with the BBC – anti-authority, anti-religious, anti-patriotism, pro-dirt and poorly produced' (quoted in Hewison, ibid.: 29). She was not alone in being shocked by the programme. When *TW3* criticized the Conservative prime minister, Sir Alec Douglas Home, in October 1963, the BBC received 600 phone calls and 300 letters of complaint (Crissell, 1991: 145).

Satirical sneering at the establishment was to find institutional form in the magazine *Private Eye*. Once again the key figures were products of the elite. Patrick Marnham (1982: 16) describes how 'The editors of *Private Eye* first met at Shrewsbury School', where they developed the skills by running the school magazine and taking part in the debating society. Public school not only provided the connections and opportunities that were to make *Private Eye* possible; it also supplied, as Hewison (1988: 34) notes, the sense of humour: the mockery of authority, the nicknames, the prejudices. These qualities were refined and developed at Oxford University, where the future editors were to reunite, after their period of National Service. These individuals were not only responsible for *Private Eye*, they also wrote for, and performed in, *TW3*.

Private Eye's politics were not animated by any particular partisan allegiance; it attacked anyone who was in power. Indeed it did not just eschew party affiliation, it disdained all commitment. As Wagg comments (1992: 263), 'The *Eye* has seldom, if ever, explicitly endorsed a political cause.' The only exception to this general rule has been the campaigns against corruption led by the socialist writer Paul Foot. But this campaigning was inspired by the general view that anyone who assumes authority or aspires to political office is somehow tainted or malign or vain, and as such is to be suspected.

Wagg (1992) traces a route from 1960s British satire to the internationally popular TV show, *Monty Python's Flying Circus*. Here the surreal humour of the Goons was combined with the iconoclasm of *TW3* and *Beyond The Fringe*. The Monty Python team were, once again, the product of Oxbridge (with the exception of their American animator, Terry Gilliam). They delighted in mocking authority figures by extrapolating wildly the bizarre logic of bureaucracy and petty officialdom.

Subsequently, the surreal satire of the 1950s and 1960s was to be incorporated into mainstream popular entertainment. Satire became a staple of situation comedies, most notably in *Yes, Minister* and *Yes, Prime Minister*. It was also used, albeit benignly, by mimics like Mike Yarwood and Rory Bremner. The sharper, more bitter satire of the earlier era surfaced occasionally in *Not the Nine O'Clock News*, in Rik Mayall's *New Statesman* and in the puppetry of *Spitting Image*. But although the satirical form diversified and established itself in the mainstream, its central joke remained the same. The new shows continued to mock *all* politicians and the business of politics generally. Satire, as Wagg argues (ibid.: 261), 'represent[s] nothing so much as a fear of politics, of confronting social issues, of "taking things too seriously"'. Despite the apparent endorsement of personal liberty in the satire, there were strong elements of homophobia (in *Private Eye*) and misogyny (in *Monty Python*).

This review of satire in Britain since the 1950s highlights several important characteristics of the genre, which, as we have noted, establish a continuity with previous incarnations of satire. The satirists tend to be men, highly educated and middle-class (like their predecessors: 'talented gentlemen'). If anything, the satire of the 1960s was even more a product of privilege. For Wagg it emerged 'from *within* the culture of the dominant social classes' (ibid.: 255; original emphasis). Hewison (1988: 34) makes a similar point: '*Private Eye* shows how the satire movement was a means of ventilating ideas rather than challenging society with some new complete blueprint. The magazine's attacks were very much in Establishment terms . . . The nicknames, the humour, the prejudices meant that this language was only understood within the Establishment, to which *Private Eye* became a parasitic attachment.' The social origins of the satirists established their political perspective.

Because British satire is marked by its disdain for politics, all politicians are seen as arrogant in their claim to know better, and hypocritical in their pretence to *be* better, than their fellow citizens. Compounding this view of politicians is a deep suspicion of the underlying assumptions of politics: the idea that there are ways of changing the course of events. For the satirist, there is no order, only chaos, a chaos that is bred in a world moved only by individual greed and pride. Such a vision sees all attempts to improve society as deluded folly. This is a perspective which is necessarily anti-democratic and reactionary, and it takes sustenance from a moral perspective which treats all deviation from narrowly prescribed norms as ripe for mockery and condemnation. It is this which legitimizes the satirists' relish in reporting adultery and homosexuality, in their assumption that all actions, however worthy, are motivated by either stupidity or self-interest. This view of politics appears to occupy a territory between populism and elitism, and to issue from 'outside' (outside the elite, apart from the 'ordinary people'). This ideology of satire is, however, caught up in the apparent contradiction between the satirists' target and their social origins. Despite their vitriol and mockery, the satirists belong to the established order. But while a commentator like Wagg sees this contradiction as invalidating the political force of the satirist's perspective, Griffin is more willing to recognize a positive political value in satire. Like Wagg, he acknowledges that satire is implicated in the system which it seeks to mock. This, though, does not necessarily destroy its political effect. 'Like all works of literature or art,' Griffin writes (1994: 159), 'satire is inescapably a product of and therefore implicated in the social, political and economic culture that produced it.' Despite this, satire can still exercise political influence by 'unsettling our convictions and occasionally shattering our illusions by asking questions and raising doubts but not providing answers' (ibid.: 160).

This discussion of satire has, so far, focused on Britain, but the points that it makes have a wider application. What the British case study is intended to show is, firstly, that in thinking about the representation of politics in mass media, we need to look beyond the formally designated areas of news and current affairs and towards entertainment. Secondly, that, in looking at entertainment, we need to pay heed to the context which makes possible the satirical treatment of politics. Thirdly, we need to note the processes and expressions that create the audiences and authors of the satire. And finally, we need to look closely at the values and attitudes contained within satire. These general points provide a framework for comparing and comprehending the satirical forms adopted in other times and places. So that it can be seen, for instance, how US television programmes, like *The Rowan and Martin Laugh-in* and

Saturday Night Live, have shared with their British equivalents a mistrust of politicians, even if their view was that politicians are ineffectual rather than malign (Wagg, 1998: 258–63). What is worth noting, too, is that in the 1950s and 1960s US satire was not the product of the privileged WASP elite. Many of the key performers – Mort Sahl and Lenny Bruce, for example – were Jewish. Further- more, US satire emerged, not against the benign torpor of the British establishment, but against the fear and division created by the communist witch hunts (Carpenter, 2000: 99). The British variant of satire can also be contrasted with the more politically radical (and sometimes more dangerous) satire that was circulated in the Soviet Union or Franco's Spain. Satirical writing has flourished in France (*Le canard enchaîné*) and in Germany (*Simpli- cissmus, Pardon, Titanic*).

One of the most distinctive differences in the form taken by satire is revealed in the contrast between British magazine and television satire and the satirical movies of Hollywood. The British form of elite satire stands in stark contrast to the more populist form adopted in the USA, as can be seen in such films as *Being There, Mr Smith Goes to Washington, Dave* and *The American President.* Each of these films works by setting conventional political wisdom or practice against 'the ordinary person' or against 'common sense'. The immorality of politics is established through the regular decencies of daily life. In contrast to Britain's elitist satire, these films mine a vein of populist satire and are the product of a very different political economy, not that of the BBC and Oxbridge, but of Hollywood (Neve, 2000).

Where British satire emanates from elite critiques directed at its own kind, a playing out of ruling class rivalries, US satire (at least in its Hollywood guise) locates its politics in populist democracy. What Hollywood satire does (albeit in different styles and with different degrees of effectiveness) is to pit the intuitions and instincts of the commonplace against the presumptions and preten- sions of the politicians and their aides. Everyday common sense is offered as a counterweight to the elite's out-of-touchness. The political ideals of the American dream act as a counterpoint to the perceived reality. In a classic of the genre, *Mr Smith Goes to Washington* (directed by Frank Capra, 1939), Mr Smith (James Stewart) is given a tour of the Capitol, ending with a scene in which a child reads the Gettysburg Address to an old man. During the course of the film, Smith is educated in the wiles of congressional life and is given a harsh lesson in cynical politics. He rebels against this conventional wisdom and takes a stand against the bosses in the name of the ordinary people. One message of the film, according to Terry Christensen (1987: 47), is that 'good men, supported by the people, can fix things up'.

Forty years later, another Hollywood innocent delivered a similar message about political life in the USA. This time the messenger was Peter Sellers' Chance Gardener in the film, *Being There* (directed by Hal Ashby, 1979). Gardener's banal homilies (taken from his knowledge of horticulture) are treated with veneration by the Washington establishment. It is another version of the Emperor's new clothes, in which the audience is invited to laugh at the delusions and vanities of their leaders.

To the extent that this theme dominates US satire, it represents politics as a kind of populist conservatism (as distinct from the elite conservatism of the British variant). It insists on judging politicians in terms of their proximity to the ordinary citizen. *The American President* (directed by Rob Reiner, 1995) continued the tradition. The political integrity of the president (Michael Douglas) is measured by his willingness to act on the principles that govern private dealings. One of the latest additions to the genre was *Primary Colors* (directed by Mike Nichols, 1998), based on the novel by the journalist Joe Klein. Borrowing heavily from Bill Clinton's 1992 presidential campaign, the film explores the tension between the personal and political, between principle and pragmatism. Despite its jaundiced view of the corrupting effects of politics, compared in the film to the fakery of professional wrestling, it nonetheless retains a sympathy for the political idea of doing best by 'the folks'. All these films, in their different ways, are defined by their evocation of populist solutions to American idealism, and by their opposition to the cynicism and deceit which are presented as the norm of politics. As such they stand in stark contrast to the cynicism of a film like *Wag the Dog* (directed by Barry Levinson, 1997), which, according to Brian Neve (2000: 27), treats the White House as the source of 'total and untraceable' manipulation.

The populist approach of US satire has, like its British equivalent, distinct political implications. In satirizing political leadership, it also forges a populist political identity for its audience. In the words of David Buxton (1990: 26–7): 'the ideology of populism, which was able to address social issues, distributes rights and wrongs while transcending class oppositions . . . The moral stigmatisation of the greed of individual members of the political and economic elite contained inherent melodrama, as well as integrating into the nation everyone who met elementary guidelines.' Satire divides society into two: greedy, corrupt individuals and honourable, ordinary people.

The point of this section has been to draw attention to the satirical representation of politics and to emphasize that the link between politics and mass media does not end with news and current affairs. This section has also asked questions about the conditions under which satire emerges, the forms it takes and the interests it promotes. This involves thinking about not only the blurred boundary between politics and popular culture, but also the form of popular culture's politics. In looking at satire, we have been looking at the politics of humour, at the ways in which jokes are expressions, not just of a sense of humour, but of a set of interests and values. Satire, though, is only one way of representing politics through entertainment. It is one example of a genre in which politics is, by definition, a central concern. It can be usefully compared with another such genre, the conspiracy film.

Politics as Conspiracy

While satire tends to portray politics as the product of incompetence and inadequacy, conspiracy films dwell upon deliberate scheming and deception. What conspiracy films suggest is that behind the appearance of democracy lies a reality in which everything is the result of the corrupt machinations of unaccountable and devious individuals or institutions. This is a world view to be found, for example, in all the James Bond films, in Terry Gilliam's *Brazil,* Robert Redford's *The Candidate* or more recently, in the Wachowski brothers' *The Matrix* and Michael Mann's *The Insider.* In films like *Silkwood* and *The China Syndrome*, the plot is built upon the idea of a conspiracy by the nuclear power industry to pervert the course of justice. In the 1960s, with Len Deighton's *The Ipcress File* or John Le Carré's *The Spy Who Came in from the Cold*, and the countless espionage movies that followed them, the conspiracy was organized by the Soviet bloc and their double agents in the Secret

Service; in later years, domestic governments, and their agents (MI5, CIA and so on) were the conspirators (as in films about Northern Ireland such as *Defence of the Realm* or about Latin America, such as *Salvador*).

The conspirators may vary, they may be power-crazed megalomaniacs, mafia bosses or Soviet spies, but the story is always roughly the same. The plot is driven by the rivalry between subterranean forces and the representatives of liberal democratic integrity. Though an element of paranoia may inform such views of the world, and though this form of storytelling may be very traditional (the Gods conspire in Greek myths), the idea of a conspiracy is not simply a myth. In the 1950s, C. Wright Mills' *The Power Elite* (1956) provided a powerful, if widely challenged, case for the reality of conspiracy. Mills portrayed a world in which all key decisions were taken by a hidden elite. Such a view continues to circulate in the popular imagination: malign forces (bureaucrats, the mafia, global conglomerates) dictate to ordinary citizens and their representatives.

In the 1950s and 1960s, during the cold war, the conspirators were often, either explicitly or by implication, the KGB and their allies. One of the most frequently cited (and arguably one of the best) conspiracy films was *The Manchurian Candidate* (1962), directed by John Frankenheimer, and starring Laurence Harvey and Frank Sinatra. During the Korean War, Harvey is captured and brainwashed by agents of communism. He is programmed to become an assassin, and to respond to commands issued by his mother (Angela Lansbury). The film is a bitter portrait of power and politics, equally withering in its views of communist and liberal democratic politics. Frankenheimer creates an atmosphere of brooding, paranoid fear. No one is to be trusted; everyone works for someone else. A similarly unnerving sense of mistrust inhabits Francis Ford Coppola's *The Conversation* (1976). In this film a private detective, played by Gene Hackman, bugs a couple who, it transpires, murder a businessman (the same businessman who has hired Hackman). It is never quite clear what and who lies behind the events that Hackman witnesses, but the film foreshadows the emergence of a surveillance state in which 'we' are all being monitored by 'them'.

The Conversation is unusual in its portrayal of an anonymous conspiracy. Hollywood prefers to identify the guilty people. In the

1970s, America's own agents became the conspirators. In Alan Pakula's *Parallax View* (1974), it was a shady business corporation; in *Three Days of Condor* (directed by Sidney Pollack, 1976) it was the CIA; and in *All the President's Men* (directed by Alan Pakula, 1976) it was an alliance of the CIA and the White House. Coppola's *Godfather* trilogy can also be read as a variant of the conspiracy movie. Oliver's Stone's *JFK* (1991) is one of the more recent – and all-encompassing – conspiracy films. The assassination of President Kennedy is attributed to the collective conspiratorial efforts of the White House, the CIA, the FBI, the KGB and several others. All these films suggest that the malign forces have to be challenged, but the only hope they offer for this challenge lies with the ingenuity, daring and integrity of the individual. Those formally responsible for fighting evil – the politicians – are in its pay or in some way morally compromised. Popular, collective action rarely appears as a solution. The people tend to be the dupes or victims of the conspiracy. In short, the conspiracy movie frames politics as the struggle between individual integrity, malign forces and popular indifference or impotence. Like satire, its view of politics is a cynical one, in which there is little hope for democracy. Or as Michael Rogin (1987: 245) says of the cold war films, 'They depoliticize politics by blaming subversion on personal influence.' In her detailed analysis of the politics of *The Manchurian Candidate*, Susan Carruthers (1998: 84) reaches a similar conclusion: the film 'refuses to accept the power of political ideas' and 'ultimately eschews politics'.

As with satire, the conspiracy film does not exhaust the ways in which politics is portrayed outside the realms occupied by news and current affairs. It is just another genre, whose conventions give rise to a particular view of politics. This is not to pre-empt the question of whether such portrayals make a difference to political attitudes and actions (see Chapter 4) except to say that, in talking about political influence, it cannot make sense to look only at news and current affairs as the possible sources of such effects. What needs to be stressed is the ways in which certain political ideologies are given space within entertainment, as within other areas of mass media. The conspiracy movie creates a world of hidden manipulators, just as satire creates a world of vain, stupid and corrupt politicians. What they have in common is a mistrust of politics itself. Entertainment, though, is not always the servant of cynicism.

Entertainment as Propaganda

Satire and conspiracy films are examples of the way entertainment articulates a cynical account of the world, but on other occasions entertainment can be used to promote political causes. One such user is the state. Through its powers as censor or sponsor, the state can try to create cultural forms that promote its interests and thwart its enemies. Before the collapse of the Soviet bloc, rock and jazz musicians were imprisoned or banned from playing music which the authorities feared would fuel criticism and dissent, while other, 'approved' forms of music were encouraged (Starr, 1983; Street, 1986). Such practices are not, however, the exclusive preserve of communist regimes. Recent research has revealed how the CIA deliberately created certain cultural forums (the magazine, *Commentary*, for instance) to promote US interests (Stonor Saunders, 2000). The FBI maintained constant surveillance of John Lennon when, following the break-up of the Beatles, he lived in the States. FBI officers sat at his concerts laboriously (and ludicrously) transcribing the words of his songs and his banter at concerts (Wiener, 1984). The birth of rock'n'roll in the 1950s inspired a moral panic and attempts to suppress it, just as did punk music 30 years later. State broadcasters across the globe have refused to play certain records for fear of the sentiments they represent. By no means all this censorship is inspired by a fear of political dissent – much is occasioned by fear of sex and sexuality – but the point is that forms of entertainment are promoted or suppressed because of the kind of attitudes and habits they are deemed to represent or encourage (Cloonan, 1996).

The state's role in controlling and using entertainment has been matched by the desire of musicians and other entertainers to deploy their talents to make political points or to organize political campaigns. There is a long tradition of songwriters who have engaged directly with politics: Woody Guthrie, Bob Dylan, Phil Ochs, Tracy Chapman, Curtis Mayfield, John Lennon, Sting, Joan Baez, Bono, Bob Marley, Bruce Cockburn, Public Enemy, Asian Dub Foundation and Rage Against the Machine. In doing so, they have drawn upon various genres: folk, blues, gospel, country, pop and rap. Pop musicians have also spearheaded political campaigns. Bruce Springsteen toured for Amnesty International; Sting campaigned to save the rainforests; Bob Geldof inspired the Band Aid/Live Aid fund-raising efforts for the victims of famine in Ethiopia; and Bono and U2 have been in the forefront of a recent campaign to end third world debt. The point is not to offer, were it possible, an exhaustive list. Rather it is to highlight the fact that politics can be as explicit a part of entertainment as it is of news and current affairs. Furthermore, this phenomenon does not end just with those cases of entertainment which are deliberately used for political effect (whether by states or by artists).

The Politics of Identity: from Soap Opera to Sport

Soap operas, situation comedies and game shows – the staple diet of TV entertainment – are typically assigned to the category of 'escapism'. This sometimes leads to the presumption that they are devoid of political content, but such an assumption is mistaken: soaps and the like are integral parts of a society's political culture. Hugh O'Donnell (1999: 226) argues that soap operas 'remain unique indexes of the societies in which they are produced'. He goes further, contending that the soaps actively embody the principles of social democracy, through their emphasis on solidarity, on concern for others, on defence of rights and on compromise and cooperation. Others have also invested soap operas with political significance, but drawn less benign conclusions about the character of their politics. Roger Silverstone, for example, points to soap opera's location within suburbia and the politics that flows from this: 'politics in and of the suburb is still, mostly, a domestic politics of self-interest, conformity and exclusion undertaken within political structures which are, mostly, barely recognised, let alone challenged. It is a politics of anxiety. It is a politics of defence' (Silverstone, 1994: 77). It is noticeable, for instance, that a soap opera like *EastEnders* is served only by small, local industries; there is neither sight nor sound of multinational business or global franchises.

These different accounts of the politics of soap operas can themselves be contrasted with the politics of another TV genre, the game show. Gary Whannel (1992) treats the game show as a metaphor for the social order: both are based on a quasi-meritocratic competition between 'ordinary people' for success that is measurable in material terms. *Who Wants to be a Millionaire?* is a typical example of the game show's proto-capitalist ethos. Whannel (ibid.: 200) writes: 'Game shows carry no polemic for a particular form of education, but they do offer a set of messages about the relation between ordinary people, knowledge and material reward.'

One of the key features of popular entertainment is the way it operates across the boundaries between the public and the private, thereby 'domesticating' politics, particularly through its emphasis on the family. For Tania Modleski (1987: 268), the essence of the soap opera, whether *Dallas* or *Neighbours,* lies with its propagation of ideas which assert the value of the family: 'It is important to recognize that soap operas serve to affirm the primacy of the family, not by representing an ideal family, but by portraying a family in constant turmoil and appealing to the spectator to be understanding and tolerant of the many evils that go on within that family.' This domestic focus is what engages the audience and organizes their responses. Christine Geraghty (1992: 139) writes of the role of family life in soaps: 'The audience [is] invited to identify with these families and to see their struggles towards family unity as a realistic reflection of the difficulties which face families in the audience.' The identities constituted through soaps, argues Geraghty, emerge through the dynamics of family relationships. Issues of sexuality – especially of gay men and lesbians – are dramatized through the family rather than through social movements organised around sexual politics.

The negotiation of identity in soaps, and their domestic politics, can be contrasted with the politics of another TV genre, the situation comedy. Mick Bowes (1990: 129) argues that the genre embodies a different ideology from that found in soaps. Where the soap opera has a developing, progressive story line, the situation comedy always returns its characters to the position they found themselves in at the beginning of the show. However, to see situation comedies as necessarily conservative is, argues Bowes, a mistake. He claims that situation comedies can and do deal with real sources of 'social unease', whether they be the constraints of class, of gender or of ethnicity, and that in dealing with these issues, they can treat them in a radical or conservative fashion (ibid.: 129–30). So, as he observes (ibid.: 133), situation comedies may revel in the triumph of the underdog, but set these achievements in 'small and badly run organizations'. Rarely do these power reversals take place in 'multinational corporations'. Humour is, by this account, highly politicized. This point provides schematic illustration in Trevor Griffiths' play *Comedians*, in which different kinds of joke are exposed as representing different points on the political spectrum, from jokes that reinforce negative stereotypes to jokes that try to undermine them. Just as music can be used as a weapon of the oppressed, so too can humour (see Littlewood and Pickering, 1998).

The politics of identity within situation comedy is explored in detail by Herman Gray (1995), who focuses upon the treatment of race within US mass entertainment. Gray is concerned with the ways in which 'blackness' is represented on television. He contends that, while these representations are necessarily contradictory and confused (there is rarely, if ever, a single unambiguous 'message'), they have typically been conservative. Situation comedies about African–American life have focused on individualist upward mobility and middle-class aspiration. 'Although blackness was explicitly marked in theses shows [*The Jeffersons*, *Benson*, *Gimme a Break*],' writes Gray (ibid.: 79), 'it was whiteness and its privileged status that remained unmarked and therefore hegemonic within television's discursive field of racial construction and representation.' In contrast, *The Cosby Show* signalled a new representation of black identity. This occurs because the Huxtable family is given an entirely different social location: 'The Huxtable family is universally appealing . . . largely because it is a middle-class family that happens to be black' (ibid.: 80). With the Huxtables being made successful and rich, 'it was impossible simply to laugh at these characters and make their blackness an object of derision and fascination' (ibid.: 81). This strength was, though, matched by a weakness, a tendency to overlook the 'disparities and constraints' that faced many other African–Americans. What Gray says about the politics of *The Cosby Show* could also be applied to rap, where examples of ambiguous and contradictory political positions are plentiful, as they are in all cultural forms (George, 1999; Rose, 1994). This discussion parallels the earlier examination of the double-edged politics of satire and, while it cannot be resolved simply either, it serves to draw attention to the ways in which mass entertainment gives a forum to political questions of profound importance.

Just as soaps and other genres constitute identities of class, sexuality and race, so another identity and another politics is constituted through sport. Sport has immense cultural (and economic) importance, and as such it assumes considerable political significance. Sport plays a role in the creation of national identities and in marking out the boundaries which serve both to include and to exclude people. The way commentators construct a notion of 'us' and 'them' can reinforce jingoism. Mike Marqusee (1994: 251) suggests that cricket, for example, 'proved the ideal vehicle for the national/imperial ideology which crystallized at the end of the nineteenth century . . . Its transitional nature made it a peculiarly suitable vehicle for "Englishness" in transition from the native heath to world dominance. As it spread through the empire, it provided the English with a global image of themselves.' In a similar vein, the Conservative politician Norman Tebbit devised a 'loyalty test' as part of his opposition to (a liberal) immigration policy. The test was to establish where you 'belonged', and this was revealed in the team you supported at international sporting occasions (ibid.: 137). The other side to this story tells how cricket is deeply implicated in the living out of post-colonial experience and in the assertion of new identities (Winder, 1999).

Sport can also be used to reproduce a gendered division of labour. Sport is presented as 'masculine', as a space which women cannot occupy. Neil Blain and his colleagues (1993: 39) write that 'Sport is portrayed on television as a man's world where women's sport is treated as being of secondary importance. Women in sport are made sense of by continually attaching supposedly feminine connotations to their activity, or portraying them as crypto-men . . . Both in production and content, football on television is a male dominated arena. The sexual division of labour is clearly articulated: men play, women watch.' Both sport itself and the rhetoric attached to it by the media serve to map out identities which in their turn fuel political thought and action.

In thinking about the way in which sport, as with other forms of popular culture, is implicated in the constitution of political ideas and identities, we need always to bear in mind the process by which this culture is itself formed. Like popular music, sport is a major source of revenue and the object of a multimillion-pound empire. Indeed, in the last few years major entertainment and media interests have transformed the availability and the character of sport across the globe. Media moguls like Rupert Murdoch have bought the rights to broadcast football, rugby union, cricket and so on. This in turn has led to the transformation of the sports themselves, altering the access to them, control over them, and the meaning attributed to them. These changes are perhaps most dramatically represented in Murdoch's decision to buy the Los Angeles Dodgers in 1998 as part of his rivalry with Ted Turner of Time Warner who had bought the Atlanta Braves. Sports teams, it seemed, had become part of the means by which media conglomerates waged economic war, and their connection to their fan base and their locality had become more tenuous.

Conclusion

This chapter has looked at the way in which a view of politics is constituted through entertainment. The way people see and experience politics is not confined to news and current affairs. It is part of almost all encounters with mass media. The form taken by politics in entertainment may be different in important ways from the form it assumes in news and current affairs, but this is no reason to ignore it. None of the foregoing discussion is intended to discount or deny the rewards which various forms of entertainment bring us. It is not meant to play down their capacity to give pleasure. Rather, it is to stress that this fun is not 'mindless'; it is not 'just a joke' or mere 'escapism'. It is to suggest that in thinking about the relationship between politics and mass media we need to look beyond the traditional corrals of news and current affairs, and to analyse the ways in which political values and the representation of politics are part of our daily pleasures. The way 'politics' emerges in mass entertainment is through the stories it tells, the jokes it makes and the motives it assumes. Margaret Thatcher once defended a comic who told a tasteless joke at a party rally: 'It is a pity if you cannot regard the remarks of a comedian as being exactly what they are: humour, and that is all' (*New Statesman*, 10 October 1997). This chapter has been an attempt to show that humour, and other forms of entertainment, cannot be dismissed so easily.

4
Media Effects

So far in this book our attention has been focused on media content and its politics. This has meant looking at the arguments about media bias, at the ways in which coverage of news frames a picture of 'politics' and at the political character of popular entertainment. These are clearly important topics in their own right, but for many commentators their interest derives from what is seen as a more fundamental set of issues. To focus on the political content of mass media is to consider only one term in the mass media–politics equation. Content matters only because it has an *effect*. 'Bias' is important precisely because of the further supposition that it blocks or distorts people's capacity to act as citizens, their ability to make political judgements and act upon them. Bias serves relations of power which thwart democracy. In the same way, popular entertainment's engagement with politics matters because of how it shapes political values and images, which in turn influence perception and experience of the world.

It is, of course, widely assumed that mass media exercise influence. It is this thought that lies behind censorship of violent films or pornography, bans on cigarette advertising, complaints about unfair political coverage, and so on. It is this same assumption that underlies public outcries about, for example, the shooting at Columbine High School in Ohio, where in 1999 two students gunned down their colleagues and teachers. Besides the call for a ban on guns, there was a call for more regulation of videos and computer games. In all these cases, the presiding idea is that media products influence media consumers. The first half of this chapter is concerned with research into the political effects of mass media, particularly as it relates to voting behaviour. The second half broadens the discussion by suggesting that 'political effects' should not be analysed in isolation. The tendency to focus on particular media texts (news and current affairs) and particular political effects (voting and agendas) provides too narrow a perspective. Instead, there is a need to look at other texts (the entertainment as well as the information) and at other forms of political expression (identity and emotions), setting both in the context of the mundane habits and practices that organize viewing and reading. This broader perspective is provided by insights generated within cultural studies, and the thrust of this chapter is that political analysis of the media needs to avail itself of the contributions being made in these related disciplines.

To gain a sense of this broader perspective, consider a famous incident from US broadcasting history. In 1938, an American radio station transmitted a report that the Martians had landed. Some listeners panicked, and started to flee their homes. The report was, in fact, part of a dramatisation of H.G. Wells' *War of the Worlds*. The programme's creator, Orson Welles, deliberately gave the broadcast the air of a real event. A seemingly regular music show was interrupted suddenly by an announcer who took the audience straight to a terrified news reporter. The journalist told of an alien landing. Every effort was made to imitate a genuine news broadcast. The programme created a mood of panic and confusion, of momentous events happening – live, on air. *War of the Worlds* evoked the same sense of news unfolding that accompanied the death of Princess Diana, only on this occasion the story was about an invasion from outer space.

That people believed that there had been an alien landing was taken by some observers to be proof of the power of mass media. For them, the panicking listeners were evidence that modern society was a 'mass society' in which new forms of communication could be used to manipulate and control whole populations. Mass society was characterized by the break up of traditional ties of family and community. Small groups and traditional networks were being replaced by the amorphous crowd. Modern production techniques created a plethora of uniform goods for a mass market. The technologies of radio and cinema created vast audiences for the same product. Without the old connections and values in place, the mass could easily be herded like a flock of a sheep. The reaction to *War of the Worlds* was one illustration of this; the idolizing of Hollywood stars was another; and the power of modern tyrants like Stalin and Hitler was a further terrifying instance. Certainly, the idea that people could be persuaded to believe that Martians had landed does seem to confirm the persuasive power of mass media. Such power is not simply a thing of the past, nor is it a problem that afflicts the less educated. In 1998, the New York art world was temporarily persuaded to believe in the existence of an artist who had, in fact, never existed. Critics and connoisseurs feigned knowledge of Nat Tate, an artist who lived only in the imagination of the novelist William Boyd. If people can be persuaded to believe in an alien invasion or a non-existent artist, how much easier is it for them to be persuaded to vote for one party or another, or to adopt one ideology or another?

It is, of course, not this simple. Even the example of *War of the Worlds* is open to other interpretations. When it was broadcast, radio was in its infancy, but it had established itself as an authoritative source of information, and people had begun to rely upon it, to believe it. What they lacked was the sophistication needed to separate the parody from the real thing, to tell irony from authenticity. They trusted the radio, and this trust was encouraged by responsible news reporting and by the absence of spoof broadcasts. Their faith was exploited by Welles, who borrowed the rhetoric of the news to create his drama. To this extent, they had good reason to believe what they heard. Talk about life on Mars had also acquired a certain (temporary) scientific credibility, so the plot was not purely a case of science fiction. Added to this, there was also cause to fear invasion, albeit not from another planet. In 1938, the Nazis were mobilizing in Europe, giving cause to a very real fear, just as others were fuelling anxiety at alleged communist infiltration of America. There was a climate of concern that made US listeners very susceptible to the suggestions contained in *War of the Worlds*. It is this focus on the *context* in which people engage with mass media that adds a further dimension to the way we think about 'influence'.

However we interpret the case of *War of the Worlds*, it should make us wary of quick and easy judgements about the effects of mass media. It may *look* as if films like *Natural Born Killers* inspire real-life murders, or that a right-wing press produces election victories for right-wing candidates, but any such correlation needs to be underpinned by a theory which connects the two, that pushes the correlation beyond coincidence into causality. The films and papers may, after all, *reflect* a set of actions and opinions rather than create them. For every confident claim that there is a clear and proven connection between screen and real violence, there are equally trenchant claims that 'there is no proved causal link between representations of violence on television and violent behaviour' (Cumberbatch, 1998: 272; see also Barker and Petley, 1997). And just as there is this debate about the effects of violence, so there is an equivalent debate about the effects of media on political behaviour. One famous example of this is the suggestion that US media coverage of the Vietnam War was responsible for the decline in popular support for American involvement. This widely-held view is, though, equally widely disputed, by those who challenge both the assumed nature of the coverage (it was not totally negative) and the actual effect of television, when compared with other sources of influence, on audiences' perceptions (Carruthers, 2000: 146–53). Given these arguments about media effects, it is time to look more closely at the ideas and evidence used in discussion of the mass media's political influence.

Seeing is Believing?

If people do not believe what they see, hear and read, it is hard to understand how the contents of mass media can influence them. If we find something incredible or the source untrustworthy, we will tend to discount them – except that this suggestion is not quite as clear-cut as it might appear. When in *Goldeneye* James Bond performs some entirely impossible stunt (like freefalling to catch a pilotless plane, climbing inside and flying to safety), we do not automatically say 'this is ridiculous' and walk out of the movie. We are prepared to believe it: 'prepared' by the context (the habits of cinema going), by our expectations (marketing hype and genre knowledge) and by the skills of the film maker (who shapes the way we watch). 'Belief' is, in this sense, a product of a complex process, a process that does not, it should be emphasized, always succeed. Films fail when the impossible is 'unbelievable'. Credibility is a matter not simply of 'truth' but of the conventions of believability within a particular genre. The conditions for credibility, and the implications of it, differ according to genre. It is important to start, therefore, with the way credibility attaches to newspapers and news broadcasting. It is not just a fact of these forms of communication.

Across different countries and different media the degree of credibility varies. Where in the UK, the broadcaster tends to outstrip the newspaper in the credibility stakes, in France and Germany it is neck-and-neck, the difference being that in France all sources are mistrusted, whereas in Germany they are all generally trusted. As regards the USA, Andrew Kohut and Robert Toth (1998) point to the variations in credibility between television and the press, and between different papers and channels. In doing so, they also note changes over time in the 'believability' of outlets like *USA Today* and *ABC News*. According to one UK survey, programmes about real-life crimes are given greater credence than news programmes, and party political broadcasts are treated with more respect than the *Sun* (Barnett, 1993). Credibility is a product of history, style and practice. It is also a product of prejudice. Ralph Negrine (1994: 2–3) notes that people's belief in what they read or see varies according to the papers they read. Readers of broadsheet papers trust them, and rely less upon television, whereas readers of the tabloid press treat their papers with scepticism and depend upon television for their news. Surveying the literature on media credibility, McQuail (1992: 209–10) reports that it has less to do with 'factuality' of the news and more to do with the perception of 'impartiality' of the *source*. The implication of this is that evidence of bias or framing is not in itself proof of influence. For this we need to look for more direct evidence of 'effects'.

Under the Influence?

Evidence for the political effects of mass media does not refer to a single thing. Researchers distinguish, for example, between effects on voting and effects on perceptions. In other words, it is possible to claim that the media affects the way people think about politics or a politician, without necessarily determining how they vote. Equally, the effects of the press may be different from those of broadcast media. More than this, we need to be aware of the different ways in which perception or voting behaviour can be affected. It may be that our views or our vote are reinforced by our media encounters; alternatively, the media may convert us from our previous disposition, or it may create a new set of preferences

(Harrop, 1986). In short, we need to be wary of simple general-isations about 'influence'. It is important to establish what exactly the influence is over.

In the same vein, we should not expect straightforward answers. A moment's reflection will indicate how technically difficult it is to prove a political effect. The first and most obvious problem is that of separating cause and effect. There is a clear correlation between newspaper reading habits and voting behaviour. For example, a 1991 MORI poll recorded that, in the case of *Daily Telegraph* readers, 71 per cent voted Conservative, whereas only 19 per cent of *Mirror* readers did so. This might seem like proof of the influence of right and left leaning papers on their respective readerships. But, of course, it could equally represent the ways in which left and right-leaning people *choose* their papers. How do we know what people would have done if they had not read one paper rather than another, especially given the many factors which contribute to voting behaviour? How do we distinguish between the effects of the many different sources of influence?

John Curtice and Holli Semetko (1994: 45–6) provide a succinct account of the dilemma that faces any attempt to identify the political effect of the press. If people's votes are the product of their socioeconomic condition, the paper they read makes no difference. Given a survey of people's voting record, reading habits and their socioeconomic background, we can investigate the con-nection between voting and reading practices by controlling for the socioeconomic factors. If there is a correlation, we may be tempted to conclude that the papers exercise an influence over votes. But if we think that votes are not determined by socioeconomic factors alone, if we think people's attitudes to particular issues are important in determining how they vote, it will be necessary to control for these in investigating the connection between the press and voting. The trouble here, as Curtice and Semetko point out (ibid.: 46), is that, while socioeconomic conditions may be inde-pendent of newspaper readership (reading a conservative paper does not make you middle-class), it is quite conceivable that attitudes are a product of the papers people read. If this is so, controlling for attitudes will be to misrepresent the effect of papers. These problems are not insurmountable, however, and we need now to turn to the research conducted on the media's political effects. We look first at research into press influence.

Press and Voting Behaviour

In an early attempt to pin down the effect of the press, Martin Harrop (1986) looked to evidence from the USA, and then compared this with the effect generated by British newspapers. He found that the main impact of the press was on voters' attitudes to certain issues, rather than their appraisal of potential political leaders (for which television was the main source). Learning about the issues does not, however, necessarily cause switches in voting intention. Indeed, the papers' most discernible effect was to reinforce voting intention. There was limited conversion effect, but some evidence of papers creating preferences among the uncommitted.

A similar scepticism about the impact of the press emerged in more recent research by Curtice and Semetko (1994), who asked whether the Conservative-dominated British press influenced the result of the 1992 general election. The idea that it had was widely touted in the aftermath of the election, not least by the *Sun* ('It's the Sun wot won it,' trumpeted its headline). John Major did indeed benefit from a late swing to the Conservative Party, but Curtice and Semetko argue that this was not a product of tabloid influence. They claim that, in fact, support for the Conservatives actually *fell* among readers of Conservative-supporting tabloids. They do, however, detect some longer term effects by which Labour papers strengthen Labour Party support, and Conservative papers do the same for the Conservative Party. The papers also, they suggest, play some part in influencing perceptions of the parties. Again this effect is detected to the advantage of both Labour and Conservative parties.

The authors reach these conclusions by monitoring change in political allegiance over time. Their assumption is that 'If newspapers do influence readers' voting behaviour, then we should find that, other things being equal, people who regularly read a paper come increasingly to share its politics' (ibid.: 46). The evidence they produce does indeed seem to suggest influence over time, but it is also consistent with a hypothesis that today people take more notice of their papers than they did in previous eras. To eliminate this latter possibility, Curtice and Semetko examine the results of panel surveys which map the behaviour of the same people over time. This allows them to separate the consistent readers from those who switch papers. This does reveal some limited newspaper effects over the long term, echoing the conclusion drawn by Harrop. They also echo Harrop's view that the influence does not produce an over-whelming advantage for either the Labour or the Conservative Party. They conclude (ibid.: 56): 'many electors still appear to view newspaper reports (and watch television news) through a partisan filter that enables them to ignore politically uncongenial messages'. What Curtice and Semetko appear to be confirming is the view that, for the most part, people read papers whose prejudices coincide with their own, or that people interpret the news through their own pre-existing value systems. Furthermore, rather than confirming the conventional assumption that a right-wing press confers a huge advantage upon right-wing parties or policies, they suggest that in terms of effect left-wing papers are better at generating support for their parties. Research into media effects on the 1997 British general election (Norris *et al.*, 1999: 168) reached similar conclusions: 'newspapers have but a limited influ-ence on the voting behaviour of their readers'.

In contrast to the minimal effects detected by these researchers, Patrick Dunleavy and Chris Husbands (1985) argue that the press has a decisive influence on political action. Their argument attacks those who suggest that papers do no more than reinforce pre-existing opinions, or that readers select messages according to their prejudices. The authors argue that a right-wing press helps to create a Conservative majority. Their research method entails controlling for those factors which would otherwise, in their view, determine voting habits. They claim to show that the voting habits of manual and non-manual workers vary according to the kind of press they read. Manual workers who read a right-wing press are much more likely to vote for the Conservatives than those who are not subject to the same kind of media exposure (ibid.: 117). In other words, the press to which people are exposed significantly influences their political behaviour. William Miller (1991) reaches similar conclu-sions to Dunleavy and Husbands', but his approach and evidence are rather more nuanced. Miller suggests that media effects must be linked to media use, and that use varies. It varies with the kind of purposes people have in using the media (whether, for example, they use the media for information or for excitement) and it varies with the conditions in which the media are used (the social back-ground of users). He also separates two sites of influence: percep-tions (how politics seems) and attitudes (what people think about what they see). In his study, Miller argues that press effects were discernible in attitudes and in voting behaviour (ibid.: 164, 176, 192–3). To this extent, he confirms the claims made by Dunleavy and Husbands, but his picture attributes less power to the press. For him, partisanship is the main determinant.

The attempt to discover the political influence of the press results, it seems, in two very different conclusions. On the one side are those who see it as having a modest long-term effect of limited political consequence. On the other side are those who see it as making a decisive difference to one political side. These conclusions are partly a consequence of different attempts to solve a methodological problem; it is also, though, the consequence of different theories of voting behaviour and larger questions about the relationship between structure and agency. Dunleavy and Husbands' 'radical' model of voting behaviour sees political preferences and interests as the product of the combined effects of social location and ideology. They argue that there is no intrinsic or necessary reason why certain practices are associated with one or other side of the political divide: why, for example, 'home ownership' is any more a Conservative or a Labour position. These questions are settled by the management of perceptions, by the creation of a political 'common sense'. A key device in this process is the media. From within this general framework, mass media inevitably assume a greater importance than they do in frameworks that explain voting behaviour in terms of issue preference or party identification. In other words, the argument about media influence involves larger questions of social and political theory as well as the specifics of elections and media coverage.

Television and Voting Behaviour

While there is active disagreement about the impact of the press, there is almost a consensus about television. There is a general reluctance to attribute substantial influence to television. There is an acknowledgement that, while it is 'informative', it is 'much less persuasive' than the press (Miller, 1991: 198–9). Pippa Norris (1996) cites evidence from the British Election Survey which demonstrates a very limited 'TV effect'. Those who watched a lot of television were marginally more likely to vote for Labour or Conservative parties than those who watched little television. One possible reason for the limited effect is the lack of concentrated attention given to the medium. Despite television's obsession with election campaigns and their saturation coverage of them, viewers appear to take little notice. In 1983, viewers watched about 14 per cent of the available coverage (Wober *et al.*, 1986). Without being quite so disparaging of television's role, Miller (1991) argues that it may be a useful source of information, but that it is not much help in forming judgements. This is partly because television, constrained by electoral law and broadcasting regulations, tends to endorse the messages presented by the parties. Television coverage reinforces ideas of party unity and popularity. And where it does seek to address matters of controversy, these do not always coincide with the voters' own agendas, and hence may be ignored. The exception to this are the 'marginal groups' who are more susceptible to media agendas (ibid.: 137). Overall the view seems to be that television is, at least in comparison with the press, a less potent source of influence, certainly where voting behaviour is concerned. Interestingly though, recent experimental research (Norris *et al.*, 1999) has shown how people can be influenced by what they see: differently skewed news reports give different questionnaire responses. However, it has not been possible to demonstrate decisively the same effect in the 'real world' of election campaigns.

So far the focus has been upon the effect of television and newspapers on voting behaviour. The evidence suggests that this is a field in which there is a great deal of uncertainty and contradiction, and that the only reasonable response is to treat all claims with scepticism. Indeed there is much to say for taking such a position, but it should not be linked automatically with the assumption that the media have no influence over politics. After all, voting behaviour is only one aspect of the political process, and we have already noted the other potential sites of influence: attitudes, information, perceptions and agendas. Over two decades ago, Colin Seymour-Ure warned of the danger of concentrating on voting behaviour to the exclusion of all else. He wrote (1974: 43): "Do the mass media change votes?" Many studies have sought to answer that question: indeed it must be the most studied question of all about the political role of the media. But . . . such an interpretation is not just unnecessarily narrow but even dangerous. For it invites the easy and superficial conclusion that if media exposure by the electorate, studied over a few weeks or months, has changed

few votes, "the effect of media on the election" is insignificant.'
While researchers have responded to such warnings by looking for
long-term changes in voting behaviour, their concern has remained
largely with the vote as the key political act. But this leaves a great
deal of politics unexamined. At the level of the individual, it leaves
untouched other aspects of their relationship to politics. It tends to
elide perceptions and action when, in fact, perceptions of politics,
while influenced by media coverage, may not translate directly into
a decision to vote for a leader or party (Miller, 1991).

More radically, Roderick Hart (1999) argues that television's key
political influence comes in the way it shapes viewers' *feelings*, the
way they respond emotionally to politics. This echoes Robert
Entman's (1997: 78) complaint that, insofar as journalists 'reduce
policy argument to a clash of simple slogans', they produce only
'emotional responses' in their audience, and not 'rational thought'.
The result, according to Entman, is almost always to discourage
informed active citizenship. In the same vein, Roderick Hart (1999:
2) argues that television's natural mode of cynical disdain 'dictates
the attitudes people take in the voting booth'. These claims are, it
should be noted, grounded not in the kind of attitudinal surveys
conducted by Miller and others, but in an account of the way
television has transformed the public sphere and framed political
discourse. What is important, for our purposes, is the suggestion
that the effects of media extend beyond the voting decision to the
perceptions of, and feelings about, the political process. This, after
all, is what was implicit in the case, made earlier, for extending the
notion of the political text beyond news and current affairs to
satire, movies and sport, arenas where feelings are shaped and
articulated. At the same time, it is necessary to be wary of Hart's
argument, which rests upon the idea that 'television' is the source of
the changes being observed. Television is no one thing, taking one
form, and run by one group of people. To this extent, 'television's
effects' have to be disaggregated. Part of the purpose of this is to
ask questions about the relationship between the content of mass
media and political action. How is it that the media have any kind
of effect?

One way of answering this is to think of media as supplying
information, where information is seen as a key political resource
which shapes people's capacity to act. Ignorance, by this account, is

not bliss; it is powerlessness. The distribution of political information is part of the mechanism by which power operates. This is the lesson of many studies of power, particular those that have been influenced by Steven Lukes' (1974) notion of the third dimension of power, the power to shape what people say they want. Such preferences are seen as the product of advertising and other forms of propaganda; that is, the management of information. Control over information is a key attribute of power and the media may be instrumental in determining access to it. Norris (1996), for example, records how different types of media generate different levels of citizen awareness. There appears to be a direct correlation between people's knowledge of politics and their media resources. It is not, however, just a matter of how information is distributed. It is about the capacity to convert and use that information, to turn it into knowledge and insight. The capacity to make sense of information is a skill, and this too is distributed unevenly. A way of modelling this capacity is to think in terms of 'cultural capital', the ability to acquire, handle and articulate information (Bourdieu, 1986; 1991).

But there is another form of capital involved: 'social capital', which describes the distribution of trust and cohesion. Robert Putnam (1995) claims that television has been responsible for a catastrophic decline in social capital, measured in terms of the networks, norms and trust that allow people to act together. Television, he argues, has been an agent of 'social disengagement', where newspapers are agents of civic responsibility. Putnam writes (ibid.: 678): 'each hour spent viewing television is associated with less social trust and less group membership, while each hour reading a newspaper is associated with more'. Television represents for Putnam a form of privatized leisure, and within this private world mistrust flourishes. It also deadens people's capacity to operate as citizens. 'Just as television privatizes our leisure time,' he writes (2000: 229), 'it also privatizes our civic activity, dampening our interactions with one another even more than it dampens individual political activities.' For Putnam (ibid.: 236–7) watching television *causes* civic disengagement.

Putnam's bleak conclusion is questioned by those, such as Norris (1996) who argue that the US data tell a different story: that television can enhance engagement, and that disengagement is to be explained by factors other than television, just as others (P. Hart,

1999) have found that the evidence for disengagement varies between national contexts. Nonetheless, the value of these arguments is the way in which they highlight the link between the capacity to act politically and the distribution of cultural resources. They shift the discussion away from a crude notion of effects to one about media's place in the circulation of power. In terms of individual political actors, this power is to be measured by people's capacity to understand, and to judge critically, political processes and the trustworthiness of others.

The question then becomes how the capacity to make such judgements is shaped and organized. It is in this context that the work of those who have explored the effect of framing on political attitudes becomes valuable (for example, Capella and Jamieson, 1997; Gamson and Modigliani, 1989; Gilliam *et al.*, 1996). Shanto Iyengar (1991), for example, shows how in establishing particular frames, news reports shape people's political judgements of responsibility and blame. In later work on public perceptions of crime, Gilliam and others (1996: 19) show how 'racial imagery in the news triggered fear of crime and a willingness to hold black people responsible for crime'. Such responses were the result of 'a mere three-second exposure'. Similar experimental results can be found in work on risk analysis, where small changes in the wording of a policy issue can produce entirely different responses. In defiance of the general scepticism about television's power to influence, but equally cautious of Putnam's style of pessimism, Iyengar asserts confidently (1991: 2): 'the only area of political life in which the impact of television has been empirically established is public opinion'. Gamson and Modigliani (1989: 2) offer a rather more hesitant version, suggesting that media discourse and public opinion 'interact'. Either way, news coverage is seen to shape public agendas and form political preferences. Iyengar wants to build upon this assumption by looking at the way television's framing of an issue influences the allocation of responsibility: who is to be blamed or praised. This research rests upon the idea that 'the primary factor that determines opinions concerning political issues is the assignment of responsibility for the issue in question' (Iyengar, 1991: 8). Where people are ignorant of, or distant from, a topic, media representations are crucial to the assignment of responsibility.

In assessing effects, Iyengar argues that coverage can be divided between that which frames news in 'episodic' terms (a concern with individual cases and events) and that which frames it 'thematically' (background and trends). It is the former which is the dominant media mode (ibid.: 14–16). The research involves subjecting groups of viewers to different types of coverage and then assessing their perceptions afterwards. These perceptions were measured firstly by reference to the 'causal' links made: how events were explained (why crime or terrorism occurred) and secondly by reference to 'treatment': how crime or terrorism was to be curbed. On the basis of a series of such experiments, Iyengar (ibid.: 67) concluded, inter alia, 'that network news stories can affect how people attribute responsibility for poverty and racial inequality'; and furthermore that episodic framing of poverty led people to see responsibility as lying with the individual, and thematic framing as attributing responsibility to society. For Iyengar, such results demonstrate how the media affect public opinion. So Iyengar joins Putnam in claiming influence for television, but differs from him in the type of influence he identifies, but both – in the way they shift focus away from voting – provide a contrast to those who insist upon television's minimal effects.

Cultural Studies and Media Influence

So far this chapter has, in thinking about media influence, pushed the case for looking more at the way media shape powers and capacities, rather than have 'effects'. What has been overlooked, though, is the context in which people relate to media. Neither large scale surveys nor detailed experiments replicate or reflect the actual experience of viewing and reading. There is, however, a considerable literature on routine audience practices, much of it deriving from cultural studies. This final part of the chapter draws attention to the possible implications of this work (and the arguments it has provoked) for future study of media's political influence. What cultural studies offers is not only an extended notion of politics, one that applies to the pleasures of popular culture, but also a way of understanding how culture is consumed and what skills and resources are applied to this consumption.

The first and most obvious debt to cultural studies comes through the idea that the source of any potential political influence cannot be confined to news and current affairs. Within cultural studies, it is widely assumed, if not always argued, that popular culture is political (see Chapter 3). This insight is less often acknowledged within political science accounts of media influence. There are exceptions (for example, Wober *et al.*, 1986) which argue for the need to recognize the full range of programmes to which people are subject. It makes no sense, they suggest, to isolate the political programmes. It is rare, though, to find this injunction being acted upon, although there is one notable exception in Richard Merelman's (1991) comparative study of the relationship between popular culture and political culture. But even Merelman does not reflect at length on the ways in which popular culture and political culture are connected.

One aspect of this connection emerges in the way that political texts (whether deriving from news or from entertainment) are interpreted. The literature on the political effects tends to treat political information as unambiguous (hence the tendency to label papers as left-wing or right-wing) and the readers or viewers as consumers of it. But if the messages are confused and contradictory, and if the audience's or readership's reception is complex, then the idea of 'influence' needs to be rethought. Certainly, the idea that the media produce a stimulus to which action and attitudes are a response is frequently called into question. The media do not produce 'messages' which are received and appropriated; rather they circulate symbols and signs which require interpretation. Gamson and Modigliani (1989: 2), for example, talk of 'individuals making sense . . . Individuals bring their own life histories, social interactions, and psychological predispositions to the process of constructing meaning.' Entman (1993: 53) talks of the 'interaction of texts and receivers'. This move owes much to arguments advanced by Stuart Hall (1980: 131) who suggests that the emphasis on interpretation 'promises to dispel the lingering behaviourism which has dogged mass-media research for so long, especially in its approach to content. Though we know the television programme is not a behavioural input, like a tap on the knee, it seems to have been almost impossible for traditional researchers to conceptualize the communicative process without lapsing into one or other variant of lowflying behaviourism.' Seeing texts as containing many different and contradictory meanings makes it impossible to think of them as operating in a stimuli-response mode. Media content has to be understood as part of a process where 'common sense' is constructed through the readings which can be made of the images and language of the text. Meaning is not to be read simply as neutral information supporting a particular world view. It also engages feelings and passions, a desire to preserve or change the world, a judgement of the way others behave and think. What is being appealed to is the idea that culture 'structures feelings' (R. Hart, 1999; Williams, 1981). This is a very different idea from that of 'influencing a vote'. Recent writing on social movements, for example, draws on this dimension of culture's role to show that popular music organises the sentiments which tie people to a cause (Eyerman and Jamison, 1998).

A further twist needs to be given to the story of media influence. Just as texts are rarely unambiguous, so interpretation of them is contingent. The conditions under which they are read or seen affects the way they are understood. Audiences do not simply 'exist', nor do they just act as media devouring machines. They have to be created and organized, and in the process they assume a particular relationship to what they see, hear and read. Public service broadcasters construct the audience as a 'public', as citizens with a variety of tastes and interests but united by a common interest that is captured in the injunction that they be 'informed, educated and entertained'. Commercial television, by contrast, constructs its viewers as 'consumers'. Programmes are designed to deliver a particular market to a set of products. The construction of audiences takes place, as we saw in Chapter 2, through the use of scheduling, modes of address, camera angles and so on. The implication of this approach is that the potential for, and the character of, media influence will vary with the type of audience. The other dimension to reception that cultural studies has emphasized is *how* people watch, listen or read. Viewing is a social process marked by a number of factors, including material circumstances, social class and gender. Observers note, for example, that men tend to take possession of the remote control; they also record that not only do women and men watch different things, they watch differently. Men tend to adopt a silent individualism, while women talk during programmes, turning viewing into a social event (Ang, 1996; Morley, 1986). The evidence about reading practices is less substantial. But even here it is possible to cast doubts on the image of the reader as a solitary actor ingesting text, from page to brain (Radway, 1991). Nicholas Garnham, however, warns that, whatever the value of ethnographic insights into reading and viewing habits, it is important to begin with material circumstances: 'patterns of media consumption remain closely tied to income levels' (Garnham, 2000: 116).

In drawing attention to the conditions under which audiences operate, and the role of the media in creating their audiences, we have moved further from any neat connection between what is seen and its effects. The detailed observations of audience behaviour and circumstance, which emphasize the socioeconomic context of reception, distract attention from what is being watched to what is going on around the television set. This shift of focus makes it hard to talk of television or the press as manipulative, or as producing profound changes of attitude. The text (and the 'biases' it contains) becomes peripheral, only one factor in the business of reception.

It would appear that this shift of focus makes talk of 'influence' and 'effects' irrelevant. There is no longer a chain that links the text (and its 'messages') to a group of attentive readers or viewers. Instead we have a set of contingent features, the particular configuration of which invests in any given text different meanings. This, however, is not the only conclusion that can be drawn. The simple models of media cause and effect may no longer work, but it does not follow that we should assume that the media make no difference to the way people think and act. It just means that understanding this process involves recognizing the complexity of people's relationship to the many texts they receive, the ambiguity of them, and the conditions under which they are interpreted. As Garnham (ibid.: 125) writes: 'media messages do affect our understanding of the world, but how we interpret or act upon that understanding is related to social position and experience'. We need to acknowledge the ways in which other (equally ambiguous or contradictory) information and experience shape watching or reading. Writing of his own experience of research into television audiences, David Morley (1992: 77) argues: 'Media communications have to fit into the fields of personal and institutional communications in which the people who constitute the audience also exist as voters, housewives, workers, shoppers, parents, roller-skaters or soldiers. All those institutions, all those roles within which people are situated, produce messages which intersect with those of the media.'

This conclusion derives, as John Corner (1995: 135) points out, from the fact that 'any "transmission" of meaning [is] a good deal more complicated than a straight linear flow'. Meaning is not a transparent feature of a text, but the product of interpretation by readers and viewers. To this extent, influence is intimately linked, for Corner, to interpretation, and interpretation is itself a product of contingent features of the experience of encountering a text. The immediate implication of this is that meanings are neither stable nor consistent, and for this reason, as Corner notes, 'the very fact of *variation* works against the idea of any uniform influence' (ibid.: 137, original emphasis). This is not, though, to rule out the idea of influence. After all, television producers work with the very purpose of creating effects – shock, laughter, sympathy – and audiences respond to them. The point is to acknowledge the *interaction* between the two, between the text and the cues it contains, and the audience's reading of, and response to, them.

The move away from a crude account of media 'effects' means that there needs to be careful reading of media texts to reveal the way politics is framed or encoded. The media are viewed, not as having a distinct influence which allows particular texts to generate particular effects, but rather as putting a set of ideas into circulation, as normalizing a set of practices and attitudes, representing 'common sense'. This common sense is not without its contradictions and ambiguities. It does not contain a straightforward message; it is open to competing interpretations, but it sets limits: it does not admit of an infinite range of readings. The capacity to deduce other interpretations is, however, dependent upon the capacity of the audience to offer an alternative account. Newspapers and broadcasters supply a resource – ideas, responses – out of which people fashion their view of the world. These resources are not supplied by news and current affairs alone; they are contained in the story lines of soap operas, in chart hits and Hollywood movies. Indeed, they are not confined to mass media. How these resources are used depends on the experiences and conditions that are brought to their reception.

This approach will not yield the patterns of influence which some political scientists seek. It will not be possible to attribute responsibility for electoral outcomes to particular papers. Nonetheless, it will be possible to provide a more coherent picture of the way in which the mass media feature in the daily routine of political thought and action. The mass media may not be the cause of votes and attitudes, but they may be responsible for legitimating the operation of particular agendas and ideologies.

The media (and especially television) exercise influence through the way in which they create a picture of the world that is 'realistic', and as such alters our perceptions and actions in relation to it. This influence may take many forms. As Corner argues (ibid.: 141), the situation is not one in which a choice exists between 'influence or no influence'. Rather it is a matter of assessing the type of influence. For Corner, the crucial determinant of political influence, given the interpretative–interactive construction of meaning, is the 'knowledge environment': the resources we bring to bear on interpretation. Corner's position represents, as does Hall's, a rejection of strictly behaviourist notions of cause and effect, and a rejection of dominant ideology versions (with their focus on the monolithic power of the text). Emphasis on interpretation argues for a recognition that texts have to be made to produce meaning, and influence is, therefore, an altogether more complex idea. This does not mean that it cannot be researched, as Greg Philo shows in *Seeing and Believing* (1990). Philo illustrates how different groups responded to news about the British miners' strike of 1984–5. Depending on their own knowledge, political positions and personal experience, viewers sometimes accepted and sometimes rejected the picture being offered by the media. Such evidence encourages talk of 'media influence', but shifts the focus away from the texts to the conditions of their circulation and reception.

This brings us to the final contribution made by cultural studies: the notion that people bring skills and resources to the judging of political texts. We have already referred to this earlier, in connection with Putnam's and Bourdieu's work, but it is important to reiterate the point that viewers and readers differ in their capacity to make sense and make judgements, of political texts. This is part of Philo's argument, but it is also made explicit in the work of others (see, for example, Garnham, 2000: 138–64) who locate value judgement in the social conditions of the judges. Taste is a product of a social process, and people's capacity to exercise judgement is a product of the distribution of cultural capital: the authority given to certain voices and interests. Mapping this power is crucial to understanding people's ability to use, and to be used by, media representations of politics. In short, talk of media influence needs to run in conjunction with thoughts of powers and capacities.

Conclusion

The implication of the cultural studies approach to audiences is that the notion of effect becomes less central. In particular, it argues that we should place more emphasis on the conditions under which readers read and viewers view. This is not just an argument for more ethnographical study of audiences, and of the way they watch and interpret television. It requires a recognition of the wider context of those interpretations. As Philo writes (1990: 5): 'Messages are situated within political and cultural assumptions about what is normal and acceptable within the society. In news production, these include beliefs about hierarchies of access, about who has the right to speak, what are the key political institutions, and what is "acceptable" behaviour.' This translates into an argument for looking more closely at the interests which organize the conditions of consumption. It means examining the political economy of the press and television, to see what interests are shaping the access and opportunities available to audiences, to see who and what is creating those audiences in the first place. Or, as McQuail (1994: 381) argues, it is evident that the media have power, and then the key questions become who gets to use or benefit from it, and who has access to media power? Even if questions remain about the nature of media power, McQuail is surely right that any analysis of it must refer to the political economy of mass media. To assume that media have no effect would be, in Garnham's (2000: 109) more trenchant formulation, to let 'media producers off the hook of any responsibility for what they do'.

PART TWO

THE POLITICAL ECONOMY OF MASS MEDIA

5

State Control and State Propaganda

In some countries, a journalist's main anxiety is that his or her expenses claim will be queried. But in other parts of the world, journalists have much more to fear. In Algeria, journalists risk their freedom and even their lives to report stories. 'Journalists are assassinated or face government censorship,' according to Omar Belhouchet, an Algerian reporter, 'that's why we can't live a normal life' (*The Guardian*, 20 July 1998). Under Algeria's military leadership, newspapers have been raided and banned, and editors and journalists have been imprisoned. Others have been assassinated by the Islamic opposition. In China, a journalist spent more than a decade in prison for advocating democracy. In Iran, a cartoonist was jailed for a year for insulting the Ayatollah Khomeni. In Syria, the journalist Nizar Nayouf was sentenced to 10 years' hard labour, during which he was hung by his feet and denied access to daylight. Even in more liberal regimes, states take people to court for the unlawful disclosure of secrets or for refusing to reveal sources. Incidents of this kind are routinely documented by the journal, *Index on Censorship*.

These cases suggest that what is reported in papers and on television is not simply a product either of 'events in the world' or of the perceptions and prejudices of individual journalists. Although events and prejudices certainly play their part, equally important are the *conditions* and *constraints* under which journalism is practised. Journalists have to be trained and provided with resources; they depend on access to technology and communications infrastructures, and their work is mediated by a vast array of other professions and processes that produce and distribute their words. This chapter focuses on one of the key actors involved in this mediation process: the state. How does the state shape the way politics is covered by mass media?

103

It is often supposed that, in a global economy, the state occupies only a peripheral role, and that what is true for economic policy is also true for communications policy. But though the state's role and relationships may have altered with changes in the political economy of the culture industries, it still remains a crucial player. Through the imposition of regulations and the granting of liberties, through law and policy, governments and their agents influence journalism. The threat of imprisonment is just one example of the measures available to the state in its attempt to shape the politics of mass media. Every state exercises some control over what journalists write or broadcast. Sometimes this control is blatant, sometimes it operates in more subtle ways, but all forms of public communication are subject to an element of regulation. For a while it may have seemed that the internet was an exception to this rule (and indeed there are those who continue to subscribe to this view), but there is increasing evidence of regulation here too. The German government has, for instance, been putting pressure on internet service providers to ban anti-semitic sites. The Burmese, Indonesian and Malaysian governments have all tried – with varying degrees of success – to control political use of the internet. The Chinese authorities made it illegal to publish 'state secrets' on the web: 'the catch is that no one in China can be entirely sure what is and what is not a secret' (*The Guardian*, 27 January 2000). Elsewhere, the libel law has been used to close defamatory sites; and incitement laws have been used against anti-abortion sites. With time, we can expect there to be more regulation of the web. After all, like every other form of public communication, the net is a part product of government policy (Winston, 1998: 321ff). The internet may offer more freedom, more open access than other media forms, but this is quite different from saying that it is, or will remain, unregulated.

Censorship

Censorship is the most obvious form of state control. In Afghanistan, the Taliban, the Islamic militia who control most of the country, have banned all television, cinema and music. The Algerian government owns many of the printing houses upon which the press relies, and it uses claims over 'the non-payment of debts' as a reason for refusing to print particular editions or papers (*Index on*

Censorship, 4, 1999: 128). In Zimbabwe, the law provides for a maximum of seven years' imprisonment for the publication of 'false' stories that are likely to cause 'fear, alarm or despondency among the public' (*Index on Censorship*, 2, 1999: 21–3). The prospect of state censorship fuelled speculation on the future of Hong Kong, following its reversion to China. This was how one Hong Kong paper imagined the future: 'being a member of the media in post-1997 Hong Kong will be like facing a gunman with his finger on the trigger. Although the gunman guarantees not to fire, the threat is overwhelming' (*Eastern Express*, quoted in Datta-Ray, 1996: 32). Typically, we think of censorship as involving this kind of direct intervention and, typically, such controls are associated with non-liberal regimes. Such expectations accord with Czechoslovakia's announcement of an end to its censorship laws in 1990, following the collapse of the Soviet bloc (Budge *et al.*, 1998: 148); they also fit the fact that, in 1981, Kuwait instituted a system of pre-publication censorship for its newspapers. But censorship can take a variety of forms, and it does not necessarily require direct intervention. A year after introducing its system of censorship, Kuwait repealed it. This did not, however, result in a free press. State censorship was replaced by a system of self-censorship which required journalists to abide by a strict code of conduct that included the injunctions not to 'damage national unity' or 'spread rumours'. Breaking the code could lead to suspension of a paper (Reporters Sans Frontières, 1993: 177–8).

Self-censorship may indeed prove to be a much more common, pervasive and insidious form of control. Recent reports about the Hong Kong media suggest that the Chinese presence has induced widespread self-censorship among journalists. Chin-Chuan Lee (1998: 57) describes 'the press's tendency to dodge political controversy, the hiring of pro-China staff to assume responsible posts, the shift of editorial tone in line with Beijing's policy, the redesign of space to reduce the paper's political overtone, the firing of high-risk contributors, the dissemination of writing guidelines on "sensitive" stories, and the placing of sensitive stories in obscure positions'. All of this has been achieved without direct intervention. While the Chinese government amended the Hong Kong Basic Law to include rules which could become the basis of censorship, these rules have not been acted upon. Rather changes in press behaviour have been achieved through a culture of fear, and through a system

of rewards (and implicit punishments) run by the Chinese authorities. By favouring certain media outlets and certain individuals
with gifts, honours and prized information, the Chinese government has created an incentive structure that results in self-censorship rather than externally imposed censorship (ibid.: 58). Chinese
censorship works through the routine practice of journalism: 'the
orthodox theory of journalism overtly defines the role of the media
as the mouthpiece, or the "throat and tongue", of the party and the
people' (Bin, 1998: 45).

China is not the only country to induce self-censorship. Writing
of his experience of editing newspapers in the Middle East, Jihad
Khazen (1999: 87) observes: 'The most prevalent form of censorship
is self-censorship. Sitting at my desk, I feel at times that I'm not so
much covering the news as covering it up.'

Censorship is not confined to non-liberal states, even where the
constitution appears to prohibit it. President Yeltsin was known to
sack directors of national television stations, despite laws protecting
freedom of speech (Budge *et al.*, 1998: 151). In France, during the
Fourth Republic, the state broadcasting station (RTF) shared its
premises with the secretary of state for information, and RTF
journalists were obliged to follow the instructions issued by the
ministry (Chalaby, 1998: 45). In the UK, coverage of Northern
Ireland and of terrorism has been strictly regulated. Examples range
from a ban on the voices of Sinn Fein representatives, to changes to
plays and documentaries about the province, to the banning of pop
songs (Curtis and Jempson, 1993). State security has also provided
an excuse for censorship. A BBC television programme on the
Zircon satellite was banned by the government on grounds of
national security, and the broadcaster's offices were raided by the
Special Branch, who removed the offending tapes.

To say that all states censor is not the same as saying that all
states censor equally. They do not. There are systems in which
censorship is institutionalized and extensive, others where it is more
covert or ad hoc. There are, after all, many ways to censor. Spain
long maintained, even after the fall of Franco, the practice of
running a two-minute delay on all live broadcasts, so that offending
moments could be excised (Vilches, 1996: 180). States ruled by
single parties, for instance, tend to impose tighter restrictions than
those in which opposition is legitimate. And some states, like the
USA, formally deny the right to censorship in their constitution,

but, as critics of the regime argue (Herman and Chomsky, 1988), this still leaves open the possibility of de facto censorship through the way in which commercial and other interests affect what counts as 'news' and what priorities are accorded it. Gerald Sussman (1997: 136) lists examples of what he sees as US censorship: the failure to cover the testing of biological weapons and the failure to report CIA involvement in Haiti. While these arguments have some polemical force, it may not be helpful to see them as a form of state *censorship*. They may more accurately be seen as a system of corporate *information management*. It is not a question of the state preventing publication of facts and images, rather of organizing the publication of other facts and images. Secrecy is a key mechanism in this process.

Secrecy

Rather than censor what threatens to become public, liberal states prefer to keep things secret, so that the issue of a ban never arises. If journalists know nothing, there is little need to censor them. As with censorship, countries vary in the way they police secrecy. The USA enshrines freedom of speech in its constitution and operates a practice of freedom of information. In theory at least, this means that journalists can have access to any official information, provided that it does not breach national security. Press freedom in France is also protected in French law, allowing infringement only in cases of defamation, bad taste and national security. The UK, by contrast, has traditionally operated a highly secretive system, and reforms have been very slow in coming (Cockerell *et al.*, 1985; Ponting, 1986). Where in the USA, the principle is that information be made available, unless there is a good reason for it not to be released, in the UK, the presumption favours secrecy. Even as the UK has begun to change the law on secrecy, partly as a result of incorporating the European Convention on Human Rights, it has remained cautious. The new freedom of information legislation still grants power of veto to ministers who wish to deny access to 'sensitive' information. Besides, there are other restrictions which maintain the regime of secrecy. The restrictions on access to information are compounded, for instance, by the oath of office taken by ministers in which they are bound to 'keep secret all

matters committed and revealed' to them (Hennessy, 1990: 344ff).
The law on secrecy was even used to prevent publication of the
costs of refurbishing the Lord Chancellor's official residence, on
which he was estimated to have spent £650 000 (*The Guardian*, 16
February 1998). During the Falklands War, the Ministry of
Defence tried to impose a virtual news blackout by refusing to
make any information available. As David Morrison and Howard
Tumber note (1988: 200–201): 'The Ministry seemed to believe that
if the press and television were told nothing, nothing could be
published.' Instead, the journalists were forced to speculate.

British civil servants are bound by the Official Secrets Acts (1911,
1920 and 1989) which make it an offence to release documents into
the public domain, even documents which are not themselves
officially labelled 'secret'. Attempts to do so have led to prosecu-
tions, albeit not always successful ones, and to imprisonment. The
civil servant Clive Ponting was prosecuted, but found not guilty, of
passing on Ministry of Defence documents about the Falklands
War to an MP. Sarah Tisdall, also a civil servant, was prosecuted
and imprisoned for leaking details of the movement of Cruise
missiles to *The Guardian* (Ponting, 1985; see also Leigh, 1979).
An aura of secrecy is further induced by other conventions and
restrictions, one example of which is the Osmotherly Rules. These
are the rules that guide release of information by civil servants to
Parliament. Such information, it might be supposed, is crucial to
the operation of democratic accountability and to the ideal of
parliamentary sovereignty. However, the purpose of the Osmotherly Rules is to 'avoid the risk of publication', a phrase
redolent of the British political establishment's attitude to the media
(Hennessy, 1990: 361–3).

The UK system may be peculiarly restrictive, but all states,
however liberal, have secrecy laws and other regulatory devices
which are designed to restrict the flow of information. Australia,
like Britain, operates a rule which prevents access to cabinet papers,
the documentary evidence of government decisions and discussions,
for 30 years (Schultz, 1998: 82). There is, though, a clear difference
between states that operate on a principle of freedom of information and those that do not. In the absence of a freedom of
information act, journalists have no right to government material;
they also enjoy little legal protection if they wish to keep secret
sources of such information. Britain may represent a particular

(and extreme) version of the use of secrecy, but all bureaucratic structures manage information in pursuit of their institutional self-interest. In the struggle for power and influence, information is a key resource, and the value of information is inversely proportional to the extent of its dissemination. Insider trading in the stock market is an obvious example of the way exclusive information yields high rewards. What is true for financial information is also true for political information.

Propaganda

Denying access to information is one device available to a state intent upon managing media coverage, but this same power can also be used to distribute it selectively. Susan Carruthers (2000: 31) records how, in both world wars, 'British propagandists recognized that their task of courting American journalists would be easier if more lenient arrangements for censorship were introduced, and if reporters were provided with easier access to the physical location of dramatic stories.' The corollary of secrecy and censorship is propaganda. The selective release of information is intended to protect and promote the interests of those in power. It is a relatively small step from this to the blatant promotion of the state and its leaders. Clearly, where the state owns and controls press and broadcasting institutions, it can use them for propaganda purposes, as was the case in Nazi Germany and the Soviet Union, and more recently in Yugoslavia under President Milosevic. All pretence at journalistic independence is essentially hollow. But even in liberal regimes it is possible to identify state attempts to use mass media for propaganda. Indeed, the argument of Herman and Chomsky's (1988) *Manufacturing Consent* is that all 'news' in the USA (and by implication, elsewhere) is primarily propaganda.

Certainly, political parties and interest groups engage legitimately in propaganda exercises. Such practice, however, is conducted at their expense, by buying advertising space, for example. (Advertising also provides governments with a weapon against the media. In 1984, the New South Wales government switched its classified advertising, worth $1.5 million a year, from one newspaper group to another, in response to some unfavourable coverage (Schultz, 1998: 81–2)). Equally, governments may seek to make the journalist's job as easy as possible by providing press releases. It is, though, important to retain a distinction between public relations as propaganda and the direct use of the press or television. In liberal regimes, it is assumed that parties do not buy or dictate a particular coverage. They are in the business of persuading or pressuring journalists to provide a certain type of copy; whether journalists deliver or not is a function of the relationship, but this relationship does not have the command structure of propaganda. There is a recognized (if negotiable) division of labour. It is when that division breaks down that the malign form of propaganda emerges – an accusation that has been levelled at Spanish governments who have used their power over television to get favourable coverage (Rospir, 1996: 195).

There are times when even direct propaganda is regarded as a legitimate part of the state's activities, and the media's compliance equally acceptable. The state is expected to issue propaganda for the public interest: to warn against the risk of AIDS, or to notify its citizens of other risks to health and safety, just as it is entitled to inform them of their rights and entitlements. This type of propaganda is legitimate in a way that promoting the party political interests of those who manage the state is not.

While these distinctions may appear to be relatively clear, they are inevitably the source of contradiction and confusion. Even in principle, it is hard to separate the public interest from the interest of the ruling party. This problem is compounded in practice by the difficulty in discerning what message any given advertisement conveys. When the Thatcher government was promoting the sale of shares in privatized utilities (a policy which had the formal backing of Parliament and the voters), the images it used – green fields, neat housing estates – were interpreted by some critics as advertising more than the new schemes; it was selling the impression of a prosperous country ruled over by a dynamic government. Similarly, when the same government introduced its new policy for helping the unemployed, it was noted by critics that the television advertisements were shown during programmes that were not typically watched by their target audience (that is, the unemployed). Rather, they were being viewed by opinion shapers and by the government's natural political allies (Scammell, 1995: 221). When the Major government launched its Parent's Charter to outline the rights of children at school, it sent the document to 20 million homes at a cost of £3 million, despite the fact that fewer than five million homes had children of the relevant school age. In other words, the advertisements were seen as a form of political propaganda rather than political information.

Direct use of state communications systems is but one way in which governments seek to represent themselves in a favourable light. Just as state systems can hide information so they can choose how to present it. They, after all, have unique access to the relevant data, and they can use their comparative advantage to release them in ways that serve their interest. In the same way, they can use 'tame' journalists as the conduits through which they release information. The relationship can work in reverse: journalists can supply the authorities with information. In the former East Germany, and elsewhere within the Soviet bloc, journalists acted as agents for the secret police, passing on information about dissidents. Mostly though, the state selects its leaks in order to generate particular kinds of copy for particular constituencies.

Governments engage in 'tactical leaking'. Unfavourable or 'bad' news can be made to coincide with other, more distracting, events. The Thatcher government released details on the length of hospital waiting lists (the worst for four years) on Budget Day when the media's attention was elsewhere. *The Guardian* (26 February 1996) published a Ministry of Defence memo which discussed the best tactics for releasing news of the MoD's decision to maintain its ban on homosexuals serving in the armed forces. The memo read: 'An in-depth one-to-one briefing on a background basis for the selected journalist for a feature-type piece to appear on the day of publication. Despite (or because of) its generally hostile editorial stance, such a piece, emphasising the depth and breadth etc of the report would probably have most effect in "The Guardian".' These techniques are not peculiar to Britain. Rodney Tiffen (1989: 97) describes very similar techniques being used in Australia; as he notes: 'Leaks and briefings are indispensable in contemporary politics.'

The Gulf War saw extensive use of the media for propaganda purposes (Bennett and Paletz, 1994; Carruthers, 2000: 39–43). In the USA, the government deliberately promoted the idea that Saddam Hussein was a tyrant ('the butcher of Baghdad') and that protecting Kuwait was a cause worth fighting for. Stories about Iraqi atrocities were actively circulated and reproduced. Gerald Sussman (1997: 156–7) claims that the US media were used to distort the truth, misleading the public over the destruction of Scud missiles and suggesting that the USA had bombed a biological weapons plant, when in fact it was an infant milk factory.

Whatever the techniques, it is clear that war pushes or leads states ever closer to using media for propaganda purposes. During the Falklands War, the UK Ministry of Defence's almost total control over information was used to feed false rumours and erroneous speculations. The ministry encouraged (or did not discourage) the spread of disinformation in order to disrupt Argentine intelligence, albeit at the cost of misleading the domestic audience (Morrison and Tumber, 1988: 205). The British government also managed coverage through the access it granted to film crews. The BBC journalist, Brian Hanrahan complained that 'My particular team, which was one of two television cameras there, were forbidden to leave ship for about ten days or so after the landings [on the Falklands] had taken place' (Harris, 1983: 130).

The distribution of information to journalists is, of course, not typically conducted in an ad hoc manner. It is part of a system, one aim of which is to maintain control. Carruthers (2000: 44) argues that coverage of government is less a direct result of the state publicity machine, and owes more to 'long-standing news routines'. In a similar vein, Sussman (1997: 256) talks of the network of institutions – 'embassies, CIA, the White House, cabinet-level department, Congress' – all of whom feed 'tips, stories and contacts to the press on a regular basis'. One embodiment of this is the 'press release'. Research conducted in the 1990s suggested that about half the articles appearing in Australian newspapers 'began as press releases' (Schultz, 1998: 56). The impact of these public relations (PR) devices is increased by dexterous use of timing: close to the deadline, 'which reduces the chances for gathering reactions and gaining critical perspective' (Tiffen, 1989: 76). Other countries are little different (Franklin, 1994). Another device for controlling content is the press conference. While they serve the same purpose, press conferences (or their equivalent) can be organized in different ways and under different rules. In the USA, there is the open, public, televised presidential press conference attended by the White House correspondents. The British version of this system is represented by the lobby, a club which allows privileged access to government information to a select group of journalists, giving them 'exclusive' copy, and at the same time allowing the politically powerful to give a particular spin to the coverage (Cockerell *et al.*, 1985; N. Jones, 1995). The British closed lobby is in direct contrast to the open system which operates in America, where briefings are on record and on camera. But even the UK system is not fixed and immutable. The lobby has operated differently according to the practice of different press officers, from the ruthless Bernard Ingham to the accommodating Gus O'Donnell, and from him to the abrasive Alistair Campbell who, as Tony Blair's press officer, has put lobby briefings on the record.

Another form of institutionalized information management is the media centre (like the Millbank complex in London). This is a sophisticated machine for promoting contact between politicians and journalists. Such organizations give institutional existence to the informal networks which manage the supply and distribution of political information. This world of contacts and casual links provides mechanisms by which political information (however (un)reliable or released for whatever motives) is to be circulated. It is this system which, one British minister complained, was being used by her colleagues to smear her reputation: 'I am amazed by how many vultures there are out there trying to pick my eyes out' (Clare Short, quoted in *The Guardian*, 13 February 1998).

A final technique used by government to control coverage is the application of pressure through close scrutiny of, and complaints about, media reporting. Governments, whether in the USA, the UK or Australia, bombard journalists with complaints about their copy, creating an atmosphere of anxious self-criticism (Franklin, 1994; Kurtz, 1998; Schultz, 1998). Such techniques are the product of increasingly close surveillance of broadcasting, but they are combined with threats about access, regulation and funding. There is in all this an eerie echo of the techniques used by the Chinese government to create the conditions for self-censorship in Hong Kong.

Regulation

So far attention has been upon what might be described as the obvious elements of state information management. Secrecy, censorship and media management represent the capacity of states to supply or suppress the flow of information available to the media. But underlying these capacities is the wider context of rules governing the use of information and the daily practices of media organizations themselves. The state is part of a *system* of news production; indeed, the state is a key part of the process by which the very idea of 'information' itself is constituted. The state establishes the forms of communication that operate within its territorial borders and regulates the content of those systems. At one level, the state is responsible (albeit in conjunction with other states) for creating the market value of knowledge. Copyright laws construct a regime of rights around certain forms of knowledge or expression. However laudable or worthy such laws are, they nonetheless act to constitute certain kinds of 'information' as a commodity to be traded, and to set limits to its use. To give one example of this, French law recognizes the right of individuals to claim copyright to their own image. This means that papers, in printing a picture of someone without their permission, may be in breach of copyright law. At a more mundane level, copyright law regulates the printing or reprinting of articles and documents, as well as designating the rights of control over those artefacts. Who owns the copyright to, say, private letters is not a trivial matter where the media wishes, for whatever reason, to publish that correspondence.

The laws of libel can be viewed in a similar way. US politicians, for example, are afforded much less protection from libel than are UK politicians. Another form of state regulation comes through privacy legislation. The ostensible purpose of such laws is to mark out areas which are protected from journalistic intrusion. The debate that such legislation engenders divides people between those who value the protection of privacy and those who see such protection as restricting excessively the possibility of investigative journalism. Also there are those who see privacy laws as working disproportionately to the advantage of the rich and powerful, rather than protecting the rights of those without access to, or resources for, legal redress.

These laws of copyright and libel, like many other such laws, help to construct the resources with which the mass media deal. The state, in this sense, constitutes the raw material which the mass media then process. But the state does more than produce the crude oil of publication, it also helps create the refinery. All forms of mass communication exist within a framework of law, regulation and rights. The ability to broadcast, to make money from the transmission of programmes, is a consequence of rules governing the use of the available electromagnetic spectrum, of cable networks and of geostationary orbits in space. Though the rules vary between countries and between media, what is involved is a matter of degree, not of kind. The conditions and the context of communication are established by the state, and by subnational and supranational authorities.

There are, of course, those who argue that the state is an increasingly marginal political actor. Two general processes are held to be responsible for this marginalization. The first is the process of technological change which, it is sometimes suggested, occurs independently of political control. States *adapt* to technical change; they do not lead it. Change is the result of an inexorable logic; one that takes us from the telegraph to the radio to the television to the satellite to digital broadcasting and beyond. The second, and related, process that appears to marginalize the state is globalization. The emergence of transnational conglomerates, empires built upon the exploitation of new technology, appears to create power bases which exist above the realm of any one nation state. As with technical change, it seems that states must adapt to the new sources of power, and in adapting they lose any claim to sovereignty and autonomy. Nonetheless, states still remain significant actors, and to the extent that they wield power, they shape the character and content of mass communication within their borders. The rhetoric of globalization and of technological determinism leads to the false conclusion that all systems of broadcasting and publishing are the same. There are, however, considerable variations, and these are marked politically – not just by the difference between democracy and dictatorship, but by differences within these general types. How any mass media represent politics is itself a product of a regulatory regime.

Broadcasting took off in the USA and the UK at roughly the same time, using similar technologies, but they evolved very different systems. The explanation for this lies in the way the state, in conjunction with the commercial interests organized around broadcasting, reached an accommodation about the way the airwaves were to be managed. The UK established a system of public broadcasting in which access to the airwaves was restricted, while the USA favoured a commercial system which allowed for the fuller use of the radio spectrum (Lewis and Booth, 1989). This is not to deny the existence of public broadcasting in the USA, nor to play down its contribution (*Sesame Street* being one of its most famous products), but its role and profile is very different from that of its European equivalents (Ledbetter, 1997).

These divergent approaches in themselves created different opportunities for state intervention and control. The relatively unregulated US system involved less government control. The UK system did not lead automatically to state control, but it did establish greater scope for influence from the political centre. The BBC was expected to provide a formal independence from the state through a system of public service broadcasting. This was to be achieved through a funding and management structure that allowed for political accountability without direct political control. Funding was provided through a licence fee charged to all those who owned a wireless (and subsequently a television set). The fee was set by government, but the responsibility for spending it was left to the board of governors, who were appointed by the government but who were answerable to Parliament.

Clearly such a system invites the suspicion that it provides an opportunity for political control, whatever the formal barriers. The state has, after all, a number of weapons in its hand. The government can threaten to withhold the right to broadcast, although this is a threat which is more theoretical than actual: the political costs are likely to be too high. More modestly, the government has the power to affect the funding, by refusing to increase the licence fee. It can also ensure that fellow-travellers and sympathizers are appointed to the board of governors. All of these weapons have been deployed, at least according to some commentators (Franklin, 1994). But it would be wrong to see the power as absolute. The weapons may not work; they are primarily negative and indirect. The power of governors is limited, and government appointees do not always deliver government policy. The threat to cut funding may not be credible, and it is notable that the Thatcher government, who waged a sustained campaign against the BBC, chose to remove uncertainty about the licence fee by linking it to inflation. There are, in any case, severe risks entailed in trying to interfere. It is not necessarily in the interests of government to be seen to be interfering in an institution that is thought of as independent and trustworthy. The government can gain more from the coverage of a respected institution than it can from one that is thought to be operating at its beck and call.

This system of public service broadcasting was also taken up by other European countries, and continued to operate into the 1970s, before giving way in a number of cases to the impact of deregulation and commercialization. The principles supporting a public service system were roughly similar: a belief in the need to recognize the diversity of a nation while providing a forum for the creation of a 'public', relatively free from the dominance of the state or commercial interests. These shared principles, however, issued in different regulatory regimes and developed at different rates. When it was proposed to President de Gaulle in the 1960s that he might consider granting French state television greater autonomy, along the lines of the BBC, de Gaulle refused because he regarded television as his weapon against the press (Chalaby, 1998: 46). Only gradually and reluctantly did he relax his grasp. The French example was not untypical. As Ian Budge and his colleagues (1998: 143) point out, there was considerable European variation in the degree of party political involvement and state financing. In the case of Germany, political responsibility was devolved to the regions rather than being held by the federal government. And in countries where there are long-standing cleavages marked by political, religious or linguistic differences (as in Belgium), these divisions may be acknowledged in the control of broadcasting. Just as the creation of public service broadcasting depends on government initiative, so too does its maintenance. Changes in state policy in Italy and Spain has made public service broadcasting vulnerable. These political shifts have also been accompanied by technological ones – satellite, cable, digital – which have limited the ability of states to determine what is transmitted within their territorial borders. They have also been powered by a shift in ideology: neoliberal governments have made a virtue of deregulation and of creating new commercial opportunities around broadcasting, which have in turn created the conditions for the rise of the new media conglomerates run by men like Rupert Murdoch and Silvio Berlusconi.

Just as there is no automatic transition from public service theory to practice, there is no necessary relationship between the system of broadcasting regulation and that for the press. Each has its own history, each is the product of competing interests and ideologies. It is true, however, that single party systems, or systems that, for whatever reason, wish to limit the expression of dissent, will tend to aim to regulate press and broadcasting (Sparks, 1998). Equally, there are liberal–pluralist systems (ones in which the market plays a significant part) where both broadcasting and the press are subject to very light regulation. But there are versions of each of these general systems that combine regulation and non-regulation, so that a regulated broadcasting system may run in parallel with an unregulated press. This can be the case even where the same principle is being appealed to, whether it is freedom of speech or freedom of expression. Each can be used to justify regulation *and* its absence.

That a 'free press' means the right of individuals to own newspapers is the result of ideology and interest. Freedom of the press was defined *against* state ownership and regulation. It was the right to set up a paper. Freedom in broadcasting, by contrast, was defined through the idea that the radio spectrum was a scarce public good whose use had to be protected for the good of all. Broadcasting is generally more heavily regulated than the press. This seems to be true whatever the type of political system, although, of course, the degree of latitude allowed in each case varies considerably (McQuail, 1992: 107).

It is not a necessary condition of a liberal democracy that the press be left largely to its own devices. This may be the case in the UK and the USA, but in Italy the state has, since the early 1980s, introduced major press legislation. Under the press laws of 1981 and 1987, the state has restricted the spread of monopoly press ownership, it has subsidized technological change and it has instituted a press regulator (Garante per l'editoria) (Sartori, 1996: 140). As Carlo Sartori notes (ibid.: 140–41), it is hard to establish the direct consequence of these laws and to make claims for their success, but they do serve to illustrate alternative models for press–state relations. Systems of media regulation appeal to principles which define the regimes that they inhabit. The most obvious contrast is between liberal democratic states and state control systems. The latter are typified by the Soviet bloc and by Singapore, both of which have operated strict regulatory codes.

The implication of these different structures of broadcasting and press regulation, and the techniques and devices deployed within them, is that changes in media policy will have a number of important consequences. These will be most obviously identified in the way politics is represented, and by the relationship between audiences/readers, journalists and political interests.

In the UK, the Broadcasting Act 1990 altered the terms on which television companies acquired the right to broadcast to the different regions into which the country is divided. Previously the franchise was in the gift of the Independent Broadcasting Authority. The allocation of franchises was conducted in relative obscurity and there were few changes in the distribution of the franchise. With the new act, the IBA was replaced by the Independent Television Commission. The ITC was given a less interventionist role, and the allocation of the franchises was set out in statute. Essentially, the award was to go to the highest bidder, provided that they demonstrated economic soundness and (in a late amendment) that they met a quality threshold. The money that was bid went to the Treasury, so the companies had to generate sufficient income both to pay for their franchise and to finance the operations of the company. The result was that the ITC had, in almost all cases, to award franchises to companies that had bid the most. Sometimes companies won with relatively small sums where there were no rivals; others had to pay a great deal; and occasionally the company with the second highest bid won the franchise, because the highest bidder was deemed to fail the financial or quality test. The bidding system had obvious consequences for broadcasters. To make money, they needed to do two things: either to cut production costs or to increase advertising revenue. Both worked against peak-time coverage of politics. Even where franchises are not distributed on this basis, as in the USA, the dependence on advertising squeezes news and current affairs, limiting its time, resources and quality (Hallin, 2000). James Ledbetter (1997: 15) notes how public broadcasting in the USA 'relies more and more on corporate underwriting and an array of commercial gimmicks for its funding; its programming approach . . . will look more and more like those of commercial networks'. Despite formal requirements to serve the public interest, a feature of almost all forms of broadcasting, the effect of commercialism and competition is felt on the coverage of politics. Rival broadcasters who schedule movies against your newscasts, or newscasts that gain audiences unattractive to your potential advertisers, put huge pressure on companies. In Britain, this is evident in the wrangling over the time of the nightly news bulletin, with the BBC and ITV each shifting the news away from peak hours. In the USA, Daniel Hallin (2000: 224) reports how, in the 1980s, 'networks were moving to eliminate the special status of news divisions, supervising them more closely and forcing them, like any other division of the corporation, to contribute to the bottom line'. Their ability to do this was partly a result of a relaxing of the Federal Communications Commission's interpretation of the 'public interest'. Insofar as news and political coverage matter to the operation of democratic societies, media policy can have profound consequences for those polities, and for the identities, interests and knowledge of those who inhabit them. To give some flavour of the ways in which media policy touches on these larger issues, it helps to consider some of the dilemmas with which states, especially in Europe, have to deal.

Parochialism or Cultural Imperialism?

A presiding concern of many European states, for instance, is the threat of 'Americanization'. But not all states are equally vulnerable, nor do they share the perception of the 'danger'. Other states place greater emphasis on issues of balance and diversity, particularly where they administer multilingual or multicultural communities. As the Euromedia Research Group observe: 'Government has been the one type of actor which has felt most responsible for securing diversity in broadcast content' (1986: 140). Achieving this aim depends upon the structure of broadcasting: where it is the responsibility of a monopoly, diversity is a matter of regulations; where broadcasting is deregulated, diversity is managed through the allocation of franchises.

Quantity or Quality?

As we have seen, it is sometimes suggested that the US system of commercially driven, lightly-regulated broadcasting diminishes, among other things, the quality of political discourse and news coverage generally. Raymond Gallagher (1989) is fiercely critical of this view. He argues that, in fact, not only do Americans get more choice of news, they also get more news. In particular, the quantity and quality of local news far outstrips that offered by the heavily regulated British broadcasting system (ibid.: 187–9). Certainly, local news attracts higher viewing figures than national, network news, but whether it still represents a *better* service is open to dispute. Hallin (2000: 224) contends, for instance, that the high ratings for local programmes dictate news values, with the result that politics is shunted into the wings, and sensation and human interest hold centre stage.

Industry or Culture?

An important dimension to the process of state regulation is the heading under which broadcasting is allocated, whether it is treated as a sub-division of industrial policy or of cultural policy. The implications and incentives are different in each case. States that emphasize the cultural dimension of broadcasting are more likely to seek to manage or regulate the content, whereas those driven by industrial concerns will focus more on consumer access and commercial possibilities, and pay less attention to content.

Political Differences?

Do the ideological sympathies of liberal democratic governments matter to the form of regulation and its political effects? While it is true that governments of different political hues act differently, it does not follow that these differences are the product of their politics. Arguably, the political structures within which they operate are more important. For example, Germany's federal structure imposes constraints on politicians' room for manoeuvre, but this does not prevent major reforms following a change of government (Humphreys, 1988).

Regulating the Future

Underlying the story of state regulation of media is a story of changing communications technologies. Systems of regulation have emerged to create and to manage new forms of communication, just as things like the Highway Code emerged to regulate the use of roads and cars. This chapter has concentrated on the established media of radio, television and the press, but, of course, these have to be taken in conjunction with emerging media forms, and particularly the internet. Chapter 10 is devoted to the political implications of the net, but it is important here to note that this technology raises a new set of regulatory concerns.

As we noted at the beginning of this chapter, there are those who have argued that the net defies regulation, that it provides a truly free public space. Certainly, there are cases where the net and satellite TV have forced breaches in state censorship; there is one television station that broadcasts in Afghanistan in defiance of the Taliban authorities (*The Guardian*, 1 November 2000; Khazen, 1999: 89–91). It is true that the character of internet-based communications makes it less susceptible to state management. In this respect the net is like the telephone, whose use is also hard to regulate, save by restrictions on access. Phone tapping, though practically possible, is a very cumbersome and costly form of monitoring. It is notable that the Soviet Union deliberately held back the spread of the telephone precisely because it was a technology that dissidents could use with relative impunity. Nonetheless there are states who, despite the technical problems, are intent upon regulating the net. China is one obvious example, where access to websites is restricted; despite this, major displays of public dissent have been orchestrated through the web. In Singapore too, the government has attempted to regulate use of the internet. And as a demonstration of the technical possibility of this, a local netservice, SingNet, asked the Ministry of Home Affairs to help it scan the computers of 200 000 subscribers, in the wake of virus damage (*Index on Censorship*, 3, 1999: 150–54). The fact that such an endeavour was feasible is indicative of the potential for state regulation.

In the West, the source of regulation is different, but no less significant for democracy. The commercialization of the web, its potential for massive investment and profit, has inevitably changed the constellation of interests which determine its use. Whatever the source of control, it is evident that the internet is a further site of regulatory activity, and one which needs to be incorporated into the overall account of the state's relationship to forms of communication.

Conclusion

This chapter began by looking at the techniques and devices that states use to manage the news and those who report it. It has ended by looking more broadly at the systems through which states regulate the general practice of mass media. It would be wrong, however, to see these two dimensions of the state as discrete and separate entities. They are closely interlinked. The system of regulation frames the context in which the state deploys its various techniques. The priorities that the state adopts and the form of regulation (or deregulation) it presides over will affect profoundly the character and content of mass media. In particular, it will shape political discourse and the constitution of the political realm.

In looking at the state, we have, though, to be aware that it is not the only important actor in establishing the mass media infrastructure. The state is itself in constant contact with the corporations and conglomerates that own the papers and cable systems and terrestrial stations that constitute the modern mass media. That is why we need to turn now to these pieces of the mass media's political jigsaw.

Before we do so, it is worth acknowledging the context in which the discussion has operated so far. The focus has been on nation states operating within the territorial boundaries. What is missing from the picture is, of course, the impact of globalization both on nation states themselves and on the systems of communication with which they are dealing. The globalization of media is dealt with in Chapter 8, but it is necessary here to make the point that, while globalizing tendencies may alter the issues and agencies with which states deal, those states remain key components of the management of globalization. The death of the nation state has been exaggerated. Or rather, it is wrong to assume that it has been written out of the script before looking more closely at the routines and activities for which it remains responsible, and which vary between states despite globalization. It is clear that globalization is a vitally important dimension of the shifting dynamics of mass media politics, but the attention given to it should not lead us to overlook the part played by states and their agencies.

6

Conglomerate Control: Media Moguls and Media Power

For some commentators, the impact of the state on the politics of the mass media is nothing compared to that wielded by the new breed of media moguls. Men like Rupert Murdoch, Ted Turner, Conrad Black and Silvio Berlusconi, and companies like News Corporation and Bertelsmann, often appear to be the main players in the emerging media order. Black's company, Hollinger International, at one stage owned 400 publications worldwide, with a total circulation of 11 million, until he sold some of his Canadian titles for $2.3 billion (*The Times*, 6 October 2000). And with the appearance of multimedia conglomerates, like the one that links Time Warner and America Online, which is estimated to be worth $120 billion, it seems that indeed the media world is now populated by a new breed of corporate superpowers. Their impact on political life is most dramatically represented by Berlusconi's rise to power in Italy on the back of his television and press empire. 'Berlusconi's control of the media resources,' writes Paul Statham (1996: 88), 'has transformed the basis for political communication in Italy.' Berlusconi may have fallen from political grace, but his spell as prime minister foreshadowed a new conjunction of the media and the political order.

Certainly, the Berlusconis and Rupert Murdochs of this world have assumed iconic status. Andrew Marr (1996: 200), himself editor of *The Independent* until he fell out with his own corporate bosses, described Murdoch like this: 'He smashes unions. He squares politicians. He keeps in with national leaders, offering them news-space and book contracts (Thatcher and the Speaker

124

of the House of Representatives Newt Gingrich, to name but two). Everywhere, he lobbies. He attacks regulations that threaten him, or tries to sidestep them . . . The world stands gaping; national leaders feel a little smaller in his presence. His power is intense.' Murdoch's impact on the outside world, it seems, is matched by his power over those who work for him. One of his ex-editors wrote: 'When you work for Rupert Murdoch you do not work for a company chairman or chief executive: you work for a Sun King. You are not a director or manager or an editor: you are a courtier at the court of the Sun King' (Neil, 1997: 197).

This chapter explores the idea that media owners wield power within and through their corporations. It does this first by looking at the nature of these empires, and at their owners and their interests; we then turn to consider their ability to influence politics through these media outlets and the restraints upon such ambitions. This discussion is not just a matter of identifying examples of influence. It has crucial implications for the debate about democracy and mass media. Put crudely, if particular individuals are seen to have power, or if certain partial interests predominate in the way the media operate, and if these individuals and interests control political discourse to the detriment of other legitimate goals and values, then this may constitute the basis for constricting their rights to own such outlets or to have influence over them. In short, important policy decisions depend upon the conclusions we draw.

Media Empires

Newspapers and broadcasting institutions sell products and services; newspapers and television programmes are commercially manufactured products, news itself is a product that has a tradeable value in the market place. Media organizations also deal in advertising space, which allows others to promote their products; in return, newspapers and television channels deliver audiences (particular demographies, tastes, disposable incomes). As commercial organizations, a key measure of their success is profits, just as it is for the manufacturers of nappies or cars. In 1986, the *Daily Telegraph*, for example, was bought by Hollinger International for £30 million; six years later, the paper declared a pre-tax profit of £40.5 million (*Financial Times*, 22 February 1996). In 1995, News

Corporation announced profits of $(Aus)1.4 billion, of which News International, the British end of the enterprise, contributed £779 million.

But while media organizations exist to make money, this is not necessarily their only motivation, and their behaviour cannot be reduced to the cash nexus. They are complex institutions. They are not simply machines either for reporting events or for making profits; they are also bureaucracies with their own internal political orders. How they are organized, how power is distributed within the organization, will have profound repercussions for the kind of product they make. Structural reorganization of any media business, whether in the public or the private sector, involves more than the implementation of a new theory of organizational behaviour. It affects the programmes made by broadcasters and the coverage provided by the papers; and it determines the distribution of power within the business and whose decisions count. Both dimensions – the commercial interests and the organizational structure – are crucial to understanding the way that the media cover, and relate to, politics. The simplest way of revealing this connection between interests, organization and political coverage is to look at the changes which the media have undergone in recent years.

According to Curran and Seaton (1997: 42–58), once newspapers were simply the product of particular political fiefdoms or interests; they then became the commercial responsibility of the so-called 'press barons'. They are now subsidiaries of vast conglomerates, which once, suggested Graham Murdock (1982: 119), fell into two categories: the 'general conglomerate' and the 'communications conglomerate'. The first had a variety of interests, which had no necessary or direct relationship with their media interests. The communication conglomerate, by contrast, 'operate[d] mainly or solely within the media and leisure industries' (ibid.). Increasingly these distinctions have become harder to maintain as the new conglomerates have spread their commercial interests ever more widely. Golding and Murdock (2000: 78) describe Time Warner as a textbook illustration of the new order: 'it is now a major international player in book publishing, recorded music, feature film production and exhibition, satellite and cable television programming (through the CNN news channel, the Home Box Office and Cinemax movie channels, and the Cartoon Network), and animation, video games and children's toys'. And now, in its alliance with America Online, it has a major interest in the internet. Such corporate histories are marked by increasing concentration of ownership, even while the number of media outlets has expanded over time. Pluralism of choice is no guarantee of pluralism of supplier. The apparent diversity of media alternatives is belied by the facts of ownership. Through its various outlets, Time Warner supplied in the late 1990s 120 million readers with books and comics and 23 million subscribers with their cable service (Sussman, 1997: 127). In Australia between 1987 and 1993, according to Julianne Schultz (1998: 83), 'Rupert Murdoch's News Limited moved from being the smallest newspaper company to publishing more than 60 per cent of the nation's newspapers and holding a monopoly in four capital cities.' In Britain in 1992, News International had 31 per cent of the daily readership (split between three titles) and 36 per cent of the Sunday readership (shared by two titles). By 2000, the top three media conglomerates controlled more than 80 per cent of daily and Sunday newspaper sales in the UK (*The Guardian*, 31 October 2000). Reuters dominates the global competition between news suppliers, leaving its rivals a poor second (Boyd-Barrett and Rantanen, 1998: 4).

But, in looking at such concentration of ownership, we need to draw attention to two elements of this situation. The first concerns the conditions which allow the concentration to occur. Despite commercial and market incentives for concentrating ownership, none of this is inevitable. Markets can be, and are, regulated. Governments can impose restrictions on the ownership of newspapers and can act against monopolies (as the US authorities did against Microsoft in 2000 and as the European authorities did in blocking the addition of EMI to the Time Warner–AOL merger). The same levels of media concentration are not necessarily to be expected in Australia as in the USA or in the UK. Concentration is not just a product of free market competition; it is a product of regulations (or their absence). Besides, there is no natural law which dictates that the press be organised through a (regulated) market. It is conceivable that the right to print papers could be distributed in the same way that broadcasters obtain a franchise to broadcast. You could have public service papers just as you have public service television. Equally, there are those who argue the reverse: that conglomerate control is much more limited and much less worrying than state regulation (Beesley, 1996).

The second important aspect of concentrated ownership is that the conglomerates who dominate are not necessarily part of a cosy cabal. Although they may have interests in common, they are also rivals. This is most evident in another politically sensitive matter: the notion of fair competition. In the UK in 1997–8, News International started a price war, in which *The Times* cut its cover price. The exact costs of these ploys are hard to discern, but it has been claimed that weekday editions of *The Times* were losing between £57 000 and £74 000 each day (£2.9m–£3.8m each year), and that the Saturday *Times* was losing over £750 000 each issue (£38.5m–£49m a year). News International countered these suggestions, arguing that the balance sheet was complicated by the fact that the increased circulation allowed the company to recoup a great deal in advertising revenue. But a rival newspaper magnate, Conrad Black, argued that *The Times* could not have been breaking even *before* the price war, let alone afterwards (*The Guardian*, 1 June 1998). Whatever the actual facts, the pricing strategy had direct consequences for other papers, who had to follow *The Times'* example, or risk being priced out of the market. News International's ability to engage in this competition was possible because of the vast profits amassed by its parent company, News Corporation. Its intention was to weaken its rivals and to increase its own market share.

So, while the media conglomerates have interests in common, they are also in conflict with each other. Which takes precedence – the common interest or the competition – is a matter of considerable importance, and will be resolved differently according to the perspective taken: liberal theorists will stress the competition, corporatists the cohesion. To get closer to understanding corporate behaviour and its political implications, we need to ask what other motives, besides the rivalry and the pursuit of profit, drive these corporations.

News Corporation is a classic example of the new conglomerates that dominate the mass media industry. It owns terrestrial television stations in the USA and Australia; it owns cable and satellite television stations in the USA, Latin America, Europe, Australasia and Asia. It has also invested in film studios in the USA and Australia. It has controlling interests in newspapers and magazines and book publishing across the globe. It also has money in a variety of other business, including record companies and computer concerns. These new entities are marked by the way they interconnect types of media and the systems of delivery, marketing and distribution. The merger of two media groups in Britain – MAI and United News and Media – created an organization with the following interests (*The Times*, 9 February 1996):

Television and entertainment	19%
Business media and information	26%
Regional newspapers	10%
National newspapers	15%
Advertising periodicals	10%

The Germany-based conglomerate Bertelsmann AG has interests in record companies, television, radio, film, multimedia, books, magazines, newspapers, offset printing and much else. There is a strong incentive to link them: to get the papers to help sell the books and the films; and the films to promote the music company. At the same time, multi-sector ownership creates disincentives for papers to investigate topics that adversely affect other branches of their empire. When the publisher HarperCollins, a News Corporation company, decided not to publish the ex-governor of Hong Kong Chris Patten's book, it was reported (*The Guardian*, 26 February 1998; *The Observer*, 1 March 1998) that this was because Murdoch feared it might affect adversely his media interests in China. 'Kill the book,' Murdoch was reported to have demanded (*The Guardian*, 2 March 1998). But while this story, which Murdoch himself denies, received extensive coverage in rival papers, it attracted only belated attention in *The Times*. For the columnist Francis Wheen this was evidence that *The Times* was being used to improve relations with the Chinese authorities, as News Corporation sought to expand its business in the Far East. A sign of the success of this strategy, according to Wheen, was evident when President Jieng Zemin allowed 'the film *Titanic* into Chinese cinemas, to the delight of 20th Century Fox (prop. R. Murdoch)', an event which the *Sun* honoured with a review of the Chinese premiere (*The Guardian*, 20 October 1999).

As the conglomerates' interests reach out in so many different directions and across ever larger areas, so inevitably they become entwined in politics. Berlusconi's rise to power has, in this sense, a logic to it. Here was a media mogul who became Italy's prime minster, and who made extensive use of his various media outlets in his campaign. His Fininvest channels were filled with advertisements for his party, Forza Italia (Statham, 1996: 94–6). Once in power, he was not only in a position to oversee his own three private television channels, he was also able to influence the conduct of the three state television channels. One of the presenters from Fininvest was appointed to the Parliamentary Culture Committee (*The Independent*, 9 June 1995). Meanwhile, his advertising company had a 65 per cent share of the television advertising market (Statham, 1996: 91). In short, the new media corporations bring together a particular set of commercial and political interests. But to what extent do the latter take precedence in the character of media content?

Ownership and Control

There is no neat divide between commercial and political power. As we have already seen, the opportunity to exist as conglomerates depends, in part, on government policy on monopolies. It is also apparent that commercial decisions have a political impact, through the effects, for instance, of closing a newspaper or amalgamating media interests. But at the same time, commercial power – executive decisions about what to buy or sell, what product to manufacture – does not translate directly or simply into politics. If we want to claim that owners play a direct *political* role, we need to look more closely at the operation of power within media organizations.

The economic interests and incentives of the new media conglomerates are crucial to explaining elements of their behaviour, but they do not necessarily account for a paper's politics. There is no simple correlation between economic interest and the political content of papers or the pressure they put on governments. The fact that we have seen the decline of the press baron, whose interests were traditionally linked to politics and to exercising influence, does not mean that press ownership as a source of power died with Lords Northcliffe and Rothermere. Berlusconi is testimony to this, but equally he may be the exception to the rule. There is a widespread assumption that other media moguls use their power to engineer political ends. The activities of men like Murdoch are the constant object of political attention and of policy questions. Murdoch has been demonized by some, and lionized by others. He is seen as the source of malign political influence, or the model of entrepreneurial genius. Either way, he is more than a figurehead for his empire; he is believed to wield power in pursuit of political goals. It is exactly this thought which inspires the suggestion that the extent and nature of this control needs to be counteracted through legislation designed to limit cross-media ownership or to protect editorial independence. But does it make sense to think and react like this? To answer this question, we need to reflect upon the nature of media power, and then about how it is used.

In considering relations of power in mass media, it is useful to distinguish between the types of influence which might be involved. Murdock (1982: 122) identifies two forms: allocative and operational control. The first applies to the general strategy of the conglomerate – its merger and acquisition decisions, its financial plan and the use of its profits. Operational control is exercised at a lower level (that is, within the general strategy set through allocative controls). Allocative power is typically held by the company's board (which is, in theory, responsible to the shareholders).

Murdock (ibid.: 123–4) argues that, in the debate about ownership and control, two alternatives have emerged. On the one hand, there is the view of those who focus upon the exercise of 'power' and who see decisions as the consequences of its use and distribution. Against this view stand those who shift the analysis to the larger structure within which 'decisions' are located, and talk of the constraints that determine outcomes. These two positions return us to the familiar debate within the social sciences between structure and agency. Is social change to be understood as the product of individual decisions and actions or as the consequence of structural forces which are indifferent to the individuals who are caught up in these forces? Murdock (ibid.: 125) is unhappy with this dichotomy, and argues that a proper understanding of control in mass media needs to recognize both dimensions.

This is not the same as saying that the dichotomy can be made to disappear, as Anthony Giddens (1979) does with his notion of 'structuration'. Rather it is to recognize that notions of structure and agency (and the tensions between the two) are a necessary part of any attempt to explain social action (Hollis and Smith, 1991a; 1991b; Dowding, 1994). This is a version of Karl Marx's powerful idea that people make their own history, but not in circumstances of their own choosing. What this suggests is that we need to combine an understanding of individual rationality (agency) – what it makes sense for someone to do – with an appreciation of the context and institutional forms (structure) in which they act. This approach focuses on what Colin Hay (1997) calls 'context-shaping' power or what Bent Flyvberg (1998) describes as power's capacity to define the 'reality' on which rationality works. Power is seen as setting rules and constraints within which actors, with different resources and capacities, act to realize their goals. Both individuals and structures are relevant. The general features of the media economy – the market, the state regulatory structure, the corporate structure – organize and prioritize a range of alternatives and possibilities, but within this context individual and collective actors operate more or less effectively to realize their interests.

The implication of this approach to power is that we need to focus on the incentive structure under which control is exercised. Murdock (1982: 125–9) again detects two competing perspectives. The first locates power within capitalism: power is exercised in pursuit of the interests of the capitalist class. The second locates power within industrial society, and the incentives are generated not by the larger economic context, but by the particular features of the industry's organization. Common to these perspectives is the view that managers (editors, advertising executives and so on) rather than owners are the decisive actors, and that managers are motivated by the benefits which the organization provides, and not by the need to realize profits on capital investment. A crude distinction between the perspectives can be drawn by asking whose interests predominate in corporate decision making. In the first, profit is central, and hence considerable power is attributed to the source of those profits (advertisers, for instance); in the second, the emphasis is on other measures of success (sales and ratings), pushing readers or viewers to the fore in policy decisions. Murdock's purpose in introducing these differences and distinctions is not to establish a final, definitive view of the distribution of power in the mass media, but to produce a framework or set of questions which enable us to reflect on the character and form of that power.

In this chapter, we are examining power *within* media organizations, rather than the power these organizations have over society more generally. As a way of focusing the general discussion of media power and of exploring the framework suggested by Murdock, we concentrate on a particular example of (alleged) media power, that of Rupert Murdoch. This is not to suggest that Murdoch is unique; the record of other conglomerate leaders tells similar stories (see Tunstall and Palmer, 1991). Rather, examining one example provides a richer picture of the nuances of power and influence, and Murdoch stands out as the figure whose power has become an international obsession. As will become apparent, there is only so much that can, in fact, be said about Murdoch's power, and such analyses need to be supplemented by a focus on organizational process rather than on individual authority (more structure and less agency, as it were).

The Power of Rupert Murdoch

People think of Rupert Murdoch as powerful, in the sense not only that he is the head of a major corporation, but also that his power is not confined to commercial decisions and to weighing up purely economic costs and benefits. Murdoch is assumed to wield political power, to use this power to influence what his papers say, what voters think and what governments do. As one biography says of him: 'His main titles have rarely strayed far from the right-wing fundamentalism in which he now so passionately believes' (Belfield *et al.*, 1991: 4). To attribute this kind of power to Murdoch is also to attribute motive, to suggest that he has a reason for influencing his papers. More than this, it is to attribute a *political* motive to him, one which may either conflict or coincide with his commercial interests. It is, after all, conceivable that his commercial concerns override everything else. In other words, his only interest is in the bottom line, and although this may have profound political consequences, it is not those consequences that explain or motivate the decisions. The political line is of no particular interest to him, except insofar as it serves his commercial interests. Alternatively, his political interests could be such that he is willing to sacrifice commercial gain. As a way of capturing the implications of these alternatives, consider the support given by Murdoch's papers to Tony Blair's Labour Party in 1997. This backing could be seen either as a result of reading the popular mood (or their readers' mood), as a consequence of his own personal preference for Blair over John Major, or a consequence of his expectation that Labour was going to win, and that his business interests would need government support.

It might be supposed that a simple test of the motives of owners is whether they run their enterprises at a profit or at a loss. If the latter, it might be assumed that their interests are political, not commercial. When Lord Thompson owned *The Times* the paper incurred considerable losses; similarly, in the early 1990s, News International reported a loss of £266 million. But such evidence does not provide incontrovertible evidence of political motives. Losses can have commercial value: a loss-making enterprise can be set against tax or its losses may be a consequence of some larger commercial purpose. It is only if neither of these apply we can talk of political interests taking precedence (assuming that neither incompetence nor other commercial explanations account for the losses). Where papers do make a profit, it does not follow that only commercial considerations matter. Even where media corporations make profits, it cannot be assumed that this represents the motivation behind every corporate decision. Different motives may coexist. The decision by Harper Collins to drop Chris Patten's book contract might be an example of this, if it was, in fact, done to protect another part of the News Corporation empire. Because conglomerates involve so many different interests, it is impossible to talk of a single motive extending over all decisions.

Beyond the immediate commercial interests, there lie a more diffuse set of interests which can encompass the well being of the media generally or capitalism itself. We could see Murdoch as operating to promote the interests of capitalism generally (even where the costs of this support may entail some short-term commercial loss). The problem with this line of thought is that, as rational choice theorists have pointed out (for example Downs, 1957; Olson, 1971), there is no way that a single actor can guarantee the success of the system, and that it is rational to free-ride on the efforts of others. It would, therefore, be irrational for Murdoch to believe that his actions alone could preserve capitalism (however much he has to gain from its survival). Alternatively, insofar as owners wield power, this power may be exercised to promote certain side benefits (non-commercial ones). It is conceivable that media organizations provide gratification for the owners' vanity or grant them social status and access to certain social circles. The late

Robert Maxwell was often assumed to be as interested in political influence as he was in commercial gain (Bower, 1988). It does seem, however, that such motives hold little attraction for Murdoch. One of his editor's, Andrew Neil (1997: 199), claims that Murdoch was uninterested in 'the approval of the Establishment', and that he 'turned down a knighthood and a peerage'.

Whatever is the case, any analysis of the power of Rupert Murdoch must include an account of his interests and of the ends he seeks to realize. Even if we are able to rule out vanity and social climbing, we are still left with the problem of disentangling the political and the commercial. Insofar as it is possible to do this, there remains a further task, which is to establish the means available to him to realize these interests. There is no necessary link between ownership and control, and in a large corporate structure there may be many centres of power. As a first step, it is best to begin by looking at the claims made about Rupert Murdoch's access to power and his decision to use it for political ends.

The Appointment and Removal of Editors

Rupert Murdoch's media power has commonly been linked to his power to hire and fire editors. He refused to renew the contract of the editor of *Village Voice*, the New York paper, when he took it over. His relationship with Harold Evans at *The Times* was marred by arguments over budgeting and politics. According to his biographer, Murdoch was concerned that Evans was 'spending freely but not always consistently', while Evans complained that he was kept in the dark about 'his formal editorial budget' (Shawcross, 1992: 246). They also differed over editorial policy (ibid.: 251–2). In the end, Evans resigned. His resignation has been seen as an indication of the fact that Murdoch wants editors who echo his politics. Certainly, the appointment of Andrew Neil to edit the *Sunday Times* seemed to confirm this view. Neil appeared to share his proprietor's political instincts. They worked together for a long time and, when their partnership ended, the cause was less a matter of political ideology than one of corporate and journalistic interests. The *Sunday Times'* pursuit of the Pergau Dam affair, a story about the alleged misuse of funds by the Malaysian government, threatened Murdoch's business interests in that part of the world. Eventually, Neil moved to New York to work in one of Murdoch's television companies. Other editors and employees of his companies testify to Murdoch's power to hire and fire (see Curran and Seaton, 1997). But what is central to the argument is the extent to which these decisions are the result of *political* judgements.

Involvement in Editorial Policy

Several anecdotal reports record how Murdoch would intervene directly in the content of his papers. Here is a typical one: 'Murdoch could not stop interfering. In 1982 he said to Fred Emery, home editor of *The Times*: ' "I give instructions to my editors all around the world, why shouldn't I in London?" ' (Belfield *et al.*, 1991: 77). From the same source, it is claimed too that Murdoch told journalists on the *Chicago Sun–Times* that they could not criticize President Ronald Reagan. (Robert Maxwell, when he owned the *Mirror*, actually rewrote columns of which he disapproved (Bower, 1988: 298–9).) In the 1970s in Australia, Murdoch's support for the Labour Party took the form of writing a party press release, which subsequently became a news item in his papers (Tiffen, 1989: 148). At the *Sunday Times*, Neil (1997: 222) describes how, after the paper had been printed, Murdoch would 'lay the paper on the lectern then noisily turn each page, stabbing his finger at various stories or circling them with his pen. He had the uncanny knack of zooming in on the paper's weaknesses.'

It is also assumed that the political line taken by the *Sun* and by his Fox TV channel in the USA (which was very critical of President Clinton) were the direct product of Murdoch's intervention. The decision that the *Sun* would support Tony Blair in 1997 was made, it seems, in the face of the opposition of the paper's political editor, Trevor Kavanagh. But not all his papers are subject to the same interference, at least according to the leading actors. For example, Peter Stothard, editor of *The Times*, described Murdoch's involvement like this: 'He has an influence in the sense that if you have known him for a long time you understand that he has good instincts about the way newspapers work. You are aware of that intelligence in the background and it does spur you on because he is a great encourager of risk . . . He does ring up from time to time and asks what's going on. He listens a lot. There is a lot happening here in London that he wants to know about. He is interested in politics because he likes to know what's going on. But the idea that he is constantly on the phone is wrong' (*The Guardian*, 28 June 1993).

Murdoch himself confirmed this view, at least in relation to *The Times*, if not for the *Sun*. Asked in 1995 if his papers would support the Labour Party, Murdoch replied: 'Look, what will happen exactly is this. *The Times* and *Sunday Times* will support whoever the editors wish to support. The *Sun*? I'm sure the editor will consult with me and I will have some input into that' (*The Guardian*, 22 May 1995). As editor of the *Sunday Times*, Neil claims that only once in 11 years did he have to submit an editorial for approval before publication. This was when he wrote about News International's industrial dispute with the print unions, caused by the decision to move its papers from Fleet Street to Wapping. Neil (1997: 132) claims the only change made was for 'legal reasons'. He says that 'he never barked orders to change what I was planning for the front page', and though Murdoch tried to get the paper to back Margaret Thatcher in the struggle for the Conservative Party leadership, he did not complain when the *Sunday Times* supported Michael Heseltine. At the same time, Neil (ibid.: 203 & 222) notes that, despite his 'hands-off' approach, 'Murdoch was always uppermost in the editor's mind. . . . sometimes he would leave you wondering if you had done anything right; . . . other times, when he liked the paper, you felt you could walk on water.' Allegations about Murdoch's influence, according to these accounts, extend from direct instructions over what can and cannot be said, through to the creation of a culture in which a certain norm becomes part of the established 'common sense' of the paper, to the view that he had little or no impact.

Commercial Policy

It is apparent that Murdoch has been involved in key matters of general strategy. It is inconceivable that the price war would have been launched without his agreement, just as *The Times'* revamping of its layout in 2000 required prior approval (if only because of the costs incurred). When the *Sunday Times* wanted to introduce a books section, it was opposed by the advertising department, but with Murdoch's backing it went ahead (Neil, 1997: 215). Murdoch himself admits that he pays close attention to the budgets of his papers and acts to cross-subsidize the losses. News Corporation has invested heavily in digital broadcasting and has bought into sports teams in the USA. News Corporation has a 100 per cent share in the LA Dodgers, and a 20 per cent share in the NY Knicks and the NY Rangers, and, crucially, owns the television rights for 17 National Basketball Association teams, 12 National Hockey League teams and 20 major league baseball teams. Not only do all these decisions have profound implications for the company's interests, it also affects its bargaining power and the relations it has with, among other things, the political economy of the countries with which it does business. It is hard to imagine that these allocative decisions are taken without Murdoch's direct involvement.

So, in summary, there appears to be evidence of Murdoch having access to, and making use of, the levers which direct the course and content of his media outlets. But there is one question which always has to be asked. Does he use these powers to pursue a particular political line? Certainly, one of the claims made about Murdoch's media power is that he wields it on behalf of conservative causes. This was why he supported Margaret Thatcher and attacked Bill Clinton. His biographer William Shawcross (1992: 154), however, casts some doubt on such claims. He recalls how in its early Murdoch days, the *Sun* opposed 'capital punishment, apartheid, racism and the Vietnam war'. In 1970, the Murdoch press backed Labour (in the UK and in Australia) and, in 1972, it supported striking British miners. But whatever the party political sympathies his papers displayed, Shawcross suggests that the defining feature of Murdoch's politics was his mistrust of 'the establishment'. It was this that led him to appoint Andrew Neil to edit the *Sunday Times*. Neil was an anti-establishment figure himself, a young outsider, someone who represented the modern meritocracy and opposition to traditional power. This general political position was not, of course, inconsistent with his support for Margaret Thatcher, nor was it entirely inconsistent with support for Tony Blair (as a challenge to the Tory establishment).

While Murdoch has been involved in editorial policy, argues Shawcross (ibid.: 184), he has not done this at all times and in all places. When he replaced the editor at the *Village Voice*, he did not replace her with a more conservative editor and he did not influence coverage (even tolerating – albeit grudgingly – criticism of himself). Shawcross also contends that the pressure to remove Evans from *The Times* had less to do with Murdoch, who initially was supportive of his editor, and more to do with the journalists' dislike of Evans' style (ibid.: 245–54). With Andrew Neil, Murdoch agreed contractual terms which gave the editor considerable protection. If he was to be fired, he would be paid two years' salary (rising to three years after two years in the job); besides, as an unconventional appointment, Neil was more difficult to remove without Murdoch losing face. Similarly, when asked about his dealings with the Chinese authorities and the decision to drop Chris Patten's book, Murdoch refutes the story told about his involvement: 'No. I was never asked to back out of the Patten deal. As far as I know, they [the Chinese] didn't know he was writing a book. It was done very clumsily by HarperCollins' (*The Guardian*, 29 November 1999). This does not demonstrate that Murdoch had no involvement in the decision to drop Patten's book, but it does raise doubts about the motives and responsibility for that decision. Certainly, there is a danger in making too much of the anecdotal evidence, or of assuming that the anecdotes all point to one conclusion. The ambiguity stems, in part, from an approach to power which seeks out such examples. It runs the risk of focusing exclusively on the individual actor and too little on the context in which they act. One way to counter this slant is to look at other, rival sources of power.

Readers and Viewers

Readers and viewers certainly matter to the rhetoric of mass media. They help to legitimate the activities of journalists: sales and ratings are taken as indications of popularity and of public interest. The underlying assumption is that mass media reflect the tastes of those who buy their papers or watch their programmes. It follows that, for sound commercial and political reasons, owners and editors cannot afford to ignore their customers. So, for example, the reason for News International outlets taking the line they do may have more to do with the shifts in the opinion of readers and viewers than with the whims and prejudices of the corporate executives. To ignore public opinion is to risk commercial punishment. When the *Sunday Mirror* published pictures of Princess Diana working out in an exclusive gym, the paper's readership fell by 250 000; just as readers of the *Sun* boycotted their paper in protest at the way it covered the death of Liverpool football fans in the crush at the Hillsborough stadium (Snoddy, 1992).

Individual incidents do not, though, represent a complete picture. After all, such power is exercised only belatedly and occasionally. To claim that consumers are a significant force means establishing a mechanism by which their preferences can be registered on a regular basis. Such arrangements do exist; there is the letters page, the feedback show, the publication of public opinion and telephone polls, the phone-in, talk radio and so on. In the USA, there has been an attempt to systematize this form of public participation under the guise of 'civic journalism', where journalists take their agenda directly from the revealed preferences of the public (Clark, 1997).

There are, however, limits to the impact that these forms of popular involvement can have. Reader boycotts have had very little sustained effect, and depend upon the coordination of some other agency. Equally, the regular forms of participation (the letters page, the phone-in) are carefully mediated by media professionals. Civic journalism has been much criticized for actually limiting, rather than extending, the critical function of journalism (Grimes, 1997; Jackson, 1997). Certainly, individual consumers can achieve very little, especially as the decision not to buy a paper may be taken on any number of grounds (of which politics may be the least). Nonetheless, it is important not to see this state of affairs as a fixed and inevitable condition of relations between audience/readers and their media. Rather it is a result of the way that the relationship is organized and structured. Put simply: readers could exercise more power if there were established systems of accountability, or if – as happens in some community radio stations (see Lewis and Booth, 1989) – listeners are subscribers or contributors. It is only where such systems of audience or reader participation do not exist that the media remain largely impervious to popular demand and more susceptible to the expectations of their advertisers (their paymasters in default of some other form of financial support).

Advertisers

All papers depend upon advertisers, but not all papers depend equally. Crudely, tabloids depend more upon income from their readers, while broadsheets depend more upon advertisers. Commercial television depends overwhelmingly upon its advertisers, as do the free papers. The local press depend upon local advertisers. According to Franklin (1994: 42), the local press in the UK derives 25–35 per cent of its income from advertising, the tabloids derive 30 per cent; and the broadsheets 70 per cent. But does this dependence, however large, actually influence the politics of the paper?

Such links are hard to prove. There are, after all, an infinite number of stories that are *not* covered, and to show that a particular one is not covered because of a fear of offending an advertiser would require evidence of pressure. The journalist Blake Fleetwood claims that a piece he wrote for the *New York Times* about Tiffany's jewellery store was subtly changed, and was accompanied by a much blander editorial than the story warranted, because Tiffany's was a major advertiser (*Washington Monthly*, September, 1999). In a similar way, the *New York Daily* found itself in conflict with one of its advertisers, Bell Atlantic, after the paper had run a piece critical of the company. These instances do not demonstrate a systematic pattern of influence, although there have been reports of advertisers exercising direct editorial control, either by demanding to read copy before placing advertisements, or by the merger of news and advertising departments (*Medium Wave*, BBC Radio 4, 4 January 1998). In October 1999, the *Los Angeles Times* published a 164 page supplement about the Staples sports arena. The supplement raised $2 million in advertising, which, it turned out, was split between the sports arena and the paper (*The Guardian*, 3 January 2000). The effect of this episode was to call into question the editorial independence of the *LA Times*. Such examples, however, remain relatively rare, and in any case they do not exhaust the ways in which the connection between the advertiser and political coverage may operate.

The political influence of advertisers may be identified, not in the specific content of any given magazine or paper or programme, but rather in the *kinds* of stories that appear. The sections into which papers are divided will often owe much to the kind of advertising they want to attract. Car, homes and garden, and travel sections all provide hooks with which to tempt advertisers. Attracting advertisers also depends on being able to deliver the audience/readership they seek. This may be detected in various ways. It may result in a general shift away from 'hard' news to human interest stories. The media outlet has to create an environment that disposes its readers/ viewers to consume. More precisely, it has to create a bridge between consumers and advertisers. As the chief executive of a UK television news service explained the conditions under which he worked: 'The dynamic is really news attracting the kind of audiences that advertisers want to buy, and the channel controllers sitting there saying "I want those kinds of advertisers, I need this kind of content. I need the news to deliver this kind of audience"' (*The Times*, 12 March 1999).

The logic of this does not automatically work against the coverage of politics. As Colin Sparks (2000: 275–6) points out, insofar as the affluent reader or viewer has a taste for, or interest in, detailed coverage of politics, 'it makes very good business sense' for media outlets to provide such coverage. But, according to Michael Schudson (2000: 178), this logic works only where there is a concentrated, elite audience. Where the audience is of a different kind, the logic results in a quite different conclusion. When in Britain the main evening newscast on ITV was moved from 10pm to 11pm, the channel earned a reported £70 million more in advertising revenue (while losing two million news viewers), because the programmes now running at 10pm were more attractive to advertisers (*The Times*, 3 March 2000). The media outlet has to be attractive to advertisers, and a measure of this attractiveness is the ability to reach a particular market. If the paper can show that it has a readership from a certain social category, advertisers who want that market will use such an outlet. This type of relationship will dispose the paper or programme maker to address some topics and not others. And, to this extent, advertisers set an agenda for the media, which is political insofar as it recognizes certain interests and excludes others.

From this it is possible to derive an argument for the conservatism of the broadsheet press. The advertisers that they want to attract will be, in turn, after an affluent readership. Such people are likely to have an interest in maintaining the status quo. Hence it is possible to trace a line from advertising to political disposition but, in doing so, it is important to bear in mind other pressures and constraints. The tabloid press also takes a conservative line without having the same dependence upon advertisers. Besides, there are instances when papers have chosen to ignore their advertisers. When one advertising client complained to Rupert Murdoch about a *Sunday Times* story, Murdoch simply banned the client from advertising in his paper. In an ensuing conversation with his editor, Murdoch asked how much the lost account was worth. 'About £3 million,' he was told. 'Fuck him, if he thinks we can be bought for £3 million,' came the reply (Neil, 1997: 201).

Sponsorship of programming adds another dimension to this issue. While rules govern sponsorship (what can be sponsored and how), the need to attract sponsors undoubtedly has an impact on the kind of programmes that are made. This, though, constitutes a system which is relatively transparent. Audiences are notified of the sponsor and might be expected to connect content and the product. Nonetheless, the need for sponsorship can have an impact on the type of programmes made (it is easier to get sponsorship for drama than for documentaries). Insofar as advertisers and sponsors are important to the revenue of media outlets, they will have an indirect effect upon coverage of politics. The measure of this will not simply (if at all) be the political line so much as the *presence* of politics itself. The need to attract advertising revenue leads to a tendency to marginalize politics, and to adopt a populist approach to scheduling and news coverage, in which 'hard news' makes way for 'human interest' stories. These trends can be identified and mapped (see Curran and Seaton, 1997) and can be used to indicate the possible – if not irrefutable – influence of advertising on the content of media. To this extent, advertisers and sponsors, like readers and viewers, represent a counterweight to the influence of owners.

Conclusion

This chapter has explored the way in which corporate interests shape the coverage of politics. Its main focus has been on the role of owners in this process, if only because this is where much discussion of power in the media begins. We have looked at the way media conglomerates have changed over time, and how these changes translate into particular corporate interests. We have then examined in more detail the incentives, opportunities and actions of an individual corporate executive, Rupert Murdoch, to see what can be said about their power to influence the coverage of politics. This was followed by a review of the other interests and actors that might rival those of the owner: advertisers and consumers. Running through this discussion has been an important linked theme: the location and character of media 'power'. In particular, should that power be understood as an attribute of individual agents or as a feature of structures and processes? From one perspective, attributing power to individuals like Murdoch is to miss the larger context which shapes and makes possible their actions. Individuals do not have power, structures do. Against this perspective stands the suggestion that, while structural factors may shape the roles which individuals fulfil, and hence constrain their thoughts and actions, they are still required to interpret these roles; no two people do this in identical ways. To this extent, power is an attribute of individuals.

Ideally, the two approaches should be combined in detailed examinations of particular processes and decisions. The form and extent of control over media outlets cannot be the subject of sweeping generalizations. As our discussion of Rupert Murdoch makes clear, the exercise of power is complex and open to competing interpretations. Central to any account of power in the mass media must be an acknowledgement of the way in which this control is mediated. Both the internal structure of the media outlet and the wider political structure within which those outlets are situated act to channel the flow of political influence. The degree to which the editor is beholden to those above him or her can be affected by the constitution of the paper. Ownership of media outlets is also subject to political regulation that can determine the interests and opportunities of owners. These can be influenced by government restrictions on cross-media ownership and by judgements on unfair competition and antitrust legislation. Markets are politically constituted systems; they do not exist as autonomous entities. Media power is a product of political decisions, values and processes. So in thinking about the political consequences of media ownership we need to examine the commercial interests of media conglomerates, the practices of owners and the policies of government. We need to be constantly sensitive to the conception of power that underlies the discussion. This same injunction applies as we turn to another source of potential power: journalists and editors.

7
Watchdogs or Lapdogs?
The Politics of Journalism

Liberal democratic regimes place great store by their journalists. It is they, as reporters or interviewers, who provide the information upon which citizens rely; it is they who act out the rituals of accountability when cross-examining politicians. But is this trust warranted? Do journalists practise their profession as autonomous agents? Are they independent servants of political truth and the public interest? Or are they the hired guns of particular political and commercial interests? Certainly, if ownership is the source of media power, it follows that editors and journalists must be beholden to the interests and patronage of their proprietors. Such assumptions, as we have seen, are supported by the anecdotal accounts of witnesses to proprietorial intervention. If, on the other hand, owners are only one of the many sources of influence acting on editors and journalists, we need to look more widely to see if there are other constraints on their freedom and independence.

Among the obvious sources of pressure on journalist are parties and political actors. There have been reports, for instance, of UK government ministers trying to influence appointments made to editorial positions in the national press (*Sunday Telegraph*, 10 May 1998). More typically, journalists are frequently portrayed as the willing victims of the skilful manipulation practised by political spin doctors and public relations professionals. A fascinating account of their triumphs (and failures) is found in Howard Kurtz's *Spin Cycle* (1998), a vivid picture of spin doctoring in the Clinton White House. The spin doctors, 'the men in the dark' as one British politician described them, are presented as the architects of political coverage.

Indeed, the spin doctor has become a cultural icon, a symbol of the new cynicism about modern journalism. Instead of the knights in shining armour of *All the President's Men*, where the journalists Carl Bernstein and Bob Woodward exposed the corruption of President Nixon's administration, we now have the cynical manipulators of *Wag the Dog*, leading gullible journalists to half-truths and bare-faced lies, or the smooth charm of Michael J. Fox in *Spin City*, desperately trying to protect his stupid, self-serving politicians from public ridicule.

What all of these claims – about the influence of owners, governments or spin doctors – are suggesting is that journalists are the lapdogs of partial interests, not the watchdogs of the public interest. This chapter is an attempt to assess these claims by looking at the influences operating on journalism and at the interests which organize its practice. We begin by examining claims made for the power of spin doctors, and ask whether, in fact, the focus on the spin doctor is not distracting attention from more important trends in journalism, in particular, the alleged demise of investigative journalism and its replacement by 'real life programming' (docusoaps and shows like *Big Brother* and *Survivor*) and 'dumbed down' news. What is revealing about this debate, I want to suggest, is the way it draws attention to the question of how journalism operates: is it the product of individual adherence to a professional code or is it the result of a process, led by market forces and commercial pressure, in which individual initiative and skill has relatively little impact? These competing models of journalism have important consequences for the way we understand media power and for attempts to change its distribution.

Spin Doctors

'People would be horrified by the degree to which journalists prostitute themselves,' remarked one spin doctor. He went on to claim that, when he was spinning one story, 'I had final clearance of the picture, headline and all copy of a supposedly "un-PR-able" newspaper' (*The Times*, 10 April 1998). Books, television documentaries and acres of print are devoted to the spin doctor and to his or her powers. The suggestion behind all this coverage is that it is these people, not the owners or the advertisers, who control what the media say (or do not say) about politics. What appears as a 'news story' can sometimes be nothing more than a minimal rewrite of a press release. Certainly, it is relatively easy to spot the work of PR departments and spin doctors as the same phrases or approaches occur in stories in different papers. Such examples encourage the conclusion that the news which appears in papers or on broadcasts is not the product of independent journalistic endeavour, but is instead the carefully crafted product of the public relations industry and, in politics, of the spin doctor.

'Spin doctoring' refers to a number of activities and individuals. It refers to the 'gatekeeping' of journalistic access, granting or denying interviews, as well as to the briefing of interviewees on what to say and what not to say. It also includes the glossing of stories or speeches to journalists, pushing particular lines or interpretations. 'You have to be economical with the truth sometimes,' a spin doctor once explained (*The Guardian*, 6 October 1997). It means creating good photo-opportunities, or making sure that journalists and photographers are in the right place at the right time. It involves the writing of the speeches, and of the accompanying press releases, and it extends to pressuring or persuading journalists, through threats and flattery, to represent your client favourably. Spin doctors do not, after all, only work within the confines of traditional party politics; almost every organization, from the most upright of businesses to the most radical of social movements, employs people to sell them to the media. They may not be called 'spin doctors', they may work in 'public relations' or count themselves as a 'spokesperson', but their job is roughly the same: to make sure that the coverage their organization or client receives is the coverage they want.

In *Spin Cycle*, Kurtz (1998: 78–82) tells a story which neatly illustrates the art and the guile of spin doctors. In 1996, President Clinton and his wife Hillary had been on a world tour. Mrs Clinton had been reluctant to give interviews, and kept journalists off her plane. Having maintained her distance, she eventually relented and granted a brief interview to two journalists, who were invited to join her in the cramped confines of her car. Unprepared and awkwardly perched, the journalists listened to Hillary Clinton outline her views about welfare reform. One of them picked up on Mrs Clinton's use of the phrase 'formal role' when talking about her responsibilities, and interpreted this as meaning that the First Lady was to take a prominent place in the Clinton administration (she had taken a back seat after the failure of her attempts to reform health care).

When the story hit the street with the headline, 'Reinventing Hillary', the White House reacted immediately, denying that Mrs Clinton had ever said what she was quoted as saying. The piece was 'trashed' by the spin doctors. Even when the journalist proved her report was accurate by playing the tape, the White House spokespeople kept challenging the story. A day later, when the pilloried journalist met Hillary again, the First Lady is reported by Kurtz as remarking: 'Don't worry . . . Your story's fine.' Political news is rarely a simple product of politician and reporter, but is actually an artifice crafted by many intermediaries.

Some spin doctors remain anonymous, lurking in the background, others assume star status. In the USA, the names of Mike McCurry or Don Baer become regular features of news broadcasts and press stories; just as did Jamie Shea, NATO's press secretary, during the Kosovo war; and just as did Bernard Ingham, Charlie Whelan or Alistair Campbell in Britain. Whatever their public profile, the assumption is that these people are not just aiding the production of political news; they are making the news. When Whelan resigned as press secretary to the chancellor of the exchequer, Gordon Brown, his memoirs secured banner headlines in the *Mirror*: 'I SPUN IT MY WAY'. Critics of spin doctoring see such claims as proving that people like Whelan distort and manipulate the political process, making impossible the mechanisms of accountability that are central to the democratic process. This was one of the central themes of the film *Wag the Dog*, in which wars and weapons are invented simply to distract attention from the president's misdemeanours. In Britain, the suspicion is that Alistair Campbell, the prime minister's press secretary, is more influential than his political master, or that Whelan was more important than his ('Chancellor Whelan' was one paper headline) or that Mrs Thatcher played up to the image of her created by Bernard Ingham (Harris, 1990; N. Jones, 1995). There is no little irony, therefore, in reading these comments from Ingham, who was himself once the object of such criticism: 'Campbell and Whelan are more concerned by a story than its veracity. They bully journalists, they reward and punish. Whelan, I think, is a very dangerous man. . . . They are getting a free ride from a press which seems transfixed. But it's short term. The chickens will come home to roost, or this is no democracy' (*New Statesman*, 24 October 1997, p.13).

But are these fears justified? Spin doctors themselves argue that they are merely expediting the process of disseminating news and information. Furthermore, some journalists, far from seeing spin doctors as intrusive bullies, acknowledge that 'it is part of the job of reporters to have their ears bent by them' (*The Independent*, 3 October 1997). There is, too, in the rhetoric about the influence of spin doctors, an assumption that there has been a radical change in the management of news. But politicians and others have always sought to get favourable coverage, and all that is different now is the method rather than the practice itself. Todd Gitlin (1991: 129–32) argues that many of the targets of current anger about political coverage and media manipulation have a history that can be traced back to the mid-nineteenth century (and arguably the strategy, if not the means, originate earlier, in the writings of Machiavelli). Whether or not spin doctoring is a new phenomenon, and whether or not it is a cause for alarm, it might be argued that to focus upon it is to distract attention from the larger picture.

The argument about the power of the spin doctor tends to focus on the relationship between these individuals and the journalist. It does not say much about the context in which this relationship takes place; that is, the political economy of the media. The increasing need to generate advertising revenue has caused an expansion in the space to be filled. The more space there is, the more copy is needed to fill it. When space was limited, the opportunity for discrimination was greater, and the balance of power favoured the editorial staff; but as the space has expanded, so power has moved in the other direction. The same effect occurs with the expansion of media outlets and with the emergence of 24 hour news services. There is also a pressure to provide copy that is attractive and accessible. One journalist complained that competition between newspapers was leading to a 'shift downmarket on at least the news and features pages . . . The emphasis is on attracting marginal and younger readers who are believed to be less interested in reading about "heavy" politics – that is policy rather than personality' (*The Guardian*, 20 September 2000). Neatly crafted sound bites and photo-opportunities fit neatly with this new order. Popular attention cannot be assumed amidst the noise of competing outlets; journalists have to grab attention. Together, these factors conspire to create work for the spin doctor.

Spin doctoring, therefore, can be seen as the product of a larger set of changes, and the arguments about its effects have to acknowledge these factors. Fighting the influence of spin doctoring, if it is acknowledged that this needs to be done, cannot simply be a matter of stiffening the sinew of journalists so that they can 'stand up' to their would-be manipulators. Rather it is a matter of considering the wider trends affecting changes in the media generally. The logic of this argument can be explored further by looking at another dimension of the politics of journalism: the decline of investigative journalism and the so-called 'dumbing down' of news coverage.

Investigative Journalism and the 'Dumbing Down' of News

Discussion of the fate of investigative journalism is intimately linked to the idea of 'dumbing down'. The former evokes a time when journalists devoted themselves to uncovering serious cases of corruption. The deceptions of President Nixon and Henry Kissinger over the bombing of Cambodia, the local government corruption that marred the North East of England in the 1960s, the 'Iraqi Loans Affair' in Australia, the cavalier disregard for health and safety by Western firms in developing countries – these are the proper topics of a responsible investigative journalism. 'Doorstepping' celebrities and politicians caught up in adulterous affairs, revelations about the life of their children, or claims about their sexuality: these may emerge as a result of investigation, but they are at best exercises in trivial sensationalism and at worst gross abuses of privacy. They represent a devaluing of journalism, which is compounded by a set of news values that place the world of showbusiness and human interest stories above those about corruption and poverty.

In many ways, the notion of the investigative journalist epitomizes the popular ideal of the profession. It is enshrined in the image propagated by films like *All the President's Men* or *The Insider*; it was evoked in the press's relentless pursuit of the allegations made about Bill Clinton's political career (from Whitewater to Monica Lewinsky). The ability of journalists to investigate, rather than merely to report information given out at press conferences, is often presented as a key defining feature of mass media in a democracy. It addresses the 'watchdog' function, the role of journalism as scrutineer of officialdom and elected representatives. The job of the journalist is to expose corruption and deceit in public office, to act as a key mechanism of public accountability in a democracy. For journalists to operate like this, they have to be able to extract information from people who do not want it revealed. For this, journalists need resources and they need to be free of direct commercial and/or political pressure. But investigative journalism does not just happen; it is not just a matter of journalists following their 'natural instincts'. Investigative journalism has to be organized and resourced. It depends on trained journalists, supportive editors and a substantial budget. The history of investigative journalism in Australia, culminating in programmes like *Four Corners* and *60 Minutes*, tells of the particular coincidence of circumstances, opportunities and resources (Schultz, 1998: 166ff). It is not the tale of heroic loners.

In recent years, it has been suggested (Doig, 1997) that there has been a decline in investigative journalism. The heyday of the 1960s and 1970s, when newspapers and television programmes exposed the Thalidomide and Watergate scandals, when miscarriages of justice were pursued and resulted in the release of the innocent, is now past. Newspapers no longer commit resources to exposing these stories. Broadcasters that once scheduled current affairs programmes at peak viewing times now move them later and later, or scrap them entirely. Those that remain concentrate less on politics and more on consumer issues, and what once were revealing documentaries are now docusoaps. 'Bad TV is driving out good, as the satellite and digital wastelands encroach,' remarks David Leigh, himself once an investigative journalist for the axed *World in Action* (*The Guardian*, 9 December 1998). In the USA, there has been talk of a 'crisis in journalism' and particularly a 'crisis of tabloidism'. Journalism, it is claimed, is being dominated by 'marketing' and 'demographics'; it is these interests that determine what is covered and how. Journalists are now perceived, not as watchdogs, but as lapdogs (*Columbia Journalism Review*, April 1998). Gitlin (1991: 123) writes of election campaign coverage as a case of 'reporters dancing attendance at the campaign ball while insisting that they were actually following their own beat'.

It is highly unlikely that politicians are now less corrupt than they used to be, and that therefore there is less to report. An explanation for the decline in investigative journalism has, there-fore, to be sought elsewhere. We need to look to the impact of changing social attitudes, increasing competition and so on. In particular, we need to look at the conditions which establish and promote particular types of journalism. Putting the problem like this is to assume that the changes in journalism have less to do with the individual practitioners and more to do with the struc-tures which shape their working conditions. To explore the implications of, and the assumptions behind, this account of journalism, it helps to look more closely at competing accounts of journalistic practice.

Models of Journalism

There are many ways of conceptualizing 'journalism', each of which makes different assumption about the sources of power that shape political coverage. Some versions of journalism make it susceptible to influence, others make it impervious. Three models are set out here.

Journalism as Observation

The novelist Christopher Isherwood once compared the art of writing to photography: 'I am a camera,' he wrote. A similar metaphor is evoked by the rhetoric of journalism. The job of the journalist, it is suggested, is to observe events and to report the experiences of others. The journalist is a mere cypher. The training manuals and the codes of conduct, which the professional journalist is expected to observe, do much to propagate this idea, as does the strict demarcation that is maintained between opinions and facts, between editorial and news pages. In their *Guide for Journalists*, Eastern Counties Newspapers (ECN, n.d.: 7) proclaim: 'Our papers are independent of all political parties and must be seen to be impartial and unbiased.' When accused of bias, media outlets are quick to respond. The BBC's editor of the *Nine O'Clock News* dismissed a complaint of racism in his programme's treatment of a story by saying: 'Our coverage was balanced, accurate and of the usual high standards of integrity expected by our viewers' (*The

Observer, 20 February 2000). The style of reporting is intended to reinforce such claims. It must be impersonal, dry, matter-of-fact. It is not personalized, richly embroidered or highly emotive: 'Stories can be written in a lively and interesting way without using adjectives . . . A good story does not need to be dressed up or overwritten. The facts will speak for themselves.' (ECN, n.d.: 13). It was Reuters who evolved the convention that an absence of adjectives ensured 'unemotional' coverage and suggested objectivity (Read, 1992: 371). A similar rhetoric is embodied in the saying that 'the camera does not lie'.

No one who holds to this view of journalism would claim that reporters record *everything* they see and hear. They have to make judgements about priorities (what is the important detail) and about news values (which stories matter). These judgements are, however, established by the professional codes and training which define journalism. In March 2000, ITN successfully sued the magazine *Living Marxism*, which had suggested that two ITN journalists had fabricated a news report. There was some criticism of the fact that a major news organization had taken on such a small outlet (which subsequently was forced to close), but the justification was that the integrity and credibility of ITN's reports were at stake. In their coverage of the 2000 presidential election, the US news media rushed to 'call' the result, to be the first with the news. They got it wrong, and their credibility was seriously dented. Papers appeared with the banner headline 'BUSH WINS', when, at the time, he had not won. Journalism depends on the belief that it tells the truth, which is why sanctions are taken against those whose lies are publicly exposed: one US newspaper columnist was sacked because she made up the fact that she had a terminal illness; another was fired for falsifying quotations.

The professionalization of journalism enables it to resist the blandishments and bullying of interventionist owners. If newspapers did not cover the news, or if they skewed it to favour their proprietor, they would lose credibility. If one paper consistently operated a different set of (partial) news values, it would look odd on the news-stands. In short, news content is a product of the combined effect of events in the world and professional practice; it is not the product of the will or whim of the individual journalists (or, for that matter, the owner).

Journalism as Subjectivism

Against this objectivist view is the claim that journalism is subjective. It is the product of the prejudices of the individual writer.
This argument depends, in part, upon the claim that objectivity is
an incoherent idea or an impossible stance. Every story is written
from a 'point of view', which inevitably favours one set of interests
or actors over another. Journalists are individuals both in the sense
that they have different views and in the sense that they have
different skills. (For a survey of journalists' private attitudes, see
Henningham, 1998.) This means that any two journalists may
interpret the same event differently, and some may do it better
than others, by being more resourceful or eloquent than their peers.
A classic representative of this model of journalism is Hunter S.
Thompson, once feted along with Tom Wolfe as an exponent of the
'new journalism' (Thompson himself preferred the expression
'gonzo journalism'). In a typical passage from *Fear and Loathing
on the Campaign Trail '72*, Thompson (1973: 236) demonstrates his
own distinctive approach to political journalism: 'For a variety of
tangled reasons – primarily because my wife was one of the guests
in the house that weekend – I was there when McGovern [at this
stage running for the Democratic nomination] arrived. So we talked
for a while . . . and it occurred to me afterward that it was the first
time he'd ever seen me without a beer can in my hand or babbling
like a loon about freak power, election bets, or some other twisted
subject . . . but he was kind enough not to mention this.'

This version of journalism derives its sense of integrity from the
'honesty' with which it chronicles the subjective responses and
experiences of the reporter. There is no pretence at Olympian
objectivity. The wider assumption is that, while every news report
contains a bias of some kind, these biases are randomly distributed
across and between media outlets. If subjectivity rules, it is at least
plausible that the owner can affect what gets written, to the extent
that they are responsible for selecting journalists who share their
prejudices. But equally, if the value of journalism lies in the
distinctive voices it supplies, skill rather than political values may
count for more in the selection process. In any case, owners tend to
be involved only in the selection of editors, and it is unclear whether
they, or the editors they appoint, would want journalists for their
prejudices rather than for their journalistic skills. Where the first

model of journalism puts the emphasis on professional values and suggests that, like the ideal of the scientific experiment, the results are indifferent to the party doing the job, this second approach stresses the individual's contribution to the outcome. Both, in their different ways, suggest that ownership is largely irrelevant to the political character of coverage.

There is an element of truth contained in these models, both of which share a notion of journalistic autonomy. But what is missing in these accounts of journalism is an explanation of why journalists come to write about one thing rather than another. Rather, the attention is upon *how* they write about a given event, not why that event is selected over any other. It might be countered that they simply report 'events' out there in the world, but of course what counts as 'an event' is not self-evident. An event, or at least one worthy of news coverage, has to be defined as such, and any definition is necessarily contingent and fluid. What is an 'event' to the London *Times* is not necessarily one for the New York *Times*. On the same day, different papers and programmes report different stories. The explanation for this cannot lie with the events themselves, or with the journalists reporting them; it must lie with the process which identifies and prioritizes the stories to be covered. This is the argument of the third model of journalism.

Journalism as Structured Activity

In this final model, 'news' is not the product of some unanticipated event to which news reporters respond. It is pre-planned and anticipated. News is the product of the availability, source and distribution of material resources and interests. Edward Herman and Robert McChesney (1999: 198) report that in 1996 NBC news made the Olympics its most covered story of the year, while for the other network news programmes the Olympics were not in the top ten. 'Perhaps it was a coincidence,' they remark caustically, 'but NBC had the US television rights to the Olympics.' News, and what journalists cover, is a product of the distribution of corporate interests. This has become, according to McQuail (1992: 106), a much-quoted 'law' of journalism. But commercial interests are not the only factor at play. Changes in media technology also shape the character of news coverage. The development of electronic news-gathering technology (ENG) reduced the cost of, and increased access to, pictures of events. When this is combined with portable satellite systems, news editors can get stories from the 'front line' as they happen. What this does to television news values is to change the criteria of newsworthiness and to put the emphasis even more upon the visual.

Often, if there are no pictures, it is not news. Susan Carruthers (2000: 211) gives the example of two events in Iraq in the early 1990s, both involving death and persecution. One was the Shia rebellion, the other was the plight of Kurdish refugees. As it happens, the first cost more lives, but it was the second that appeared on the nightly news, because there were cameras to record it. There were no cameras for the Shia rebellion, and so it was not news. Earthquakes on the other side of the world do not happen (in the sense that they do not appear on the news) without film footage; events in East Timor during the 1990s went largely unreported in the West because, it was suggested, film crews and journalists could not operate safely there. There are limits to this argument. The availability of images matters for some stories (especially foreign news), but not for all. Other stories, about the economy, for example, are 'news' even without an accompanying illustration. A hike in the interest rate is news, even if the only picture is a library photo of the Bundesbank or the Bank of England. What all this suggests is that journalism is the product of a process shaped by technology and values and interests that operate independently of those journalists formally responsible for producing news.

According to this perspective, to explain the character of journalism, we need to look at structural rather than individual factors. The rush to call the 2000 presidential election result owed much to the competition between the networks to establish themselves as the market leader. To understand journalistic practice, we need to look at the pressures on the editorial budget brought about by price wars and other commercial factors, such as the need to attract advertising. Advertisers may want lifestyle features, rather than investigations (especially of their clients). Equally important will be the political pressure from parties and politicians who through their techniques of media management seek to shape the news. The implication of this perspective on journalism is that the fate of investigative journalism lies with managerial decisions (and the material interests behind these decisions) about how to allocate resources. Schultz (1998: 192) describes the economics of Australian investigative journalism in the 1980s: 'At the same time as editors at the *Sydney Morning Herald* were saying they could not afford a team of three investigative reporters, *60 Minutes* was prepared to let producers and researchers work on major items for several months.' Andrew Neil (1997: 56–7) tells of his decision to axe the *Sunday Times*' Insight Team (often thought of as the embodiment of the investigative journalism tradition (Doig, 1997)). This executive decision had nothing, says Neil, to do with the 'far left politics' of the team's leader, but was made because they were only working on 'second rate investigations'. Whatever the truth, the restructuring of the paper affected the kind of stories it carried. The explanation is not to be found in 'events' in the world – there is always something to investigate – but rather in terms of the political economy of the media.

This third perspective on journalism rejects the two main premises of the other ones. Journalism is necessarily selective and partial, but the selectivity and partiality are not the product of individual values and skills or professional codes. Instead this structuralist model sees coverage as the product of a news-generating process. Understanding the content of news, therefore, means studying the structures that organize it: the division of labour and distribution of resources, the technology and the hierarchy within newsrooms. 'News' is, by this account, what the organization determines it is. Rather than news events creating news stories, we have a situation in which newsrooms create news stories. Take, for example, the distribution of foreign correspondents. All news organizations take decisions about the allocation of these reporters – about the number of staff, about whether they are on a permanent contract or stringers, and about which countries they are allocated to. The effect of these allocations is to shape the news from which the outlet selects. As far as readers and viewers are concerned, nothing happens in countries without foreign correspondents. The character and quantity of foreign coverage is shaped by the general size of the budget and then by its allocation. Jeremy Tunstall (1996: 339–40) shows how the 'upmarket' daily papers in Britain have increased their foreign staff, from around 70 two decades years ago, to more than 100 in the 1990s. The 'downmarket' tabloids, by contrast, employ no foreign correspondents at all, while they used ten 20 years ago. Also important is how these correspondents are distributed. Tunstall (ibid.: 347) reveals that they are concentrated in Europe and North America. Africa gets much less attention, and what it does get is heavily skewed towards South Africa. This is an example of a general phenomenon, one which we encountered in discussing the representation of politics: news is a product of its sources. William Gamson and Andre Modigliani (1989) talk of the 'sponsors' of news – official sources, interest groups and so on – to explain the form taken by the coverage.

If one factor shaping the practice of journalism is the deployment of journalists and their sources, another is the allocation of resources. Stories cost money, and with a limited budget news organizations have to determine what they can *afford* to cover (or put another way, what they cannot afford to ignore, because of the ratings and advertising income they need to generate). In 1970, reporting the war in Vietnam cost Reuters £40 000 per annum (Read, 1992: 382). A disillusioned ex-member of the BBC's *Newsnight* current affairs team wrote: 'I know how budget cuts and management fads have neutered Newsnight: I've lived through the process. I have seen the most well-resourced, creatively gifted and filmically talented programme-makers turned, through sheer force of cost-cutting, into an understaffed, overworked team whose first thought must now always be the bottom line' (*The Guardian*, 16 February 1998). Budgetary factors are not the only ones shaping the news; organizational changes have an impact as well. The managerial structure is important in determining which priorities and interests dominate the scope and character of news coverage. This may be evident in the organizational distribution of power: how editorial decisions are taken and who is involved – the way the 'total newsroom' of US papers involves both marketing and editorial interests. As director general of the BBC, John Birt reorganized the structure of the corporation, creating, among other things, a new management structure for news and current affairs. This, argued Philip Schlesinger (1987), had the effect of altering the news priorities with which the BBC operated. But organizational factors may also be apparent in the more mundane relations of reporter and sub-editor. In the UK, sub-editors typically have the autonomy to rewrite stories; in the USA, reporters are expected to approve the changes. Whatever the arrangement, it affects 'the news'.

In the structuralist view of journalism, it is possible to see a place for proprietorial intervention, not (as in the second view) through the selection of journalists, but through the organization of the news machine. Insofar as owners (or their interests) play a crucial role in setting budgets, allocating space and so on, their actions frame the way journalists operate. These factors may not affect the particular character of any one story, but they can set the framework within which all stories exist.

Even changes in the political regime itself can affect the practice of journalism. Liu Hong (1998: 32) reports that, before the process of economic liberalization, 'all newspapers in China had the status of the emperor's daughters. They did not have to worry about their dowries or marriages. Most papers received their subscription from the public purse . . . It made no difference whether people wanted to buy the paper or not.' Journalists were answerable only to the communist authorities. However, when economic reforms were introduced in the 1990s, the incentives changed to make journalists more responsive to their readers (or the *perception* of their readers). Again the suggestion is that journalism is shaped by wider structural factors.

The full implication of this, argues Michael Schudson (2000), is that we need to view the organization of journalism from a variety of perspectives, not just the political economy one offered here, but also one deriving from the sociology of organizations – the daily routines and habits of news production – and one deriving from a cultural account of the values and world views that construct 'news' itself. These perspectives give added weight to the general sense of journalism as part of an embedded process.

But because journalism is constantly being constructed and reconstructed, we have to be conscious of its changeability, and of the possibility that journalism itself may be eliminated in the same way that it was formed. Journalism as a career has already been overtaken by public relations. Added to this, politicians are increasingly interested in finding ways of reaching audiences that do not involve journalists: by appearing on chat shows or by using the internet. Research by Dooley and Grosswiler (1997: 43–4) argues that 'new political media are precipitating an awareness, at least among some mainstream political journalists, that their jurisdiction over political news reporting is in jeopardy'. Whether or not such fears are confirmed, the suggestion remains that the wider context of journalism is the key focus for any predictions for its future.

In default of these wider changes, it remains important to see how resource allocation, and the commercial interests that underlie it, directly affect the way politics is covered. In Britain, 30 years ago, political coverage was primarily a matter of reporting directly the proceedings of parliamentary life. Now the emphasis, as we saw in Chapter 3, has shifted to the commentator and the columnist (Tunstall, 1996: 282) It is the commentators who command the space and the kudos. Their stock-in-trade is to pass judgement on the political story (with its own heroes and villains), telling us how it began and where it will end. The political commentator is, therefore, instrumental in establishing a picture of politics in which personality is as important as principle. This development in political coverage is a product not simply of the changing agenda and interests of the writers, but of the pressures and interests that caused them to be appointed and to be allocated space. These include the shifting commercial incentives and interests of the newspaper industry which squeeze out direct political reporting, because it is costly and cannot rival broadcasting coverage. Besides, attracting advertisers pushes the agenda away from political stories to 'human interest' ones, a trend that is itself compounded by the way in which the flow of political information is increasingly managed and controlled. In short, it is possible to see the rise of the political columnist and political commentary as the product of shifts in the political economy of the media.

The third model of journalism places the emphasis on the effect of the political economy within which journalists operate. In this respect, there is a useful parallel to be drawn between the organization of journalism in the media industry and the organization of other industries. This is to reinforce a theme that runs throughout this book: the need to see the coverage of politics as a commercially mediated cultural activity. At the beginning of Chapter 6, we noted that media industries are producing products and services, and that their practices have to be understood in the same way that other businesses are understood. But these conglomerates are also producing culture, products that have meaning for the way people identify themselves and others. Our understanding of the behaviour of these organizations needs to reflect this fact. One implication of this might be that we need to take account of research into cognate cultural industries, whether Hollywood or the record industry. Recent work by Keith Negus (1999), for example, has pointed to the ways in which record companies organize themselves to support particular musical genres (and to marginalize others). 'News' can be understood as a genre in the same sense, and we can see how changing corporate strategy can affect the conditions for different types of journalists (artists). The columnist is, after all, a performer. The idea that journalists be seen as sober-suited versions of the pop star may seem faintly ridiculous, but then to look at the salaries paid to newscasters is to remind ourselves that they are celebrities at the very least, and more often than not 'stars', no different in the way they are made and marketed by corporate strategy from Julia Roberts or Phil Collins. The marketing of the performers is intimately linked to the marketing of the content, and just as Hollywood plot lines are shaped by corporate strategy, so are the stories told in the news.

Conclusion

It might be supposed that, if journalism is structured in the way that the third model suggests, the prospects for reform are limited, that attempts to counter 'dumbing down' are bound to fail. This conclusion is not warranted. Rather, what the third model does indicate is that the answer to the problem does not lie in eliminating spin doctors or in the good intentions of journalists. Reform has to focus on the conditions of journalism. The arguments for regulating journalism are discussed in Chapter 12, what needs to be noted here is that legislation can make a difference, insofar as it shapes the conditions under which journalism is done. But it is equally important to address the market conditions under which media operate and the regulatory regimes that apply to them. As Alan Doig (1997: 206) writes: 'Any revival of investigatory journalism . . . must work within a very different environment than that which promoted investigative journalism in earlier decades.' By this he means that the revival must address the commercial pressures that make 'ratings and profit' of greater importance than 'performance and the public interest'.

Nor does the third model absolve journalists of responsibility for what they report and how they report it. There is still a place for journalistic ethics. The structuring of journalism shapes the *role* which its occupant has to fulfil, but the role is not so tightly defined as to straitjacket its inhabitant. Roles are *performed*, and individuals have the scope to interpret the rules and conventions which define their activity. To this extent, journalists are in a position to make judgements about what it is legitimate to say or do in the pursuit of a story. In return, society is entitled to pass judgement on how that role is fulfilled and to require different standards. What those standards should be are discussed later. For now, we end by recalling the experiments in 'civic journalism' which were mentioned in Chapter 6. Civic journalism was an attempt to improve the quality of election coverage, and to counter the political management of news. The coalition of media organizations in North Carolina created a common agenda, based upon the priorities of their readers and viewers. Politicians were required in interviews to address this agenda, rather than their preferred one (Clark, 1997). The results were not always viewed as successful, with critics complaining that civic journalism was essentially conservative and uncritical (Jackson, 1997), but the point is that the North Carolina experiment represents an instance of the way in which the organization of news gathering directly shapes the output. Civic journalism underlines the argument that the capacity of journalists to play a democratic role is not simply a matter of individual integrity or of the willingness of reporters to resist the pressures applied by spin doctors. Journalism's ability to serve democracy depends on the allocation of resources and the organization of its practices.

8

Dream Worlds: Globalization and the Webs of Power

Mass communication has existed for little more than the average person's lifespan, and yet in that short time we have moved from what now seems the most basic of radio communication (the crystal set) to the apparent sophistication of digital broadcasting (and the possibility of interactive television). We have yet to experience the full consequences of these latest developments, but we can be sure that, 70 years from now, people will look at our system of communication and think of it as being as primitive as we now regard a valve radio. Of course, it will not just be the technologies that change. It will be the way in which people relate to these new forms of communications, and how these relations order their sense of themselves and the others to whom they are linked. You can, after all, change the amount people talk, and who they talk to, just by rearranging the furniture in a room. What, then, might be the effect of altering the entire system of communication? For Edward Herman and Robert McChesney (1997: 136), though the effects of media globalization may, in the short term, be 'benign or positive', in the longer term it threatens 'democratic politics'.

Later chapters of this book explore some of the implications of future technologies for democracy and political activity; this chapter concentrates on one particular process and its effects: globalization. The political importance of a globalized media can be measured in a variety of dimensions. Firstly, globalization can describe the power and reach of the new media conglomerates. Secondly, it can point to changes in the ways in which national governments and nation states operate. Thirdly, it can be identified in the shifts in the way citizens of those states view themselves and others. Global media have introduced viewing publics to wars and famines; audiences have become party to international negotiations and virtual participants in acts of diplomacy and peace keeping (Carruthers, 2000: 197–205; Curran, 2000: 136–7). Governments, the UN, relief agencies and others have all used the global presence of television crews and reporters to shape political agendas and policies. Whether this has created a 'global village' or cultural imperialism is a subject of much debate, but it is clear that perception of the world and access to it have been transformed, and in this and other ways globalization affects the relationship between mass media and politics.

Signs of the global media enterprise economy are already familiar ones. They can be seen in the world wide presence of corporations like Disney and Sony, News Corporation or Reuters, organizations which appear to have a stake everywhere. This is not a new phenomenon; arguably it is the continuation of the legacy of empire; nonetheless recent changes have been rapid and far-ranging. In the early 1990s, CNN transmitted its rolling news to 137 countries (*The Economist*, 2 May 1992: 26). Now CNN is part of the vast Time Warner conglomerate, and as such is part of an even vaster organization following the merger with America Online. This conglomerate has a stake in vast tracts of mass culture, from the Hanna-Barbera cartoons to *Time* magazine, from *The Matrix* to *Batman,* from Madonna to Metallica, from P.D. James to Sidney Shelton. Back in 1994, the cable company Viacom paid $10 billion for the Hollywood studio Paramount, adding to its ownership of MTV (Music Television), the publishers Simon & Schuster, Beavis and Butt-Head cartoons, the Blockbuster video chain, and Virgin Interactive Entertainment (Herman and McChesney, 1997: 77–81). At the time, the chairman of Viacom described his company as a 'global media powerhouse of unparalleled proportions' (*Independent on Sunday*, 6 April 1994). Since those days, these conglomerates have been joined, and sometimes dwarfed, by the other new global communications players. Companies like Vodafone-Mannesman operate vast mobile phone networks (estimated value in 2000: $261billion); and in the next generation of their products, they promise to supply images and websites in the way they now offer voices and text messages.

Towering above these massive conglomerates is the Microsoft empire (estimated value in 2000: $577 billion) created by Bill Gates, which has been the gatekeeper for almost all forms of computer-based communication, colonizing the internal software of computers and their capacity to communicate with each other. Microsoft has bought into UK cable networks (NTL and Telewest), interactive television (NDS) and into DX3, which is involved in encryption of music for the web. In 1998, Microsoft was investing in technologies which enable viewers to use their televisions to surf the web; they also forged a deal with British Telecommunications to give them access to the link between mobile phones and the internet (Golding and Murdock, 2000: 80).

All these ventures reflect an ambition to provide a complete media package. Indeed, what these organizations represent is an ability to control cultural production – whether news or entertainment – whenever and wherever it takes place. They are the warlords of commercial and cultural global domination; they are the new emperors. Or at least this is how they seem. This chapter is an attempt to assess the extent of this power and the implications of globalized mass communications for the politics of media. Importantly, the politics involved apply, not only to corporations and governments, but also to the cultural politics of identity, space and place. But first we need to look at the conditions and processes that have been bracketed together in the idea of globalization. Globalization did not just appear, driven by some law of nature; it had to be made to happen.

A History of the Future

It is impossible to separate the notion of globalization from the possibilities created by technological change. Indeed, the story of mass communications is inextricably bound up with the story of technical innovation, and this is as true for global media as for anything else. What is important, though, is how the tale is told. It is relatively easy to get agreement about the innovations that have mattered and what they involved. First there was radio, the capacity to transmit sound over distance, without the need for any physical connection, and with the signal available to anyone with a receiver; and then there was television, which added pictures to the sound. Both were a development of the technologies of the telegraph and the telephone, themselves the inheritors of work in electromagnetism and electricity.

These technical changes were marked by more mundane, but no less important developments in component technology: the replacement of the valve by the transistor, opening up the possibility of portability and reliability, as well as cost reduction. From here the path led to integrated circuitry and the microchip, crucial to the creation of the computer and satellite technology, which were themselves dependent on theoretical work in mathematics, philosophical logic, astronomy and so on. And later still, this knowledge and technology have been harnessed to create, with innovations in computer language, the worldwide web and the so-called 'digital revolution'. The latter promises new one-stop media: 'As a consequence of the digital revolution practically every product of the media – including books, films, sporting events, phone calls, archives, videos and newspapers – can be digitized; that is converted into the 1s and 0s of computer code. These can then be dispatched – at the speed of an encyclopaedia per second – across a worldwide network of optical fibres'(*The Guardian Outlook*, 13 May 1995). Meanwhile, the internet is already seen to herald an order in which not only the way we communicate, but the way we organize our lives will be radically overturned. Central to this transformation has been the compression of geographical distance, so that financial markets in New York, Tokyo and London are a keyboard stroke away from each other. Vast areas of land and of populations are covered by a single geostationary satellite. The Asiasat satellite, for example, reaches 38 countries and 2.7 billion people; as such, it has access to 40 per cent of the world's TV sets. In short, new technologies appear to be creating new possibilities for communication and new forms of existence.

But while it is relatively easy to get agreement about the key technologies and what they make possible, there is much less of a consensus about *why* it is happening and therefore what interests and processes are implicated in the changes. Sometimes it is made to seem that we are in the grip of a process of (natural) evolution, and that we need only to adapt to this changing order, reluctantly at first perhaps (worried by what it is doing to the world we know), but soon embracing it (and then wondering how ever we managed without it). This kind of interpretation of events is associated with writers like Ithiel de Sola Pool (1990) who see each wave of technological invention as building progressively upon its predecessor. It makes no sense to resist. We have to accept the political, social and cultural changes that new technologies bring in their wake. For de Sola Pool, this means the acceptance that, if new forms of communication technology destroy or make redundant national borders, we need to give up our quaint affection for a world of sovereign nation states.

This way of thinking about the development of communications can be labelled technological determinism. It assumes that technology is driven by an inner scientific logic, a logic of progress in which each stage adds to its predecessor, enabling people to do more than they could before. To defy this logic is to act irrationally: it is to refuse the opportunity to improve the quality of life; it is to deny the inevitable. The only reasonable response is to adapt. This is a view that has a strong intuitive appeal. There does indeed seem to be a logic to technical change, one that takes us from the transmission of sound to the transmission of pictures. It is hard to mount arguments against technologies which appear to give us more of what we already have, especially if it is cheaper, faster, more reliable. Who would swap their digital receiver for a valve radio, their car for a horse? It is easy to succumb to the pressure to adopt, and adapt to, each new development. To be without television and radio in developed countries is to be cut off, to be marginalized. Groups, like White Dot, who campaign for the abolition of television, seem from this perspective to be anachronisms, no more in touch with social or scientific reality than flat earthers or creationists.

But however attractive the idea of technological determinism, we need to be wary of its charms. Brian Winston (1998), for example, offers a quite different perspective on these changes: they are not the product of some persistent logic, they are instead the consequence of interests and intentions; the route taken by technical development is not mapped by the logic of 'progress' but by the allocation of resources, itself the consequence of political and economic priorities.

Radio was the product of military needs, a way of coordinating the movement of vast armies. In the same way, the transistor was designed to meet the needs of submarine technology; and the integrated circuit (the microchip) was needed for space exploration and the security interests allied with it. The internet too is the product of corporate and state interests. Initially created as a failsafe system of communication to enable the US military to continue to function in the aftermath of a nuclear attack, the internet was developed by scientists who wanted to use the network of computers to communicate with each other. Only with the appearance of user-friendly computer languages has the current form of the web become possible. Similar processes are at work transforming the net's anarchic chaos of information into a highly lucrative commercial market.

Domestic access to news, entertainment and sport is not simply the consequence of technological innovation. It is the product of, among other things, commercial initiative. In 1993, the Bell Atlantic telephone company merged with Tele-Communications (TCI). The deal was worth $33 billion and created a giant communications conglomerate that could reach 42 per cent of US homes. Murdoch's News Corporation made a similar deal with the second biggest telecommunications company in the USA. The tie-up allowed Murdoch to supply films, news and much more to its newly acquired subscribers. Moves like this create the material reality that allows modern communication to exist. So it goes on: technology is the product of priorities established within the corporate and political system. In April 2000, Pearsons announced a £12 billion merger with the CLT Ufa group, based in Luxembourg. This meant that the producer of *Baywatch* and *Neighbours* was linked to 'a network of 22 television channels and 18 radio stations, creating Europe's biggest broadcasting business' (*The Guardian*, 8 April 2000). The Pearson announcement came only three months after the Time Warner–America Online merger, which linked a company which had the potential to reach a billion viewers through its news (CNN) and entertainment (HBO) outlets to another company with 20 million members in the USA alone, not to mention those in Japan, Brazil, Canada, Hong Kong and across Europe. These mergers were driven by the need to locate new markets and to have a controlling stake in new forms of media. Furthermore, they depended on the cooperation of government. 'Globalization' is, after all, as much a political as an economic phenomenon, a product of New Right ideology as well as of the 'logic' of the market. The globalized media economy depended crucially on the 1997 decision of the World Trade Organization to deregulate telecommunications. Without a liberalization of trade and other barriers, the global networks could not operate.

But this version of technical change, in which intent and interest are decisive, is itself open to criticism. It may exaggerate the extent to which the key players themselves command the outcome of research and development. Neither the technologies nor their consequences can be anticipated fully. Organizations are as often coping with the effects of old technologies as they are calling new ones into being. Technologies do indeed develop some degree of independent momentum; and while the various actors may be instrumental in instigating and regulating these technologies, they are never fully in command (Hughes, 1983). One factor in the equation, for example, is governments which, for a variety of different reasons and in a variety of different ways, also regulate systems of communication. The extent to which they succeed may be debated, but they cannot be ignored. In the same way, the use made of the new technologies is not controlled absolutely by the corporations. The music industry, for instance, became concerned by the ways in which MP3 technology (the downloading of CD-quality music from the web) threatened its source of income, just as the flood of so called 'dot.com' companies unsettled financial markets and established a new breed of corporate actor.

The degree to which the use of technology can be controlled and predicted varies from case to case. Marshall McLuhan (1994) represented this difference in terms of 'hot' and 'cool' technologies, Ivan Illich (1975) in terms of 'hard' and 'soft'. What both were trying to capture was the extent to which some forms of communications technology (the telephone, for example) allowed for considerable control by the user, while other forms (television) allowed for very little. We decide what is said on the phone; broadcasters decide what we see. In other words, the technology itself is one element in the way the story of technical and social change is told. In contemplating the future of mass communications, therefore, we should not think in terms either of technology automatically dictating the shape of the world, or of that world being determined by political will and/or commercial interest. Rather, the future is a product of complex interactions between the technical, the commercial and political realms. It is this third approach to technical change that is used here in exploring the political consequences of a globalized media. Technological change is made possible by the new conglomerates, but it is these conglomerates that give impetus to the technology, and both are dependent upon the mediating effects of political regimes and other participants in the process.

Globalization

Globalization has many different meanings, but one of the most straightforward definitions is that offered by John Tomlinson, who writes (1999: 165): 'Globalization . . . refers to the rapidly developing process of complex interconnections between societies, cultures, institutions and individuals world-wide. It is a social process which involves a compression of time and space, shrinking distances through a dramatic reduction in the time taken – either physically or representationally – to cross them, so making the world seem smaller and in a certain sense bringing human beings "closer" to one another' (Tomlinson, 1999: 165). Globalization represents the idea that traditional borders are being superseded by a system which operates at a supranational level.

The expression of this new order may be found in the *content* of communication: the same images and icons wherever you go. This is most typically illustrated by the ubiquity of Coca-Cola or of film and pop stars (Tom Cruise, Julia Roberts, Madonna, Ricky Martin, Celine Dion), but it can be represented also in the same photos of the same event appearing everywhere: the burnt Iraqi soldier in his tank on the Basra road; Princess Diana's funeral cortege; Cathy Freeman winning an Olympic gold medal. Or globalization may be identified in the system of *distribution*, with everyone inhabiting the same networks of communication: the same corporations supplying television programmes and news to everyone. Finally, globalization may refer to a system of *production* by which the control of means of communication lies with organizations that exist above and beyond individual nation states.

To draw attention to these three dimensions of globalization is not to be committed to the view that they all accurately describe changes in the world or that they necessarily run harmoniously with each other. While the same records may be distributed across the world by the same transnational corporations, those corporations are also involved in marketing particular performers to distinct markets, and even the global acts are packaged differently for different contexts. Cultural content is not standardized, rather it is customized. This is one aspect of what Roland Robertson (1995) calls 'glocalization'. Globalization is not necessarily about creating homogeneity and uniformity, although it may indeed do this; it is about the redistribution of power and about the technologies and interests that are linked to the new order.

The point of drawing attention to these three dimensions of globalization is not to suggest that they represent the complete picture, but to enable us to separate the different ways in which globalization may tie media and politics. The driving dynamic of globalization may stem from the same set of technological developments and the commercial interests that organize them, but the political consequences cannot be simply read off these facts. To assess the implications of globalization for the link between media and politics, we need to focus on two issues. The first is the effect of globalized media on the powers of national governments, the formal sites of legitimate political power, to regulate media in the name of whatever political interests those governments claim to represent. The second, and related, effect is on the cultural politics of identity, on the way in which the 'people' are constituted and reconstituted in global networks.

These two aspects of globalization are nicely captured in two stories about Rupert Murdoch's attempt to bring India within his media empire. The first is an account of a trip he paid to India in the mid-1990s. Alan Rusbridger (*Guardian Weekend*, 9 April 1994) wrote: 'He [Murdoch] kept all his appointments, attended all his lunches, gave numerous interviews and made a big impression all round. "He had India eating out of his hand," said Tavleen Singh, a leading columnist with the Indian Express. "It was like the visit of a head of state."' This story tells both of the way in which Murdoch's global power commanded respect, and of how he needed to win people over to his ambitions. The other story takes place four years later, when it was announced that a New Delhi lawyer had convinced an Indian court to issue a warrant for Murdoch's arrest, on the grounds that the movies transmitted on his Star channel (*Dance of the Damned*, *The Jigsaw Murders*), 'were vulgar, obscene and unfit for Indian audiences' (*The Guardian*, 9 August 1998). In this case, cultural content, rather than cultural control, was the issue. But both stories tell of the complex politics of a globalized media.

Conglomerates, Governments and Identities

Rupert Murdoch's trip to India is typical of the way he has sought to build up a global media business. He has deliberately courted those in power. Commercial success is not just a product of commercial resources; it depends on constant negotiations with governments who both need his corporations and have the capacity to set the terms under which they operate.

Murdoch's Star channel is a classic example of this. Star TV is delivered via the Asiasat satellite and has a potential reach of 45 million viewers. It gives access to seven out of the ten fastest growing economies and to markets that are worth a fortune in advertising revenue. Star's existence depends on government support or at least acquiescence. Murdoch has been assiduous in his cultivation of political leaders, without whose cooperation he could not succeed. He dropped the BBC's world service from his satellite portfolio, out of deference to the political sensitivities of the Chinese authorities, just as one of News Corporation's subsidiaries, the publishers HarperCollins, dropped their book contract with Chris Patten, and just as Andrew Neil's tenure at the *Sunday Times* ended in the aftermath of his paper's claims about corruption in Malaysia. These are taken by critics as examples of Murdoch's reluctance to antagonize political leaderships with whom he needs to do business.

The journalist John Pilger, one of Rupert Murdoch's most persistent critics, argues that the media entrepreneur goes to considerable lengths to secure the support of the Chinese regime: 'his Star TV broadcast a documentary series made by the Beijing regime, eulogising the life and times of Deng Xianoping. . . . [A] hagiography of Deng written by his daughter was published by Basic Books, a division of Harper Collins; . . . Mrs Deng was flown to Murdoch's US ranch and feted with lavish parties' (*The Guardian*, 16 March 1998). Similar claims are made for the ways in which Murdoch cultivated his links with Margaret Thatcher and then Tony Blair (inviting the latter, when he was still in opposition, to address a meeting of News Corporation executives in Australia). Not that such hospitality always delivers results. His bid to buy Manchester United FC was rejected. States have reacted against the trend towards a globalized media. One source of concern is that global products are in some way 'harmful', economically or culturally. So it is that states opt for regulation in order to protect the interests of local companies (and the economic benefits – and votes – they represent) or to protect the integrity of the national culture.

To get an idea of the fears generated by globalization, take the case of the Reuters news agency, which supplies news to commercial companies, financial markets, broadcasters and newspapers. In 1991, Tunstall and Palmer (1991: 46) noted: 'Reuters has become the biggest distributor of computer-based information services, with offices in 81 countries and fixed revenue earnings from some 200 000 terminals in 35 countries.' In 1998, the Reuters business had expanded so that it distributed news 'to over 260 client broadcasters in 85 countries' (Paterson, 1998: 79). But the issue is not just the ubiquity of Reuters, it is also what those clients get. As Tunstall and Palmer (1991: 46) explain: 'For the world's leading electronic publisher, products, technology, markets and systems are interdependent: Reuters deals in real-time information services, transaction products, trading-room systems, historical information and last (as a revenue earner) but not least, media products.' Reuters' aim is to provide 'complete information packages', but in serving all their customers, there is a danger that they satisfy none of them. Only stories with a universal resonance are carried, and those specific to particular settings are ignored (ibid.: 58). Global news, it is suggested, creates a monolithic view of the world, one in which regional and national differences are lost to view, and everybody is subsumed within a specific dominant news agenda. Paterson (1998: 80) observes another trend in the global supply of news: the concentration of control over the selection of news as Reuters and Worldwide Television News come to dominate the market.

This process of standardization and concentration affects culture as well as news, exacerbating fears about the ways in which globalization threatens cultural identity and difference. In its place, says Benjamin Barber (1997: 90), stands 'McWorld': 'With or without resistance, nations with proud traditions of film-making independence like France, England, Sweden, India, Indonesia and Japan are in fact gradually succumbing to the irresistible lure of product that is not only predominantly American but, even when still indigenous, is rooted in the glamour of the seductive trinity sex, violence and money, set to a harmonizing score of American rock and roll.' Globalization, it is argued, produces homogeneity: the same ideas and values, the same films and songs, carried to all parts of the world.

This process squeezes out local culture. In villages in India, in rooms lit by 20 watt bulbs and warmed by open fires, people watch satellite TV: 'We began with MTV . . . A touch on the zapper brought us *The Bold And The Beautiful*, a sub-Dynasty American soap . . . Zap, and suddenly the features of famed British telly-chef Keith Floyd . . . Zap, and we have skiing on Prime Sports' (*Guardian Weekend*, 9 April 1994). Don Ayteo of MTV boasts: 'We've revolutionised the way Indian kids devote themselves to leisure . . . We've created a youth culture where there was simply none before' (quoted in *Guardian Weekend*, 9 April 1994). Howard Stringer of CBS told the Royal Television Society: 'The new media giants that win control of UK broadcast properties may view them as cash cows whose resources are to be wrung dry – and invested elsewhere in their global empire. Or they may prefer to replicate for Great Britain shows that they have already produced elsewhere – and thereby reap enormous cost advantages over native competitors. Your country could become a backend market for companies that can produce bland, generic, all-purpose, trans-cultural programming more cheaply than you can produce your own distinctive programming' (quoted in *Independent on Sunday*, 21 February 1993).

Because they are worried by such developments, governments in Canada, France and Scandinavia have erected tariff barriers and imposed quotas. Their intention has been to protect local economies and cultures. So it is that rules have been established to limit the number of foreign imports to be shown on a channel or about the provision for, and supply of, news coverage. The French persuaded the EU to introduce a Directive which required that 51 per cent of TV output came from Europe and that the WTO deregulation of telecommunications left untouched domestic support for national cinema. Canadian governments have introduced quotas to guarantee space for Canadian music and have blocked US investment in Canada's media and culture industries. This approach is not confined to the West. Governments in Singapore, Malaysia, Saudi Arabia and Iran have banned satellite dishes (Sreberny, 2000: 113). Not that such injunctions always work: piracy and illegal technology always threaten to subvert state power (Held *et al.*, 1999: 371). Despite this, governments continue to try and control what their citizens can see or hear (or should be prevented from seeing or hearing).

Where broadcast systems are based within the borders of a nation state, governments have been able to regulate the content of broadcasts, although this depends on the constitution of the country concerned: the US Constitution's First Amendment protects content in the name of a free press. But where states still retain the right to control, their power to do so is nullified if the transmitter is based elsewhere or if the corporation providing the service has, by virtue of its commercial power, the capacity to rebuff government intervention. This is not a new problem. During the cold war, both the East and West sought to win over their rival population by taking advantage of the difficulty of controlling external broadcasts (the USA, with the help of the CIA, set up Voice of America, Radio Liberty and Radio Free Europe (Stonor Saunders, 2000)).

These attempts at regulation are partly about economic control and partly about cultural character. The latter, for example, explains the French concern over the integrity of their language and concern about 'imported' words. (This is one aspect of a more general worry about the fact that English has become the dominant language of the global village.) Concern over economic control is expressed in the subsidies for French cinema. Both aspects represent efforts to protect a particular notion of national sovereignty and to assert the capacity of nation states to operate with relative autonomy. Insofar as governments, for whatever reason, cannot impose regulations on new forms of communication or on their corporate backers, a degree of national sovereignty, and by implication national identity, may be lost.

Not only does globalization threaten to alter the capacity of states to control communications within their borders, it also affects the relationship between states. In particular, there is a trend towards information inequalities. Less developed countries (LDCs) struggle to participate in the new global system. In 1990, sub-Saharan Africa had 3 per cent of the 2.1 billion radios in the world; Latin America had 8 per cent, Asia 30 per cent, Europe 27 per cent; and North America 29 per cent (*The Economist*, 2 May 1992). And to the extent that these LDCs do participate in the world media market, they do so within delivery systems created and maintained by the global corporations (Malm and Wallis, 1993).

The limited space available to geostationary satellites has been monopolized by the powerful players. If information and communications represent a capacity to participate in the making of the new world order, inequalities in the distribution of media resources constitutes a form of disenfranchisement.

But are these fears of globalization warranted? There is a real danger of getting caught up in the rhetoric and the hype, and in overlooking the more mundane features of mass communications. India is a vast and disparate country, with nearly 20 different languages, and with many religious and social divides. Is it realistic to see mass media corporations, however large, imposing a single culture? It is certainly important to resist the idea that there is an inevitability about the process. Malavika Singh, an editor and programme maker, argues: 'You can't stop it, but you can counter it. Because other cultures have succumbed to Murdoch, it doesn't mean India will be the same . . . India is a 5,000 year-old culture and it's not going to take the shit' (quoted in *Guardian Weekend*, 9 April 1994). More prosaically, Michael Tracey (1985: 34) has argued that it is 'simply untrue to say that imported television programmes, from the U.S. or other metropolitan countries, always have a dominant presence within an indigenous culture. Certainly, they do not always attract larger audiences than homemade programs, nor do they always threaten national production.' And while Tracey wrote this some time ago, more recent evidence from China and Japan (De Launey, 1995; Zhao and Murdock, 1996) accords with his general point that Western culture does not automatically find an audience.

States do find ways of countering or mitigating the effects of global culture. Just as different states organized the same broadcasting technology into different regulatory frameworks, so they have developed strategies for deflecting globalizing tendencies. Governments have imposed limitations on cross-media ownership. They have imposed quotas and introduced subsidies to ensure that local and national cultures are represented and encouraged. Even where populations are exposed to the most global of cultural icons or images, there is no guarantee that they will be transformed into a uniform mass, blessed with a single set of tastes. The way the culture is used and interpreted is not determined by producers and distributors alone, but is the consequence of local contexts and conditions (Scott, 1997).

Global cultural networks have, in fact, made possible a cultural politics of empowerment. This has enabled the coordination of protest of the kind that was seen at the World Trade Organization meeting in Seattle in 1999 and in the 18 June Carnival Against Capital earlier that same year. It has facilitated the creation of alternative sources of news and information, the new technologies making possible independent reporting of events that challenge the official version. It has also led to greater cultural hybridization. Some of the responses to globalization have been informed by the idea that each country or nation state is marked by a single, monolithic culture which has to be protected like a rare endangered species. But if it is assumed that all cultures are mongrels, made up of components taken from each other, then the need for regulation is felt less strongly and the prospects of globalization are less fearsome. But these other aspects to the globalization process are not purely self-sustaining; they too – like the major conglomerates – depend on the mediating role of the political authorities. In this instance, they depend on the existence of some form of public sphere, a forum within which views can be exchange and debated.

Typically, it is public service broadcasting that has provided this public sphere. Public service broadcasting is supposed to regulate access (what programmes, which views), not in terms of commercial or political power, but in terms of some principle of pluralism and diversity. There is much disagreement as to whether public service broadcasting can and should serve democracy in this way, but our immediate concern is with whether, whatever its costs and benefits, the public service form can survive the globalized order. The Canadian Broadcasting Corporation cut more than 3000 jobs between 1995 and 2000, and cut a mainstay of its schedules, *Midday*. Similar pressures are being felt in Australia and Europe, leading Tracey (*New Statesman*, 24 July 2000) to conclude that 'public service broadcasting now seems to be a corpse on leave'.

Certainly, the new mass media make it much harder for public service television to continue in its current mode. With the proliferation of channels, the notion of the 'public' itself is being reconstituted into a mass of special interest audiences. Digital television creates the possibility of 200 channels for each home; not only that, it also allows users to customize the schedule to accord with their particular preferences. This makes it very much more difficult to talk about 'the viewing public', since there is no guarantee that people are watching the same thing at the same time. The TV executive Barry Cox argues that digital television 'will intensify the fragmentation of audiences . . . Broadcasting becomes narrowcasting – the distribution of content to small, niche audiences' (*Prospect*, November 1998: 16). In its original incarnation, public service broadcasting was an attempt to address the differences between people and their commonality. Different tastes were catered for within a single schedule on a single channel, or a small number of channels. With the proliferation of channels, audiences become increasingly segmented as the channels also seek to find niches to fill. The net effect is to erode the central pillar of public service broadcasting, the 'public' itself. This is overlaid by the erosion of the nation state which also served to frame or bound the public (although it is not necessary for publics to be tied to nation states).

A second tenet of public service broadcasting is its independence from commerce, or the preservation of a distance between commerce and content. But through the combination of channel proliferation and deregulation, the broadcasting environment has been changed so that, even if public service broadcasting is sheltered from commerce, it still has to compete with it. In the face of commercial competition, public corporations like the BBC are being squeezed out by, or are forced to emulate, their rivals. This can be measured by the struggle over the right to cover certain events. Public service broadcasters struggle to compete with the commercial sector in their bid to hold onto major sporting events, which are crucial not only to ratings and the legitimacy of the public sector, but also to the notion of a 'common culture' and the identity which grounds it. The effect of competition can also be witnessed in the type of programming, in the pressure to move news programming out of peak viewing hours or to introduce tabloid news values (Franklin, 1998; Hallin, 2000). It seems probable that in years to come, public service broadcasting, if it continues to exist, will be reinvented as a minority service.

If public service becomes a marginalized feature of the new media order, what replaces it? For some, the future is imagined as media which service a monolithic cultural and economic order. Such a vision derives from a focus on the economic power of the new multimedia conglomerates and the idea that their commercial strength is deployed to standardize the content of their cultural product: that news and entertainment are processed and packaged like McDonald's hamburgers across the globe – except, as anyone who has seen *Pulp Fiction* knows, even McDonald's varies according to location. There is another vision to be evoked of the impact of globalization on mass media: a world marked by chaos and diversity. For Danilo Zolo (1992), the new communication technologies have the effect of speeding up the pace and increasing the complexity of the modern world. Citizens' experience of politics and of society is derived directly from mass media, and is no longer mediated by church, school and trade union or professional association. At the same time, this encounter with the world is marked by a proliferation of information, but little explanation. This experience creates a sense of chaos and complexity which generates in people a sense of fatalism and despair.

In the face of this diversity of media forms and this chaos of cultural signs, the temptation might be to conclude that power has devolved to the consumers, to the operators of the remote controls, video players and set-top boxes. Manuel Castells argues forcefully against such conclusions. While 'decentralization, diversification and customization' may be the new media order, this does not, Castells (1996: 340) argues, 'imply loss of control by major corporations and governments over television. Indeed, it is the opposite trend that has been observed during the last decade.' The possibility of this apparently contradictory idea is central to understanding the character of globalization and its implications for the connection between politics and mass media. Globalization can describe centralized control and resources, which stand in defiance of the powers of national governments, but the global corporations deploy their resources to particular audiences. In Castells' phrase (ibid.: 341), we live, not in a global village, but in 'customized cottages globally produced and locally distributed'. This does not mean, however, that as customers we 'demand' the goods that the conglomerates produce.

Perhaps most importantly of all in getting globalization into perspective, we need to remember that the 'world' that we have been examining only covers a small part of the world's surface. As Sussman observes (1997: 231–2), for the third world, the 'digital revolution' is as remote as the nearest phone: Manhattan has more telephone lines than there are in all of sub-Saharan Africa; the

80 per cent of the world's population who live in less developed countries have only 30 per cent of the world's newspapers. What Sussman is pointing to is the imbalance in the media economy and the webs of power which it constructs. Unequal access to the means of communication is reflected in slanted representation. As Chris Paterson (1998: 96) concludes in his study of the global news agencies: 'Television coverage of the developing world is already deplorably infrequent and misleading. The developing world appears now to be more excluded from contribution to the global flow of television news than it has ever been.'

Conclusion

This chapter has tried to pin down some of the globalizing trends and currents which are shaping the form of modern mass communications, and to trace their impact upon the politics of mass media. We began by looking at the changing technologies that are integral to, but not determinant of, these trends. We then moved on to consider the twin effects of globalization, first on national governments, and then on culture, before ending with some reflections on future developments. Globalization has established new forms of media power brokers, who pose fundamental problems for the regulation of mass media by nation states. The need for regulation stems from the fact that the impact of globalization is felt economically and culturally. Globalization does, though, also represent possibilities which may challenge that order, but such possibilities cannot be viewed as somehow 'inevitable' features of the changes being wrought. They depend on the way the opportunities offered by new media are taken.

In thinking about this, it is important to bear in mind this injunction and prediction from Tore Slaatta (1998: 338): 'New media will not make old media disappear . . . But they will probably have an impact on their production technology, their distribution and potential markets and thereby also their contents, but these impacts need to be analysed empirically. The impact of new media on collective identity formation will in the foreseeable future remain modest, and will probably first of all make existing organizations and institutions, like national media, parties and civil society groups, become more efficiently able to network within existing boundaries of the nation-states.' This is sound advice, and for this reason it makes sense to look in more detail at the political implications and arguments which accompany this changing order, to start thinking about the political principles and values that are threatened by, or might be incorporated in, the changing order.

PART THREE

MASS MEDIA AND DEMOCRACY

9

Packaging Politics

In the last part of this book, the focus is upon the relationship between mass media and democracy. This is an issue that has been present throughout. After all, why else are people interested in media bias or corporate ownership, if not because of the worry that systematic distortion or monopoly control thwarts or denies the capacity of citizens to judge and respond to the exercise of power? The next four chapters confront directly the question how, in a democracy, the relationship between the political process and the mass media should operate. Each chapter considers a different dimension of the relationship. We begin with the phenomenon known as the 'packaging' of politics.

'Packaging' refers to the idea that public representations of politics are increasingly being managed and controlled by parties and politicians, through such people as spin doctors. The effect of this, it is claimed, is to diminish the quality of political discourse, to 'dumb it down'. Political arguments are trivialized, appearances matter more than reality, personalities more than policies, the superficial more than the profound. The blame for this state of affairs is typically directed at the politicians and at their professional cohorts, and at a supplicant media which conspires in the erosion of democracy. A telling image of this state of affairs is the annual White House dinner for the press corps, at which the massed ranks of the fourth estate give a rapturous reception to the president.

Why do such things matter? Why is the content and character of political discourse important? The simple answer is that these are central concerns for democracy. If it is assumed that democracy is a viable and desirable political form, there are certain conditions that have to be met for it to be realized. 'Rule by the people', the most basic of definitions of democracy, depends upon the capacity of 'the people' to form judgements about what policies or representatives they want, and about whether those policies or representatives have delivered what they promised. Formulating such judgements depends upon, first, information (about politicians and their actions) and, second, the opportunity and skill to convert this information into a coherent assessment. Those who complain about the 'packaging' of politics are arguing that political information is being presented in ways that seriously hamper the capacity of citizens to reach well-informed judgements about what is done in their name. The process of packaging describes a system in which access to political information – about what, for example, politicians are 'really' like – is highly controlled. So the debate about packaging touches on the profoundly important political question of democracy, and for this reason it deserves to be examined carefully.

The discussion about the packaging of politics begins with the observation, made on both sides of the Atlantic, that we have witnessed an explosive rise in the number and the influence of media consultants and image makers, people who are seen to have changed the style and techniques of political communication. Evidence is plentiful: the ever-larger advertising budgets of parties and governments (an estimated $1 billion was spent on advertising for the 2000 US presidential campaign); the ubiquity of advertising personnel and skills in the promotion of politicians; the pre-eminence of photo opportunities and sound bites in election campaigns. Some 30 years on from Joe McGinniss' *The Selling of a President* (1969), we are no longer talking of the marketing of a single actor, but of the transformation of politics itself. This transformation is couched in terms of 'modernization' or 'Americanization' or 'mediatization' (Swanson and Mancini, 1996) and it is seen to herald a world in which we have 'packaged politics' (Franklin, 1994) or 'designer politics' (Scammell, 1995). The result of these changes, it is sometimes suggested, is an 'electronic commonwealth' (Abramson *et al.*, 1988) or a 'new political culture' (Clark and Hoffman-Martinot, 1998).

While there is some consensus about what changes are taking place, there is no agreement as to how they should be judged. For some, they are to be greeted positively, as a rational adaptation to contemporary realities. For example, Liesbet Van Zoonen (1998b: 196–7) writes that the popularizing of political communication 'should be seen as an attempt to restore the relation between politicians and voters, between the people and their representatives, to regain the necessary sense of community between public officials and their publics'. This welcome for new techniques is often accompanied by the claim that media management techniques have, in any case, always been part of politics (Abramson *et al.*, 1988; Kavanagh, 1995; Rosenbaum, 1997; Scammell, 1995). The new political techniques of the electronic era are merely an extension of a well-established tradition of politics, which is to adopt and adapt to the prevailing forms of communication.

Against these generally positive views, there are others who, though recognizing the continuities, view current developments more warily. Todd Gitlin (1991: 129, 133), for instance, is concerned that an American politics which has always been 'raucous, deceptive, giddy, shallow, sloganeering and demagogic for most of its history' is now covered by a media that is obsessed 'with speed, quick cuts, ten-second bites, one-second "scenes" and out of context images', and is therefore intolerant 'of the rigors of serious arguments and the tedium of organized political life'. In a similar vein, commentators on recent British general elections have argued that now images dominate the word, and that the contest is fought over competing *appearances* (Deacon *et al.*, 1998). In a similarly worried tone, Danilo Zolo (1992: 162) comments that 'the penetration of advertising techniques deep into the political system' marks the creation of a world in which 'telegenicity' becomes a key political criterion.

In order to advance this debate, it is important, first, to review briefly the key changes in political communication that are held to represent the 'packaging of politics'. Only then can we assess the issues that divide observers.

Packaging Techniques

The idea that politics is being 'packaged' trades on the thought that parties, individual politicians and governments are developing ever more effective ways of using the media. There are many examples of this, and what follows is just a selection.

Interviews

The political interview is a staple part of politics and political coverage. For the media, it is a cheap method of filling space, while also providing some prospect of excitement through its gladiatorial structure and some version of accountability through its conventions of cross-examination. For the politician, it represents an opportunity to articulate a view or to promote a policy initiative. Ostensibly, the interview is built around a dramatic tension in which both sides have reputations at stake. But 'the interview' does not represent a fixed and permanent phenomenon. Over time it has changed greatly, as politicians have become less wary and aloof, and interviewers have become more assertive and less deferential (Day, 1991). And as formats have changed, with one-to-one exchanges being joined by phone-ins, chat shows and their ilk, so we have seen the emergence of new conventions and rules for the interview.

What is most important here, however, is the way in which politicians and their aides have tried to control the conduct of interviews, creating conventions that favour them. Their efforts have focused on such things as interview technique (not breathing in at the end of sentences to avoid interruption), staying 'on message' (saying what you want to say, not what the interviewer wants you to say), how to sit and dress (the semiotics of posture and fashion). They have also become more determined to set the ground rules. This begins with who is to be interviewed and under what terms: whether live or on tape (the former giving the control to the interviewee, the latter to the editor), whether alone or with others. All of these issues touch upon the balance of power between interviewer and politicians, and are deployed in order to tip this balance towards the latter, to enable them to say what they want (Harris, 1991). The intention is to make the interview a platform for the politician which, according to the critics of packaging, is to deliver propaganda rather than to be made accountable, or at least to reduce political communication to a form of PR, in which journalists become mere cyphers.

One symptom of this trend is the 'sound bite', a single phrase or idea which is intended to be the sole message of any exchange between interviewer and interviewee. As the BBC journalist Nicholas Jones (N. Jones, 1995: 12) has written, 'In their pursuit of publicity even the humblest and most obscure MPs have had to become slaves to the soundbite, capable of encapsulating their arguments in a few short, sharp sentences suitable for inclusion in a broadcast news bulletin.' Another sign of the decline of the interview is its use to impart apparently trivial or superficial information. Witness the penchant of politicians to appear in settings which relieve them of direct political scrutiny: Bill Clinton on MTV, Tony Blair on the *Des O'Connor Show*. Both contenders for the American presidency in 2000 agreed to appear on chat shows hosted by Oprah Winfrey, Jay Leno and David Letterman. During the 1996 Russian presidential election, Boris Yeltsin's wife Naina was interviewed for a news item. According to the *Financial Times* (10 April 1996), 'she cooed about the president's personal virtues, which apparently include washing the dishes and cooking Siberian dumplings'. Not to be out done, Al Gore and George W. Bush revealed their favourite sandwiches (peanut and jelly), breakfast cereals (Wheaties) and fast food (tacos).

But the political use of the interview does not end with the style and content. It continues into the organization of access, to the strategic placing of pronouncements. Both President Clinton and Prime Minister Blair evolved strategies for circumventing some media outlets and favouring others – choosing, for example, to use the internet, or to concentrate on regional media sources, rather than national ones, or to favour journalists who reach particular audiences/constituencies.

Images and Appearances

Politicians do not deal only in words. Back in 1967 one of Richard Nixon's speechwriters explained that it was 'the image' not 'the man' that mattered. In similar vein, Margaret Scammell (1999: 729) argues that parties and candidates '*must* attend to political image if they want to be serious players in the political market'. Parties work at 'branding' themselves to create a distinct image that provides a simple key to the party's general stance or values. The advertising executive Winston Fletcher (*The Guardian*, 23 October 1997) said of Tony Blair's New Labour: 'it is clear that the establishment of New Labour as a trustworthy brand name was a textbook marketing operation'. (In the summer of 2000, with the party slumping in the polls, one of the architects of New Labour wrote that the 'New Labour brand has been badly contaminated' (*The Guardian*, 20 July 2000).)

Over time, politicians and parties have increasingly devoted their attention to generating images (rather than detailed policy proposals). This process begins with personal appearance and dress, and continues into the way party conventions and conferences are

designed. It is evident in the way political advertisements increasingly mimic the conventions of commercial advertising; it is
blatantly demonstrated in the crafting of sound bites and photo-
opportunities. In many ways, the latter two are the most important
because they are intended to appear in regular news broadcasts, and
as such acquire the legitimacy and veracity of *news* as distinct from
propaganda (although, as Kathleen Jamieson (1992) points out,
party advertisements can themselves (by design or default) become
part of the news because they provoke a particular political
controversy). Whatever the format or forum, the intention is to
create images and slogans which are easily recognized or digested,
and which spark a series of associations that crystallize a political
response. It is important to note that these practices are not
confined to political parties. Interest groups and social movements
also deploy them; indeed, they are among the most skilled practitioners of 'branding', as they are of the exploitation of celebrities to
promote political causes (supermodels against fur, pop stars for
relieving third world debt, film stars for an independent Tibet).

Celebrities

Pursuit of attractive and appropriate media images has also led
politicians, parties and other political actors to use more indirect
means to reach their ends. In her campaign for a seat in the US
Senate, Hillary Clinton attracted the support of Nicole Kidman,
Tom Cruise, Robin Williams and Robert de Niro. Not only are the
stars a useful source of funds (Mrs Clinton's Hollywood friends
helped her raise $3 million), they also help to establish her image,
by lending their charisma and popular appeal. Politicians have
increasingly linked themselves to actors, musicians and sports
stars. They do this by making awards or issuing invitations to
them, or by appearing on stage or in settings where celebrities are
also gathered.

So it is that we have pictures of President Bill Clinton playing
saxophone on television, or Prime Minister Tony Blair welcoming
Noel Gallagher to 10 Downing Street, or President Nelson Mandela
posing with the Spice Girls, or Germany's Chancellor Gerhard
Schroeder on stage with the Scorpions rock band. It may be that
these political leaders are genuinely keen to do such things, that

they really want to play the sax or chat with Sporty Spice, but they also want us, the voters, to know about these meetings. They want the pictures on the front page or on the television news. After all, they could arrange to meet the stars in private; they could choose not to go to showbiz parties. They and their advisers calculate that the resultant pictures will encourage voters to see their (would-be) leaders in a new light. Of course, they sometimes miscalculate. When Blair's deputy, John Prescott, attended the Brits 1998 music industry awards, he was the unhappy recipient of a bucket of water, thrown over him by Danbert Nobacon of the rock band Chumbawamba. A picture of a soaked and angry Prescott was in all the next day's papers.

The practice of associating with celebrities is not new. In the 1930s in Britain, society hostesses courted sporting heroes and popular performers like Noel Coward (McKibbin, 1998: 30–1). These figures became adornments to the socialite's lifestyle and markers of their reputation. The only difference between then and now is that the stars are intended to enhance political reputation rather than social status, and that rather than promoting elite values they are promoting populist ones.

The use of showbusiness to convey certain images in the media does not end with mere acts of association. Politicians have also taken to emulating the stars. Bill Clinton's saxophone playing was echoed by Tony Blair posing with an electric guitar and Boris Yeltsin singing on Russian television. Reporting on the Philippine National Elections, James McEnteer (1996: 114) observes: 'Many political rallies resembled talent shows. At one such event, a senatorial candidate danced a cha-cha, another sang ditties in dialect, and a third offered a baritone rendition of "More than the Greatest Love I've Ever Known". Instead of discussing social or economic issues, candidates literally gave the voters a song and dance.' In the New York Senate race in 2000, Rudolph Guilliani appeared at one rally dressed as John Travolta in *Saturday Night Fever*. (Guilliani later retired from the race, but not because of this particular offence against good taste.) While other politicians are reluctant to go this far, it is evident that the mannerisms, gestures and styles of popular culture are appearing ever-more attractive. The intention is to create an aura of 'popularity', to borrow precisely from the relationship of trust and admiration that is associated with figures in popular culture – from newsreaders to pop musicians. It is no coincidence that Clinton took coaching from newscasters, figures who appear as objects of trust in the popular imagination.

Spin Doctors, Media Consultants and Advertisers

The adoption of celebrities to acquire glamour and popularity is no more inevitable than it is risk-free. It has developed as a result of the advice and ingenuity of a new breed of political advisers and consultants. Why have Hollywood directors been hired to make political propaganda: for example, Hugh Hudson (*Chariots of Fire*) and Stephen Frears (*High Fidelity*) for the British Labour Party; Spike Jonze (*Being John Malkovich*) for Al Gore? Why are comedy writers like John O'Farrell (*Spitting Image*) hired to supply jokes for political speeches? Such initiatives stem from a new stratum of media managers within the political process, people with expertise in polling, advertising, marketing and public relations. Their task has been to revamp party images and to get politicians the coverage they crave, and their brief extends to negotiating the terms of interviews, providing press releases (and discreet leaks), devising sound bites and arranging photo-opportunities. Their aim is to manage the media in such a way as to enhance the image and message of the parties they serve.

This is how insiders in the White House described their job to the journalist Michael Kelley (*Guardian Weekend*, 20 November 1993, original emphasis): 'the day is composed not of hours or minutes, but of *news cycles*. In each cycle, *senior White House officials* speaking on *background* define *the line of the day*. The line is echoed and amplified *outside the Beltway* to *real people*, who live *out there*, by the President's *surrogates*, whose appearances create *actualities* (on radio) and *talking heads* (on TV). During the *roll-out* of a new policy, the President coached by his *handlers* . . . may permit his own head to talk. There are various ways he might do this, ranging from the simplest *photo-op* to a *one-on-one* with a media *big-foot*.' The importance attached to this work has made its practitioners key actors in their party's power structure. Party organization and strategy have been reshaped to accommodate their authority and respond to their advice (Kavanagh, 1995).

New Conditions, New Politics

Before considering the significance for democracy of this way of operating within the political realm, we need first to establish the wider context in which such techniques emerge. What are the forces and interests driving these developments? The answer to this question lies in changes within both the media and politics.

Imitation or modernization

One explanation for the emergence of new political techniques is that parties and politicians copy each other. Such a thought lies behind the often debated claim that politics is being 'Americanized' (Negrine, 1996). Hence the suggestion that politics in Europe, for instance, can be seen as an imitative response to the American example. It was widely reported, for example, that both the British Conservative and Labour parties spent time observing their US equivalents and drawing upon the experience and expertise developed across the Atlantic (Butler and Kavanagh, 1997: 56–7; Kavanagh, 1995: 29–30; Norris *et al.*, 1999: 58). The same is claimed for German politics (Schoenbach, 1996). But aside from the question of whether the techniques being adopted are drawn from the USA, there remains the issue of why such techniques evolved within the USA in the first place. The explanatory task is just moved back one stage: to why the originator of the technique came to this solution and what prompted the imitator to adopt it. To answer these questions, the focus needs to be on the incentives and opportunity structures operating within political parties and political systems, rather than on some notion of political fashion.

In their international survey of such changes in party practice, Paolo Mancini and David Swanson (1996) argue that these innovations have to be understood as a process of *modernization*. The new communication techniques, though associated with 'Americanization', are essentially to do with managing social complexity, the key indicator of modernization. The transformation is not seen as a form of Americanized global culture in which everyone does politics the American way. Rather 'Americanization' is linked to a particular set of professionalized campaigning techniques. These techniques are aimed at addressing the social complexity caused by the breakdown of old hierarchies. 'Old aggregative anchors of identity and allegiance in traditional structures,' write Mancini and Swanson (ibid.: 8–9), 'are replaced by overlapping and constantly shifting identifications with microstructures that themselves are always entering into changing patterns of alliances with other structures in search of more effective ways of advancing interests.' The new forms of political communication are designed, according to this analysis, to address common problems of social complexity caused or exacerbated by the decay of established narratives and structures.

Rational Choice

One way to focus on these modernizing trends is to explore the pressures on parties to adopt particular techniques. This pressure can be captured in the logic of rational action. The democratic theorist Anthony Downs (1957) argued, long before anyone spoke of political 'packaging', that rational voters have little incentive to study manifestos or pore over politicians' speeches. The costs of acquiring and digesting this information are much greater than the benefits to be gained by a vote based upon it. It makes much more sense to rely upon free information and 'brand images'. If voters are loath to dissect the words and policies of politicians, then impressions become very important. Judgements based on how people *look* are – for the voter – easily acquired. Such logic lies behind the tendency for parties and politicians to try to create particular images and impressions. Hence there is the talk of 'branding' rather than of policy detail, a practice which echoes the branding of commercial goods (Klein, 2000).

Pippa Norris and her colleagues observed exactly this move during the 1997 British election. They write (Norris *et al.*, 1999: 59) of how Labour realized the need to devote as much attention to symbols as debates, that the party had come to the belief 'that style was as important as substance'. The chosen style 'was a deliberately "non-political"' one. This alternative 'style' owes much to the populist conventions of popular culture (pop videos, advertising, chat shows). The need for this derives, in part, at least, from the pressure created by rational action in a world where information is costly and imperfect. But why does this logic kick in at a particular time and in a particular context? Why did the British Labour Party take so long to adopt the practices that were commonplace for the

Republican and Democratic Parties? Part of the answer may be found in the changed media environment: with an increasing number of media outlets, the audience's attention cannot be assumed, and more effort has to be made to grab it. But the answer may also lie in changes in the political context.

Dealignment

Are there political circumstances in which voters become more susceptible to a 'packaged' form of party communication? Claims about a widespread political dealignment would seem to provide such a context. If old ties of party and class loyalty have been eroded, and if the traditional material basis of political choice has been replaced by a post-materialist politics, then, the argument might run, issues and images become more salient in determining party preference (Clark and Inglehart, 1998; Crewe and Sarlvik, 1983). Prior to these changes, party loyalty was guaranteed by a process of socialization, rooted in established class interests. Party choice was a product of class affiliation. Now, with class dealignment, party choice is a matter of individual policy preference. If this is the case, perceptions of parties and of the policies they advocate become crucial to party political strategy. Parties cannot rely on traditional ties; they have to sell themselves.

The mass media represent a key forum, and advertising a key language, for this sales technique (see Scammell, 1999, for an overview of this trend). Within this account of voting behaviour, media representations become central elements in the formation of allegiance. However, not all theories of voting behaviour place the same emphasis on the media, and some are sceptical not only of the degree of dealignment but also of the impact of the media on political behaviour (Curtice and Semetko, 1994). In a sense, though, this is not the issue, since what is important is not whether, in fact, the media affect behaviour, but the *belief* about the media's influence. Party elites believe in the importance of creating particular images, and act on this basis in reforming the party structure. Even so, while the belief may be as important as the reality in accounting for the internal logic of political actors, these beliefs only identify a general approach (the focus on image and on the party's 'branding'); they do not show how the strategy is to be realized. This depends on the available technology.

Technological Mediation of Politics

The penetration of television into domestic life, and the widely held view that television is now the main source of political information, are seen to create the drive towards parties' strategic focus on mass media (Negrine, 1994). So it is argued that, for example, Silvio Berlusconi's Forza Italia party, the archetype of the new style of mediated politics, adopts the tools of PR because they fit the new form of political communication (Seisselberg, 1996: 721). More than this, though, it is argued that the formats provided by television, its particular character as a medium, have shaped the mode of address adopted by the parties. Mass media not only play a decisive role in communicating political ideas and setting political agendas, they also serve to reinforce the personalization of politics. This is because 'the format of television favors personalization' (Mancini and Swanson, 1996: 13). By this it is meant that, as Abramson *et al.* (1988: 83) contend, television 'focuses the viewers' attention on the personal qualities of political figures'. Or as Joshua Meyrowitz (1985) argues, television by its nature – its use of close-ups, its intimate tone – works against a declamatory oratory and leaderly aloofness. Political communication is forced to take on the style of television's naturalism, and to adopt the codes and conventions that television demands. The result is that television 'has changed how politics is conducted and how it is received'; it is now conducted in terms of personality and received in private (R. Hart, 1999: 2).

The modern politician is required to seek support, to become 'popular', through the private reception of their personality. What this in effect means is that they have to become *celebrities*. The mass media create individuals as celebrities, whether they are serial killers, soap opera stars or politicians. The notion of 'celebrity', according to David Marshall (1997), sets the terms of political popularity. 'Celebrity' is itself a direct product of the popular culture of film, television and pop music. It is this pressure which lies behind the adoption by politicians of the formats and icons of popular culture. Politics takes on the generic conventions of the medium, politics becomes melodrama through the recounting of personal anecdotes, interviews become therapeutic encounters (R. Hart, 1999: 25–9). In other words, the medium used by modern politicians requires that they adopt the language and style of packaging. The plausibility of this argument rests upon seeing the medium as determining the message, and as seeing the resultant message as qualitatively different from that which came before. We return to the issue of the qualitative change marked by packaging later; here we remain focused on the explanation for the turn to packaging. The story is not just about the medium itself, but about the interests behind it.

The Commodification of Politics

The medium and its conventions need to be understood in the wider context of the political economy which affects both politics and the media. One central theme of this larger setting is the idea of the 'commodification of politics', the way political communication is shaped by the commercial interests organizing mass media. Nicholas Garnham (1986), drawing upon Jürgen Habermas' account of the commercialization of the public sphere in an earlier era, suggests that mass communications are now organized around advertising. The 'public' is now the 'market', and media now address and constitute citizens as *consumers*. Marshall (1997: 205) echoes this thought when he argues: 'The product advertising campaign provides the underlying model for the political election campaign. Both instantiate the prominence of irrational appeal within a general legitimating discourse of rationality. Both are attempts to establish resonance with a massive number of people so that connections are drawn between the campaign's message and the interests of consumers/citizens.' By this account, the use of advertising and of celebrity endorsements is less a pragmatic adoption of communicative conventions, and more the enforced denial of full political participation and debate. The suggestion is that it is the political economy of communications, rather than the logic of party strategy, that is responsible for packaging. But even if we adopt this version of the rise of a packaged politics, we need to be able to explain why politicians adopt particular genres and styles of communication.

It Takes Two: Pliable Media

All the efforts of spin doctors and others would be wasted if the media were not susceptible to spin, if they did not use the photo opportunities or sound bites being provided. And just as there is a history to the development of these techniques by parties, so there is a history to the media's receptivity to the various blandishments of the parties.

One reason for media to be compliant is the political pressure upon them. We have already discussed (see Chapters 5 and 7) the pressures put upon journalists by spin doctors: the pressure to take a particular line or to interview a particular politician in advance of the programme; the threats and abuse if this pressure fails (Phillips *et al.*, 1993). Importantly, though, the ability of parties to apply pressure varies with context and political system. In the USA, the constitution's protection of free speech and the absence of a national broadcasting institution (like the BBC) would seem to make broadcasters less vulnerable than their UK equivalents, where political patronage and regulation represents a credible threat. German media are less vulnerable than the British because of the different news values in place – German coverage is less obsessed with 'balance' and more with 'objectivity' (Esser *et al.*, 2000; Semetko, 1996). Some systems guarantee airtime for politics (for example, Britain and France), but others do not (for example, the USA). In France there are also strict restrictions on the images that can be used in representing candidates (Negrine, 1996). Different regulations (or their absence) affect the kind of influence politicians can have.

Another possible reason for media compliance is the impact of commercial pressures. Packaged politics fits into the agenda of media who are acutely conscious of the chill winds of the market. Competition for readers and viewers, like the competition for advertisers that underlies the need to boost sales and ratings, reduces the resources available for investigative journalism and increases the incentives for accepting pre-packaged material. It also fuels the demand for 'human interest' and celebrity stories. Neither the resources nor the interest exists for serious analysis. Packaging, by this argument, fills the gap left by the shifting priorities of the media (Franklin, 1994: 49, 71). It is an argument, however, that needs to be used warily. It can be claimed that, in fact, market-based broadcasting is less inclined to succumb to politicians' blandishments and that it is state-regulated systems which are most easily exploited by parties (Semetko, 1996; Semetko *et al.*, 1991). Market competition does not allow the media to indulge the parties in the desire for bland coverage. Either way, the extent to which 'packaging' is a characteristic of media–politics relations is dependent not just upon political actors, but also on the willingness of media outlets to play the same game.

The packaging process also relies on the willingness of 'celebrities', and the organizations who produce them, to collaborate in this process. It is important, therefore, to see how changes in the business of creating celebrities – the culture industry – also have a bearing on the emergence of new forms of political communication. Although parties have drawn upon expertise within advertising for some time, there has been a reluctance on the part of youth and popular culture to associate itself publicly with political parties and explicitly political causes. Pop stars may have joined ad hoc campaigns, but typically these have fallen outside the formal political arena or command almost universal support (Live Aid, for example). But in recent years there has been a marked increase in the involvement of stars in politics, not just as benefactors but as endorsees and as political actors in their own right. The explanation for this cannot rest simply with the political consciousness of these performers, but must also take account of the changing popular economy of popular culture (Frith and Street, 1992).

This is perhaps best illustrated by the movement of rock music into the mainstream, and its increasing function as a form of corporate leisure (tours by the Rolling Stones have been sponsored by Microsoft and their music has been used to promote Microsoft products). The political role played by rock performers (like Bob Geldof, Sting and Bono) is a product of their new status as popular entertainers, not as dissident radicals in exclusive sub-cultures. Changes in the political economy of the culture industries (the individuals and interests produced by them) are important in explaining why celebrities become incorporated into the business of political communication. Silvio Berlusconi's domination of the Italian television market is just one example of the way in which cultural power and political communication become linked (Seisselberg, 1996).

Spinning Elections

So far attention has been on the 'packaging' techniques available to politicians and parties and on the competing factors that have contributed to their adoption. None of this, however, tells us much about the outcome of this relationship, about what sort of political coverage emerges. Is there evidence that the intentions behind packaging are realized in the representations of political actors?

A number of commentators have drawn attention to the 'personalization' of politics, to the way in which leaders, rather than parties, dominate the coverage, and to the way in which those leaders are represented as much by their character as by their ideology. In Sweden, for example, Kent Asp and Peter Esaiasson (1996: 84) note that while the attention devoted to leaders has remained high but static since the 1970s, there has been a change 'in the sense that there has been a focus on party leaders as private persons'. Klaus Schoenbach (1996: 104) observes a similar trend in Germany, while also pointing out that the concentration on the personal and personality is a product of party and media interests, rather than those of the electorate (who remain more concerned with issues). Polish TV used alleged personality flaws to wound an aspiring presidential candidate (Jakubovicz, 1996: 145). In the case of the UK, research (Billig *et al.*, 1993; Deacon *et al.*, 1998) has also revealed the degree to which the parties' chosen representatives have been allowed to dominate election coverage, to the exclusion of the other members of those parties. The media tend to reproduce the images and ideas which the parties wanted, a fact reflected in the extent to which the election agenda owed more to party initiatives than to popular concerns. The public's own agenda – the issues it identifies as 'important' in opinion polls – are not the ones that dominate the screens. In the 1987 and 1997 elections in the UK, the media agenda was indebted more to the parties' choice than to the public's (Miller, 1991: 63; *The Guardian*, 7 April 1997; *The Times*, 10 April 1997).

More generally, it is suggested that the whole tone and character of political coverage has fallen into step with the packaging process. Writing of the USA, Dan Nimmo (1996: 40) talks of the prevalence of 'the ahistorical and nonhistorical packaging of campaign information'. He points to the emergence of the 'factoids' that replace facts themselves. Factoids are 'pithy assertions of facts widely treated as true even though supporting evidence is not available'. The net effect is a 'virtual politics' made up of a 'media-created, politician-manipulated reality' (Swanson and Mancini, 1996: 270).

All these different arguments support the contention that the packaging process has changed political coverage. However, this conclusion has to be hedged by the acknowledgement of cross-national variations. As Holli Semetko and her colleagues (1991) note, countries vary in their susceptibility to political pressure, and, within any given country, there are distinctions to be made between types of media. Their evidence suggests that in the UK television is more vulnerable than the press to the art of spin doctoring. Television tends to carry more sound bites than does the press. The same research also reveals that UK television is more vulnerable than US television, in part because American television has a stronger incentive to placate its advertisers and sponsors. Political coverage has to be assessed in terms of its capacity to attract viewers, rather than to honour statutory public service duties. This militates against allowing too much time and space to politicians and parties, and to the pre-digested copy they offer. Semetko and her colleagues identify a number of factors which account for variations in political coverage and susceptibility to packaging. These include (a) the strength of the party system: the more disciplined the party the more able it is to control coverage; (b) the extent of broadcasting time: the more time there is to fill, the more easy it is for parties to determine what is included; with less time, the journalists are more able to impose their agenda on coverage; and (c) regulations: systems of regulation tend to favour politicians and hamper media. These factors are important in establishing a clearer, contextualized perspective on the packaging process. They do not, however, provide an answer to the debate that underlies this topic: does the packaging process distort and damage democracy?

Fear of Packaging

Implicit in the argument about packaging is the claim that it is harmful to democracy. One of the most eloquent statements of this argument is provided by Bob Franklin. In his book, *Packaging Politics* (1994), he charts the changing habits of political leaders and representatives as they attempt to deploy the mass media to their advantage. This relationship has, of course, been documented elsewhere, most obviously in America (for example, Jamieson, 1984). What distinguishes *Packaging Politics* is not its British focus, because there are precedents for that too (for example, Cockerell,

1988; Crewe and Harrop, 1986; 1989), but its synthesis of the different trends and processes at play in the complex relationships between politics and the media.

Franklin is not concerned just to document the changes, he also expresses a disenchantment with the emerging media practices and their consequences for democracy. This is most evident in the book's title, which draws on the idea that to package politics (in the same way that products are packaged) involves some diminution in quality, marked in part by the tendency to give form priority over content. More strongly, 'packaging' suggests that, rather than the genuine item, we get an artificial or inauthentic product. Franklin's book is a critique of the quality of political discourse and of the interests that rule political communications. 'Packaging' is linked to 'marketing', and both carry the suggestion that in this context they describe lesser or debased activities.

Parties are, by this account, rapidly becoming, in effect, commercial companies whose raison d'être is to market a political cause. As Statham (1996: 91) writes of the effect of Berlusconi's party on Italian politics: 'Forza Italia operates along the lines of a commercial company, extending the logic of product marketing to the political sphere.' Zolo (1992: 162), generalizing from the Italian experience, notes the ways in which advertisers are employed to apply 'the criteria of commercial propaganda to political communication', and that the result is 'the penetration of advertising techniques deep into the political system'. 'Packaging' implies that political appearance counts for more than political substance, that form subsumes content. It suggests too that, by the packaging of politics, political discourse is simplified or standardized, and that the balance of power and responsibility shifts from the traditional actors – from politicians – to advertising executives or media consultants.

So it is that Franklin writes (1994: 13) of the way in which 'skilled and highly paid marketing and communications professionals create favourable media images for politicians and their policies'. The result is that 'the attractiveness of the marketed image of politicians and policies has become at least as influential in winning public support as an understanding of the policy itself' (ibid.). What citizens need to understand, suggests Franklin, are parties' *policies*, and the images convey only an inaccurate or superficial version of them. What is happening to policies, the argument goes, is also happening to politicians. They have lost their capacity to reflect upon politics; they have become people who, in the words of Ken Livingstone, 'think in sound bites' (quoted in Franklin, ibid.: 5), just as central government and political parties are increasingly tempted to 'sell' their policies and themselves through advertising and the tools of public relations.

Franklin's critique echoes the work of other commentators, such as Meyrowitz (1985) and Roderick Hart (1999). Mass media impose, with the help of the parties and others, their own logic and interests on political communication. What Franklin and others articulate is a general complaint about the ways in which politics is represented. For these critics, the quality of politics, and democracy in particular, is being diminished because inappropriate criteria – appearance, slogans and images – are dominating political discourse. But are they right to take up this position?

Repackaging Politics

Is packing politics as damaging as it is sometimes made to seem? There are three issues to be raised in assessing the argument about packaging: the cultural context of media–politics relations, the incentives for (and effects of) packaging, and the possibility of separating form and content.

The Cultural Context

There is a danger of treating 'packaging' as a unique phenomenon posing a specific problem, when, as we have already seen, it is better understood as one symptom of a larger set of changes captured by the idea of 'modernization'. This point can be reinforced by looking more closely at the sound bite and the fear it arouses. Rather than seeing it as a substitute for thought, the sound bite can be seen as just another means by which politicians try to accommodate themselves to the medium in which they operate. This is, in one sense, no different from the way in which we all tailor our language to our audience or our setting, and politicians have always operated this way. The adoption of the sound bite could thus be seen, in Scammell's words (1995: 17, 272), as 'rational electioneering'. The sound bite is just one in a long line of techniques that have been adopted by politicians. The current worry about packaging is, therefore, a reaction to change, on a par with the reaction that greeted the replacement of vinyl by the CD.

But even if the sound bite marks a qualitative change (rather than a purely technical change), it needs to be understood as part of a wider cultural shift. Ken Livingstone 'thinks in soundbites' because this is the form of address his generation of politicians have learnt. Livingstone is 'a child of the sixties', when popular culture became the medium of politics, when symbols and gestures, images and signs, were the currency of politics (McGinniss, 1969; Nimmo and Combs, 1990: ch. 2; Scammell, 1995: 50–51). The sound bite is, in this sense, just another version of the slogan and, like the slogans of the 1960s, it is tailored to the medium; it deliberately exploits the techniques of marketing and cultural expression which the medium makes available. This is not necessarily to excuse or celebrate it, but rather to see it as part of a larger cultural trend, from which politics is not immune. Liesbet Van Zoonen (1998a: 49–50) regards the conjunction of 'modern politics with popular culture' as necessarily 'constructing the politician as a human being with her or his individual peculiarities, rather than as the representative of particular policies or ideologies'. The packaging of politics, insofar as it focuses on the individual, personalized politician, is a consequence of general cultural shifts.

Incentives for Packaging

But even if this connection with 1960s cultural politics is only tenuous, or if the adoption of it is seen as a failing of particular politicians, there are still other reasons for looking less harshly upon the packaging of politics. These have less to do with the politicians and more to do with citizens. The lesson of the rational choice theorists is that there are strong incentives for people to remain ignorant or uninterested in what their representatives have to offer. These (dis)incentives derive from the costs of information. Detailed political information is costly to research and these costs are not counterbalanced by some clear return on the investment. It is necessary, therefore, for parties and politicians to present information in a 'cheap' form and for citizens to limit their 'expenditure'. The net effect of this can be 'packaged politics'. Parties produce slogans, logos and photo-opportunities; and citizens survey the paraphernalia, making judgements on the basis of personality and style. Importantly though, this is a skill practised in any media consumption (Morley, 1992). It is what we are good at, and to this extent democracy is enhanced by our ability to deploy these skills, rather than our lesser ability to judge policy options.

Joseph Schumpeter (1943) made a similar point some 50 years before Morley when, reflecting on citizens' limited capacity for complex political judgement, he noted their sophistication in making judgements on matters of direct concern to them. Schumpeter constructs a model of democracy out of these skills by modelling democracy on the market, and making parties entrepreneurs who depend for their survival on the quality of their product. As Scammell writes (1995: 18): 'the marketing concept may possess intrinsic virtue precisely because, in principle, it makes politics more democratic'.

Separating Form and Content

For Franklin, citizens who act on the basis of images and sound bites are allowing form to get the better of content, to let the medium dominate the message. But such claims rest upon the possibility of distinguishing form and content, medium and message. And here, too, there are reasons for scepticism. Style and image are, it might be argued, rich in meanings and messages. When John F. Kennedy debated with Richard Nixon 30 years ago, it was reported that those who saw their discussion on television gave the victory to the coolly handsome Kennedy over his perspiring rival, while those who listened on radio gave Nixon the edge. This evidence is used to support the thought that images can distort people's perception of political reality. Kennedy only won because he was a smoother media operator, not because he had the better ideas. But can it really be claimed that radio is somehow 'more objective', allowing a 'truer' picture of the candidates? And in any case, given Watergate and the bombing of Cambodia, were not the viewers right to doubt that shifty television performer?

Whatever is the case, surely the point is that the two media provide *different* means of perceiving the candidates. In listening to an argument, we are not just hearing the words, but also the tones of voice, the silences and stutters; just as when we are watching, we take note of the movement of eyes and hands, the facial expressions and body language (Atkinson, 1988). The same applies to political communication. Its messages and meanings are not simply a product of the words, and this is as true for town hall meetings as for glitzy rallies. Which is not to say that there may be qualitative differences between the two, only that the differences cannot be assumed. If television's personalizing effect is to bring politicians down to our level, should we not be delighted by this process? After all, the distant charismatic leader may also be the unaccountable leader.

These attempts to dent the packaging argument are, of course, only sketched here, and can themselves be challenged, but they make an important general point about the way the argument needs to be conducted and developed. The issues raised by those who see politics as being packaged, and the attempts at rebuttal, all point to a connection between political coverage and popular culture. In drawing attention to the cultural context, the incentive structure and the inseparability of form and content, it is apparent that understanding political communication means understanding popular forms of communication generally. Political communication cannot be separated from the cultural forms that surround and inform it. Political communication is not just about conveying information or persuading people through the force of argument. It is about capturing the popular imagination, giving acts and ideas symbolic importance. This means drawing on the techniques of those who are practised in these arts: advertisers and television producers; it also means borrowing from the rhetoric and practices of the populism that popular culture embodies.

This connection with popular culture emerges from the three qualifications made to the packaging argument. Firstly, there is the thought that techniques of political communication derive from the cultural context and assumptions of their practitioners. Secondly, the creation of 'cheap information' is precisely what popular culture offers. Thirdly, the study of popular culture has revealed the ways in which style and imagery convey messages of political and cultural importance (see Hebdige, 1979). Seeing politics as a branch of popular culture is, of course, what Franklin is committed to avoiding. It is possible to read *Packaging Politics* as part of a general critique of the debasement of culture. Franklin's tone and complaints echoes those who, from the left and the right, have worried about the impact of popular culture (see Street, 1997, for a brief survey). And anyone persuaded by these critiques of popular culture are unlikely to be very sanguine about the connection between popular culture and politics.

However, even if one is generally concerned about the effect and character of popular culture, it is still necessary to acknowledge its influence on contemporary political communication. The newspapers and programmes that carry political information are themselves part of popular culture. So to establish whether or not the 'packaging' of politics is in fact deleterious to the quality of political life, we need to engage with arguments about the politics of popular culture generally. This means that even those who see the marketing of politics as having benign effects cannot see, as Scammell (1995) tends to, 'designer politics' as traditional politics conducted by other means. Politicians and parties are not simply using new techniques in an instrumental way, they are also changing their language and their priorities, and in turn the way they are 'read' by their citizens.

If this argument is right, there are certain clear implications. All politics is packaged, and the point is not to distinguish between the 'authentic' and the 'inauthentic', the 'contrived' and the 'genuine'. What needs to be done instead is to work at discriminating between *types of packaging*, to make judgements and assessments of the packages. Just as there is good and bad popular culture, so there are good and bad forms of packaging, where 'good' and 'bad' refer to the degree to which the use of 'packaging' engages people's imagination and sense of themselves. In the same way, we need to understand the judgements that citizens make as paralleling the ways they judge other forms of popular culture, most obviously soap operas (Silverstone, 1994). We need to see how, as Nimmo and Combs (1990) argue, audiences read the 'rituals' which define coverage of politics. Implicit in this is the need to look at the way audiences can be addressed and constituted, to see how different forms of political involvement can be created by the format and style of interviews, by the codes and genres of the media's political discourse (Corner, 1995). Simply, the 'packaging' of politics is determined in part by the 'packaging' of television programmes. In making sense of this, we also need to heed the context within which it is happening: the commercial and other interests which organize our papers and broadcasting. We may, in the end, conclude that politics is being packaged in ways that harm our democracy. But this is a conclusion that can only be reached once we have looked more closely at the character and quality of the packaging process, at the meanings it supplies and the responses it elicits. What follows, by way of a conclusion, is an attempt to do just this.

Conclusion: a Case Study of Packaged Politics

A year after the general election of 1997, Tony Blair appeared on *The Des O'Connor Show*. Des O'Connor is a comedian and singer (although the latter skill is as often mocked as celebrated). His show is broadcast in a prime evening slot on ITV. In front of a studio audience, it mixes chat, songs and comedy. On the night Blair appeared, the other main guest was Elton John, who sang and talked on the sofa. The show went out just as the World Cup was beginning, and the programme was dominated by football. The audience waved scarves printed with the names of the home nations; a children's choir ended the show with a World Cup song; and the guests, including Blair, were asked who they thought would win. O'Connor himself acted as an amiable, chummy host.

This was Blair's second appearance on the show. His previous visit had been as leader of the opposition, when he had promised to return if Labour won the election. Indeed, O'Connor introduced Blair as 'a politician who keeps his promises', and his entry from off-stage was accompanied by the theme tune to the film *Local Hero*. Both host and guest were in suit and tie, but Blair was the more formal of the two, both in his style and his manner (he sat upright rather than sinking into the cushions on the sofa).

O'Connor's line of questioning seemed designed to get at the 'everyday' experience of being prime minister: what were the pleasures of the job ('meeting exciting people doing exciting things'); what were the highlights (the Northern Ireland agreement); what were the perks (he hadn't got tickets for the World Cup)? This led on to questions about his 'other life': being a waiter in France, playing and watching football with 'the kids', trying his hand at tennis, renting a video, still strumming the guitar (a reference to the fact that Blair played in a group called Ugly Rumours when at Oxford). Then came several anecdotes, which included lines that might well have been pre-scripted. At a civic reception in France, his family were given a horse. 'I didn't know,' said Blair, 'whether to ride it or eat it.' Another, longer story was about his 'mother-in-law'. Though the 'mother-in-law' stereotype framed the tale (O'Connor: 'do you take her on holiday occasionally?' Blair: 'no always, its obligatory'), it was also an opportunity to assert more formal notions of family closeness. The conversation ended back at football, and Blair's empathy for Glenn Hoddle, the England football coach – a tough job, taking tough decisions which will always be criticized.

In watching Blair's performance, it seemed evident that he deployed the kind of devices that Roderick Hart (1999) characterizes as generically specific to television (the anecdote, the confession and so on), but that these were being used to develop a particular, pre-planned agenda and persona. Blair was using the opportunity to convey a number of messages, each intended to enhance or promote his political image, to 'brand' him. And it was about *him*, Tony Blair, rather than his party. Labour was not mentioned at all. One message was about his achievements, notably the Northern Ireland agreement, which appeared several times in different guises. Another was about the demands and importance of his job, revealed in his remarks about Glenn Hoddle and an anecdote about his relations with the queen. A third message was about him as an ordinary, dutiful family man: doing regular things with his children, going on family holidays. Finally, there was a message about him as a personality. The jokes evoked an air of mild, carefully contained mischievousness, teasing ever so gently the conventions of proper behaviour or respectability (at least as they are thought to apply to the politically correct politician). These messages were not simply contained in the oral text but also in the tones of voice, postures and facial expressions ('thanks' muttered through clenched teeth when O'Connor remarked that Blair looked older after a year in office). Blair can, therefore, be seen to have used the opportunities provided by the chat show to reinforce messages and images that were part of his political project.

At the same time, the format of the show, and the actions of the performers, set in motion other meanings and images. The chat show defines itself against other conversational televisual modes. It deliberately eschews the combative, confrontational mode of the standard political interview, which de facto allows politicians to deliver and defend their established theme or message, and in which the interviewer implicitly takes on the guise of the political opposition or the sceptical citizen (Harris, 1991; Tolson, 1991). The chat show also contrasts with the confessional or revelatory mode of interview. Each format defines itself against the other, and establishes particular roles and expectations for audience, interviewer and interviewee. The chat show adopts the conventions of conversation, rather than interrogation or therapy; the interviewer takes on the role of a populist friend ('what everyone wants to know is . . .') and provides a sympathetic and encouraging response to answers (at odds, say, with the scepticism of the political interviewer). It is a format which encourages informality, and in this sense seems more revealing. The viewing audience is not addressed directly, but looks, as it were, through the keyhole, it eavesdrops on the conversation (Atkinson, 1988: 171); and the tone of voice, the trajectory of the discussion, is pitched to fit into a domestic setting.

There is, though, a further dimension to this exchange and the judgements it encourages. What is most distinctive about the chat show (compared to most, but not all, political exchanges) is the presence of the studio audience. Their chorus-like commentary, although orchestrated from the studio floor, provides a set of reactions and responses which other forms of interview do not and which are only partially controlled by the two leading protagonists. Blair's asides and jokes, his choice of accent and manner, are all mediated by the reaction of the immediate audience. His control over the 'message' is further attenuated by the fact that, as Paddy Scannell (1991: 3) has noted, 'the broadcasters, while they control the discourse, do not control the communicative event'. Where a politician is involved, 'audiences make inferences about the character and competence of their elected representatives . . . on the basis of common-sense evaluations of their performances' (ibid.: 8). The politician's 'performance' is measured by a variety of criteria, all of which can have a political impact. Blair's credibility as a 'lad' is tested by his knowledge of the 'appropriateness' of comparing the footballers Michael Owen and Teddy Sheringham, just as his remarks about family life are tested for their resonance with the daily routines of the audience. Blair's use of colloquial language, of joke telling, of mimicry, are all part of the conventions of conversation. And, as with any such conversation, the speaker is constructing an identity for themselves, in part deliberately, in part by default.

However stage-managed, the chat show format provides a different way of judging the politician, a way of measuring the extent to which they 'fit' into the home from which they are being watched. Does she seem like one of us? Does he *represent* us? Van Zoonen (1998a: 61) makes a similar point about the way 'gossip' (and chat shows are a form of gossip) can reveal important things about a politician: 'a great family man (reliability) . . . being popular among and mixing with other national celebrities (charisma), or . . . fiddling with government money (integrity)'. This personalization of politics does not necessarily represent the debasement of democracy. As John Corner (2000: 401) notes, individual political figures 'serve to condense "the political"'. They do this through the persona that they create, a practice as old as politics itself. Furthermore, the construction of a political persona, says Corner (ibid.: 404), far from damaging democracy, provides 'a focus for democratic engagement and investment, a resource for political imagination and implicit criteria for judging both the ends and means of political practice'.

The point is that the chat show and other devices of the modern politician may be as revealing as more formal acts of political communication. Whether he meant to or not, George W. Bush revealed much more about himself on Oprah Winfrey's show – about his drinking, his marriage and his personal feelings – than he had in any other interview. It cannot be deduced automatically that such encounters are a sign of 'dumbing down'. We need to look closely at the texts concerned and at the reactions they induce. In short, the claim that 'packaging politics' harms democracy must be analysed, not assumed. It may even improve democracy.

10

Remote Control

The growth of the internet has been, by any standards, extraordinary: from a local secret among scientists at the beginning of the 1990s to the topic of everyday conversation at the end of the decade, from an anarchic information network for the bizarre and the banal to an entire economy of self-made millionaires and inflated share prices. The internet, it is estimated, doubles in size every year. The accompanying rhetoric has been similarly dramatic, with talk of every aspect of human life being transformed by this new form of communication. Politics has not escaped; it too is to be transformed.

This chapter is about the possible political consequences of the net. If the last chapter was about the way in which politics is being transformed by new uses of existing media, this chapter is about the political impact of a new system of communication. In particular, it considers how the web may be reconfiguring democratic participation. Traditionally, citizens have been passive recipients of political information from their papers, radio stations and television channels. They have enjoyed a modest degree of participation through letters columns, phone-ins and the like, but for the most part they have been consumers of political information. The internet appears to change all this, enabling people to become more involved, to *interact* with the political realm. This opportunity, if it is really there, has profound implications for democracy – and this is what much recent political rhetoric would have us believe.

A decade ago the Clinton administration set itself the goal of creating 'a seamless web of communication networks, computers, databases and consumer electronics' that will protect and preserve democracy (quoted in Glencross, 1993: 3). In 1995, the G7 nations met to discuss the emerging 'information society' and the White House boasted that it could be reached by the click of a keyboard, as could endless other political information resources (see Harrison, 1994). Even the British civil service tentatively opened itself to the gaze of travellers on the superhighway. In the 1994 congressional mid-term elections, an 'on-line political activist' from California was quoted as saying: 'I think that by 1996, we will begin to see some number of campaigns either won or lost because campaign operations either use or fail to use network communications and organization' (*International Herald Tribune*, 9 November 1994). A year later one presidential hopeful, Lamar Alexander, began his campaign on the internet (*The Guardian*, 1 March 1995); now all candidates have their own websites which deliver their message and solicit campaign donations.

In 2000, the chairman of the Republican National Committee reported that 'the internet is introducing a fundamental shift in terms of communications and organizations' (Nicholson, 2000: 80). A similar sentiment was echoed by the chair of the Democratic National Committee: 'Democratic candidates will have more opportunities to speak directly and personally to the American people, through venues like Internet chat rooms' (Romer, 2000: 83). By 1998, the UK government had issued a discussion document which proposed that, in the future, electronic communications would distribute information, collect taxes, administer regulations and compile statistics (*www.democracy.org.uk/groups/gov-direct/*). The same year, the government was reported as bringing 'push button voting a step nearer', following its pre-election promise to use the internet to allow people to 'participate in decision-making' (*The Guardian*, 18 August 1998; Labour Party, 1995). Election campaigns now feature 'online debates' between candidates and citizens; in Switzerland, there was a site which allowed citizens to get a 'virtual tour' of the parliament to check on the voting record of the representatives (*www.politics.ch*). Meanwhile, in Minnesota in 1998, 14 candidates for governor debated six topics, their responses were then analysed by media commentators and the issues discussed in a public e-mail forum (*www.e-democracy.org/1998*).

These developments – and new ones emerge daily – have prompted a grand rhetoric that speaks of the dawning of a new democratic order. Governments across the world have been briefed on the subject of 'Democracies Online: Building Civic Life on the New Frontier' (*www.e-democracy.org/do*). One writer predicted: 'The Net is the world's only functioning political anarchy but it could soon become a major tool for democracy' (Fenchurch, 1994: 11). A similar spirit seemed to inform Newt Gingrich's dream of a 'virtual Congress', Al Gore's talk of the 'electronic town meeting' and Italian plans for 'la citta invisibile' (*www.citinv.it*).

Many visions inspired these plans, but one predominates: the belief that the web created the conditions for an electronic democracy. With the networks in place and interactive technology to hand, people will be able to vote on issues, inform themselves on government policy, interrogate their representatives. They can become the active, effective citizens of the democratic dream. This is to move beyond using the web as just another device for packaging politics, for parties to address voters; it is to enable those voters to take charge, to talk with each other rather than with politicians (for example, *www.USA-Talk.com*). In the UK, the government created a website, 'Have Your Say', to allow citizens to discuss proposals for freedom of information legislation. The minster responsible was also available to answer questions online, and he said that he was 'keen to hear people's views on our proposals' (*www.foi/democracy.org.uk*). The idea of 'la citta invisibile' is a system in which people are elected for a term of a year during which they make proposals for reform, which can be objected to by the popular assembly. If no more than 20 per cent object, the proposal is accepted *(www.citinv.it/delibere)*.

In short, the web appears to offer the prospect of a citizenry actively engaged in politics. But is this a realistic prospect, and is it, in any case, a desirable one? Does the internet provide salvation from the malaise which afflicts democracy? Does it function, as one enthusiast suggests, as a jukebox which, because its tunes are chosen by the people, is listened to more intently: 'while some of us may dread the prospective democratization of democracy via the Internet . . . make no mistake: The full interactive potential of the Internet offers a real chance to restore some purpose to our politics by restoring some power to our people' (Bailey, 1999). Faced with such enthusiasm, we need to look carefully at the arguments and assumptions being summoned to the cause of 'electronic democracy'.

Among advocates of the idea of 'electronic democracy', two different agendas can be detected. For some, the technology represents a way of improving the existing form of (liberal) democracy. For others, it constitutes an opportunity to create a new form of democracy – or rather, the revival of an old one: the direct democracy of ancient Athens. Electronic polling offers the chance to get 'Back to Greece' (Adonis and Mulgan, 1994).

Although these are two different visions of democracy, the discussion tends to blur this distinction, treating the new technology merely as a device for improving the efficiency of existing versions. As with previous debates about the political possibilities promised by new systems of communications, the focus has tended to be on improving current practices, rather than developing entirely new ones (Carey, 1989). Since the late 1970s and early 1980s, as reports of the potential of information technology (IT) emerged, political scientists have begun to discuss the possibility of an electronic democracy or cyberdemocracy (Abramson *et al.*, 1988; Arterton, 1987; Barber, 1984; Budge, 1996; McLean, 1989; Tsagarousianou *et al.*, 1998; Van de Donk *et al.*, 1995). But despite the novelty of the technology, the debates prompted by its application have tended to divide along familiar fault lines.

This tendency to use new technologies to repeat old arguments is a product of a failure to link political arguments to technological practices. The discussion needs to be moved on: to see technology as embodying politics, and to see the use of technology as more than merely an instrument for achieving given ends; to see it, instead, as shaping the ends themselves.

Democracy and the New Technology

It makes little sense to talk of 'free speech' without reference to the methods by which (mass) communication occurs. The ability to speak freely depends on access to the means of communication, and this is not a necessary or natural state of affairs. It has to be created and organized. A coherent political theory of free speech must be attached to an account of (a) the processes by which the technology of communication itself is developed and directed, and (b) the way this technology gives form to the ideas, values and opportunities that may be imagined. Arguments about the virtue of electronic democracy, or about the relative merits of competing versions of it, must incorporate some assumption about the technologies necessary to realizing it and society's ability to control technical change, to help achieve particular ends. Only with this control is it possible to advance or delay certain forms of electronic democracy. If no such control is feasible, if technical change is autonomous, arguments about the *kind* of democracy become largely irrelevant.

This, though, cannot be the end of the story. Supplementing arguments about electronic democracy with discussion of theories of technical change creates an artificial divide between theory and practice. Technical systems and political values are not discrete entities; rather they are extensions of one another. We live through our technology; our values and our identities both shape and are shaped by it. Think of the way that technologies of mobility (the car, the plane) have changed our views of the world and our place within it. In this sense, technology is cultural; and so is political theory: it is embedded in our forms of life in the same way that technology is (Winner, 1986). Arguments about electronic democracy must go beyond questions of theory and technique, to look at the ways in which the technology constructs the kind of people and places that will form this new democracy; it must ask, what kind of citizen, what kind of public will inhabit these 'seamless webs'?

Developments in delivery systems (satellite, cable and so on), the proliferation of channels, and the tendency towards narrowcasting, are seen, by some commentators, as creating a political order in which politics is being 'domesticated' and citizenship is being privatized (Habermas, 1989; Keane, 1991; Silverstone, 1994). This process is reinforced, it is argued (S. Jones, 1995: 28–9), by the way in which new forms of communication are dissolving traditional communities and the bonds and obligations that connect them. The result is a political life marked by instrumental, individualistic self-interest, in which the 'common interest' has no place (Sandel, 1998). These pessimistic prognostications are rebutted by those who argue that this same technology is in fact creating ideal conditions for a new democratic order, one in which citizens are forging new transnational interests and in which participatory democracy becomes a reality (Rheingold, 1992; home.t-online.de/home/nddie/home~1.htm).

In an attempt to assess these competing claims for the possibilities opened up by new forms of communication, the rest of this chapter divides into four sections. The first two review the existing political arguments for and against electronic democracy. The third addresses the notion of technical change that underlies the argument, but which is rarely made explicit. The fourth tries to reconcile these two dimensions – the political and the technical – in advocating a different approach to the debate about electronic democracy.

The Argument for Electronic Democracy

Although advocates differ over their preferred model of democracy, they are linked by a shared belief in the ability of electronic technology to create the conditions for political participation. As one enthusiast writes: 'Modern communications technology can provide the means to broadly educate and enlighten citizens, to engage them in discussions of the public good and the means to achieve it, and to empower citizens in their quest for self-determination' (Staton, 1994: 31–2). For others the net provides a forum for a truly free exchange of ideas and views, unconstrained by imbalances of power and resources (Ess, 1996). Underlying such claims is the thought that attempts to guarantee full participation in modern democracies have been wrecked by four, previously insurmountable, problems: time, size, knowledge and access. In earlier eras, democratic participation was limited because of the problems of assembling large numbers of people at one time and in one place, because of the limits to political knowledge of ordinary citizens, and because of the inequalities in the distribution of resources which hamper people's access to power and their capacity to participate. Taken together, these difficulties have made direct participation and popular deliberation both impractical and undesirable.

Electronic democracy seems to offer a solution to all these problems, thereby opening up the possibility of full participation. For example, online voting has been proposed as one solution to the problem of declining electoral turnout. A wired-up world would eliminate the constraints of time because communication and participation become instantaneous. Citizens can participate at the push of a button. They do not need to meet in cold halls or travel to polling booths. Similarly, problems of size are solved because physical space becomes irrelevant. It is no longer necessary to gather people in a single place. So it is, too, with problems in the distribution of knowledge. Not only is information on any subject now widely available through the net, but access to it is relatively easy. New sources of information can compete with established ones; take, for example, the example of Matt Drudge, who was active in supplying gossip and rumour about the Clinton administration that did not appear in the mainstream press (*www.drudge.com*). The costs of information and access are dramatically reduced, and in turn organizational costs are cut. The net seems to provide a way round the practical problems posed by democracy, whatever its form; citizens can exercise their vote, deliberate on public policy or participate directly (Barber, 1984; Becker and Staton, 1981). But it is precisely this sort of reasoning which appals critics of electronic democracy.

The Argument against Electronic Democracy

There are four main lines of criticism directed at electronic democracy. The first concentrates upon the inherent theoretical difficulties within the idea of democracy. As Iain McLean (1989) points out, there are some 'problems of democracy' that cannot be solved by the application of technology. Democratic decisions are not just the product of citizen choices. It depends on how you register those choices. As the argument about proportional representation makes abundantly clear, the character of the electoral system can crucially affect the result. You get different majorities and different winners depending on whether you use single-transferable votes or a list system, whether you use an electoral college or a simple majority. What counts as 'the best' will depend upon judgements about how democracy ought to work, what interests ought to feature and what results ought to be produced. These obstacles are exacerbated by the thought that there may not be a majority among any given population. There are instead 'cycling majorities', in which any given winner is the product of agenda setting and voting rules. Where there are three policy options, and supporters for each, none of whom can command a majority on their own, then any option can be defeated by one of the others. There is no majority choice and, where one appears, this is the result of the way the agenda is set and the voting conducted (it has very little to do with the actual distribution of popular opinion). Once again, the problem cannot be solved by the expedient of the internet and the computer. Technology does nothing to solve the conceptual problems that democracy generates.

A second line of criticism derives from the assumption that, by increasing access to, and the availability of, data, information technology improves the quality of democracy. While there are powerful reasons for seeing freedom of information as a central tenet of democracy, it does not follow that all information in itself enhances democracy. Democratic decisions are not equivalent to mathematical calculations; they also involve judgements. Just because capital punishment is the popularly preferred option, it does not follow that it is right to send people to the electric chair. Nor are decisions necessarily improved by the simple expedient of acquiring more data. Just because we know the content of the human genome, it is not immediately obvious how this knowledge should be used. All decisions require a judgement, and the art of judgement may, in fact, be hampered by an excess of information (Dennett, 1986; Vickers, 1965); or rather, that information has to be examined and explored in a dialogue, not simply computed.

These first two lines of criticism lead to a third: that the kind of democracy being proposed is a debased, impoverished version. Advocates of electronic democracy sometimes treat the democratic process as a mere device for registering preferences. For their critics, this is a gross misrepresentation of the democratic ideal. 'Modern technology,' writes Michael Walzer (1985: 306–7), 'makes possible something like this . . . we might organize push-button referenda on crucial issues, the citizens alone in their living rooms, watching television, arguing only with their spouses, hands hovering over their private voting machines . . . But is this the exercise of power? I am inclined to say, instead, that is only another example of the erosion of value – a false and ultimately degrading way of sharing in the making of decisions.' Like Walzer, Jean Elshtain (1982: 108) argues that electronic political participation is equivalent to making consumer choices on the shopping channel. The key element of democracy – deliberative, public policy choices – is replaced by privatized, instrumental decisions: 'advocates of interactive television display a misapprehension of the nature of real democracy, which they confuse with the plebiscite system'. 'A true democratic polity,' she continues (ibid.: 109), 'involves a deliberative process, participation with other citizens, a sense of moral responsibility for one's society and the enhancement of individual possibilities through action in, and for, the *res publica*.' These critics argue that democracy involves deliberation and dialogue in the formation of collective goals, rather than the aggregation of individual preferences.

The thought that electronic democracy is promoting a particular, lesser form of democracy is linked to a final criticism. This is the complaint that the technologies of electronic democracy actually serve to promote the interests of the powerful. Such arguments draw on the gap between promise and practice in the operation of actual systems of electronic participation. Although access to the web and the number of sites has been increasing very rapidly (AOL claims 24 million subscribers), most people in most parts of the world do not have access. The possibility of electronic participation is premised on the assumption that access to the new technologies is universal and cheap. Accessibility has a physical and a social dimension. It is social in that the provision of terminals is of no value if people are (or feel) incapable of using them.

This state may result from a lack of training or education, but it may also stem from a sense of alienation from, or antagonism to, the technology. Such estrangement is not a failure of particular individuals, but of the way a technology is *made* inaccessible. Feminist critics of technology point to the way it comes to be designed and organized for the benefit of men and to the exclusion of women (Wajcman, 1991). Access to technology, including information technology, is socially stratified: between classes, generations and nations. Despite the huge growth of the internet, its distribution remains highly concentrated in certain states, and within particular groups inside those states. In December 1999, only 18 per cent of Britons had access to the internet at either home or work (*The Guardian*, 20 December 1999). Maps of internet traffic reveal that only a small part of the world participates (*www.cybergeography.org/atlas/geographic.html*). Manuel Castells (1996: 371) talks of the social stratification of the world into those who are 'interacting' and those who are 'interacted'. The latter remain on the receiving end of pre-packaged communications opportunities.

The physical and social barriers to access are a product of the commercial and political interests organized around the new forms of communication. These interests are not concerned with creating global or regional opportunities for political participation, but rather with preserving or protecting investments. This is what Gerald Sussman (1997: 174) calls 'the political and economic realities': 'the ventures of opportunity-seeking commercial interests and the concerns of those who would restrict public communication in the cause of security, moral guardianship, or property protection'. Sussman draws attention to the state's complicity in such developments (through its distribution of radio frequencies and the like). But what is perhaps more noticeable is the way that the key conglomerate players (Microsoft, Time Warner, News Corporation) are forging new connections that enable them to influence and exploit the development of the net. In 1999, News Corporation created ePartners, with $400 million to spend on emerging internet companies, and Rupert Murdoch announced: 'I can't agree with those who see communications technology as a divisive social force. By facilitating communications between peoples of all nations it will help bring people closer together' (*The Guardian*, 2 December 1999). It might be that Murdoch's ambition is to bring the world together in glorious harmony, but sceptics might be forgiven for supposing that he had an eye too on the profits to be made from the new global meeting place.

For these same sceptics, the net effect is that the problems of access that beset previous forms of democracy are reproduced in the new electronic order. The same imbalances and inequality of resources continue to distort participation. For all the rhetoric of participation and equality in a new electronic democracy, the reality is a system in which corporate power acts to depoliticize politics, transforming the citizen into the consumer (Weizenbaum, 1984; Zolo, 1992). Pushed to its extreme, this corporatism imagines a future electronic democracy in which the elite already knows how the citizen is going to vote because it has complete information on everyone and everything. Voting itself becomes entirely redundant because it is entirely predictable. The system of electronic participation is in fact a system of surveillance, monitoring citizens rather than responding to them. This bleak scenario chimes with Calabrese and Borchert's observation (1996: 264–5) that, while 'the discourse on electronic democracy is aesthetically pleasing', it has to be treated cautiously: 'visions of empowerment are illusory or manipulative if they do not rest on the foundation of a clearly articulated vision of government'.

Whatever vision of the future we entertain, the arguments for electronic democracy must address complex matters of power and its distribution, just as democracy cannot be treated simply as a method for registering votes. The application of a more efficient technology is not, therefore, an adequate response. Democracy requires more than the collection of information; it also entails the opportunity to reflect upon knowledge and to deliberate about the conflicting claims of public and private goods. But to assert such things is not, by the same token, an adequate response either. The discussion of electronic democracy cannot be reduced to a formal debate about the relative merits of competing models of democracy. As the preceding discussion should indicate, the argument is not just about abstract ideas, but also about the conditions for their realization. The debate has, therefore, to engage with the technology itself and its effects.

The Technology of Electronic Democracy

Accounts of the technology of electronic democracy tend to take three forms. The first suggests that it is the neutral product of disinterested scientific enquiry. The second focuses on the political interests which drive technical change. The final account claims that technology evolves as a result of its own internal logic, and is in this autonomously independent of both science and politics. Proponents of electronic democracy tend to adopt the first of these, the idea that the technology is neutral. For them, information technology provides a 'technical fix'. The 'problems' of democracy are seen as merely practical, and solvable by the application of technology.

But technical fixes are only 'fixes' because of the way the problem is defined. They do not constitute 'the' answer, but 'an' answer. Technical fixes do not solve a problem, rather they *impose a particular definition* on what the 'problem' is, a definition that invites the preselected solution (Habermas, 1971). If democracy's problems are practical, then technology may solve them, but if they are not, then technology merely reproduces them in a different form – in the same way that building motorways may simply relocate congestion and pollution rather than eliminate them.

Criticisms of the 'technical fix' approach lead to the second account of technology, one which focuses upon the interests behind the technology. Technology exists for a reason: to serve the interests of those with power. Seeing technology this way automatically raises suspicions about electronic democracy. Rather than being a way of empowering citizens, electronic democracy may as easily be a device which deskills and depoliticizes citizens, reducing their capacity to threaten the existing system (Campbell and Connor,

1986; Lyon, 1994). If this is the assumption, then the rhetoric of electronic town halls and virtual participation disguise a reality in which the corporate commercial and political interests invested in the technology are using the new possibilities for their advantage: to sustain the status quo rather than change it. Party websites may invite participation, but actually they deliver well-packaged, emollient PR (Coleman, 1998). But this version of technical change, as the product of corporate political interest, overlooks the question of how the technology itself is brought into being. The internet was not created by sheer act of will. Drawing attention to the commercial, political and military interests linked to it (see, for example, Calabrese and Borchert, 1996; Herman and McChesney, 1997), while important, does not in itself establish them as the intentional authors of the technology. They are as often forced to cope with the many unanticipated consequences of technical change as they able to plan that change.

This gives rise to the third of the three accounts of technical change. This is the idea that technology is autonomous, that it is directed by a technical rationality which is not only independent of centres of political power, but actually dictates to them. Such a view can inspire technological dystopianism (Ellul, 1964) or utopianism (de Sola Pool, 1990), both of which suggest that we can do little more than accept the inevitable technological (and subsequent social) revolution. So it is that electronic democracy is seen as the necessary outcome of general patterns of change, led by technologies which apply themselves to all aspects of human life: we do our shopping, we choose our life partner, we participate in politics, all on the web, and each of these activities is subsumed within the rhetoric and relations of consumerism (Sartori, 1989). People's connections to each other become purely instrumental and politics is affected by the same logic. Voting is treated like any other instrumental, consumer activity, having no more significance than the choice made between cereal brands in the supermarket. More than this, the infrastructure for 'online democracy' creates the same kind of manipulative devices that mark consumption generally: marketing, advertising and so on. This account of technology rests on a strong notion of determinism, which assumes that the same technology follows the same course and has the same effects wherever it operates. But the same technology can have a different meaning and different effects according to its place in space and time. The culture in which it is embedded also constitutes it. (For a fuller version of this argument, see Street, 1992.)

In short, the three views of technology – as neutral, politically chosen or autonomous – are flawed to the extent that they overlook the combination of political, scientific and cultural processes that construct the technology. The debate about electronic democracy must begin by recognizing the mutual dependence of political argument and technology. The core ideas within the political argument are themselves the product of our relationship with technology. At one level, the technology is the embodiment of certain interests and possibilities, but at another it is the bearer of effects: it changes what we can imagine and what we can want; it shapes our politics. Though we can identify the interests and choices around a given technology, these interests and choices do not design that technology and dictate its effects. Technology is not something that exists as a simple object for our use. It acts to structure our choices and preferences, but not in a wholly determinist way. The relationship is in constant flux: political processes shape technology; and it then shapes politics.

The internet is a product of military and scientific interests, but its development and use have not been controlled by those interests. It has created possibilities and problems which no one could have anticipated (who could have imagined the 'love virus' which in May 2000 brought chaos and vast losses to the world's financial capitals?). What possibilities and alternatives exist at any one time is a matter of empirical investigation, an investigation that does not end with either the technology or the political interests promoting it. Debate about electronic democracy has to avoid political idealism and technological determinism; it has to acknowledge the complex interplay of political ideas and technical practices.

Rethinking Electronic Democracy

Debates about democracy are debates about information, about how it is distributed and how it is used (see, for example, Arblaster, 1987; Lively, 1975). Any attempt to think about electronic democracy must, therefore, consider how information technologies do (and should) structure access to, and use of, political knowledge. As we saw earlier, there are those who argue that the current forms of mass communication threaten democracy by 'distorting' political knowledge, adversely affecting people's ability to perform the role of the democratic citizen and to exercise political judgement. Elshtain's talk of the citizen being transformed into a consumer is based on the thought, to misquote Oscar Wilde, that the consumer knows the price of everything and the value of nothing. In the process, politics becomes a form of market exchange; it is 'privatized', and hence what is called 'public opinion' is merely a summation of private desires (Sartori, 1989). The citizen ceases to exist as a self-conscious actor, and as such is incapable of deliberative political participation.

These gloomy prognostications recall the familiar story that accompanies almost all new technologies of culture and communication. Television destroys the art of conversation, just as the phone makes letter writing redundant, and e-mail eliminates the need for human contact. Equally familiar are the rebuttals which stress the possibilities in the technology: that technology fuels our imagination and broadens our perspective, that we can use technology and not be used by it. This argument maps a dichotomy between choice and determinism, between citizens as freely choosing agents or as consumers whose choices are pre-packaged. But instead of being forced to accept these extremes, we can see people's relationship to IT and the meaning attached to its contents as being created in the material and social context of their lives. The way technology is used, and the significance of the messages it delivers, are contingent (Ang, 1996; Corner, 1995).

The implication of this is that we need to see how systems of communication construct different opportunities for political engagement. As Schickler (1994) observes, variations in format can produce variations in types of participation. The phone-in, for example, 'seems conducive to prejudiced, sloppy thinking, and to extremely simple views of the social and political process' (Schickler, 1994: 194). Other settings may produce more coherent thought. Similarly, Langdon Winner (1994) argues that the tendency to present information in restless 'bitesize' chunks (along the lines pioneered by MTV) fragments political understanding, just as notions of community – who 'we' are – can be organised differently according to the character of the communications network (who is linked to whom, in what relationship) (Friedland, 1996). The implication of these claims, whether or not we accept their particular formulation, is that the way information is presented and organized is correlated with forms of political discourse. In other words, the citizen's capacity to make political judgements is dependent upon the way in which political information is delivered and received.

Thinking about electronic democracy has to be sensitive to these issues, but it also has to be linked to the larger setting in which that democracy might operate. As Blumler and Gurevitch argue (1995: 98): 'the media can pursue democratic values only in ways that are compatible with the socio-political and economic environment in which they operate. Political communication arrangements follow the contours of and derive their resources from the society of which they are a part.' Compatibility cannot be guaranteed. Brants *et al.* (1996: 246) point to one potential cause of tension in their study of communication networks in the Netherlands: 'Network technology has the potential to create a new public sphere which fits the social structure better . . . However, politics does not yet fit the new technology. Politicians feel uncomfortable with the different role they play in such a challenging direct democracy.' The debate about electronic democracy has to be sensitive both to the technical forms which are on offer and to the way in which representation and legitimation operate within the wider political system.

The most dramatic illustration of the connection between new technologies of communication and the wider political system is provided by what is often termed cyber-protest or e-protest. On 18 June 1999, a spate of public demonstrations erupted across the world. In London, marchers, chanting to the accompaniment of a samba band, occupied a mainline railway station, before moving on to trash a McDonalds restaurant. Similar scenes were witnessed elsewhere in Europe and in the USA and Latin America. Five months later, in Seattle, another group of demonstrators disrupted the meeting of the World Trade Organization. These two events, and many similar ones (such as the trampling of genetically modified crops), were coordinated through the internet. Websites and e-mail discussion groups provided the infrastructure for political activities which, it seemed to the frustrated authorities, had no leaders and were not dependent on hierarchical political structures. They were virtual and very real.

In October 1999, NetAid, an internet version of Live Aid, solicited donations through the web. Meanwhile, the use of e-mail by interest groups like Friends of the Earth has enabled them to develop new organizational forms which create 'networks of networks', giving substance to the familiar green slogan 'think globally, act locally' (Pickerill, 2000; Washbourne, 1999). In a similar way, the US online service, Peacenet is used to promote cross-group collaboration (Sussman, 1997: 173). Basque separatists, gays and lesbians, Canadian monarchists and others also employ the net in just this way (*www.politicsonline.com/news/*). Such examples form part of what some commentators see as a 'civic networking movement'. This is represented by 'a new anarchic political community in which traditional political identities linked to territorial and sectional interests are undermined, and new forms of politics emerge free of state coercion' (Bryan *et al.*, 1998: 6–7). Beyond this, protest is being focused on the web itself. So-called 'hactavists' – 'Electronic Disturbance Theater', 'Cult of the Dead Cow' – are committed to the use of cybersabotage. Their intention is to bring about 'electronic civil disobedience', disrupting the operation of governments across the globe (*el-democracy-owner@www.ipso.cec.be*).

It is not enough, however, just to draw attention to the way the new technologies of communication may affect participation, or to the tensions between different interests within the political system, or to the organization and distribution of access. All of these are crucial components of an adequate response to the spread of new technology, but there is yet another dimension. These matters are overlaid by the question as to what kind of democracy is being sought. As we have seen from the current debate about electronic democracy, the protagonists appeal to competing notions of democracy. There are those who favour a direct form of democracy and those who advocate a representative one. This division has consequences for the organization of the technology as well as for political practice. So in arguing about electronic democracy and the potential represented by the internet, we have not only to think about technology in its wider political context, but also about the competing notions of democracy, between those, for example, that seek to aggregate preferences and those that aim to create a forum for deliberative decision making.

Much of the literature on electronic democracy tends to assume that it is intended to serve the first of these goals. The technology is to be used to furnish individuals with more information about issues that relate to their personal interests. The objection to this form of electronic democracy is expressed, as we saw earlier, in terms of its treatment of politics as a form of market exchange and its creation of a citizen who is a privatized consumer. Although this objection is presented as a general critique of electronic democracy, it does not have this force. It is, in fact, just an objection to one way of organizing electronic democracy and one kind of democracy. Or, to put it another way, if electronic democracy is organized differently or a different model of democracy is defended, these objections collapse.

There is no reason why electronic democracy should not take another form. It could, for instance, be used to support a system of deliberative democracy. There are powerful reasons for supposing that democracies in which citizens are required to deliberate on the choices which face a society, rather than simply registering their preferences, produce better decisions (Fishkin, 1991; Miller, 1992). The point of the deliberative process is to allow people to form opinions, rather than just to express them (Miller, 1992: 67). If this is the purpose allotted to democracy, then the forms of communication must accord with it. Citizens must not only be able to interrogate databases and acquire an expertise of their own, they must be able to reflect upon this knowledge in dialogue with their fellow citizens. This means that the hierarchies which tend to protect forms of expertise have to be broken down. At the same time, it is not just a matter of increasing access to information and allowing for discussion. There has also to be the opportunity for deliberation, which requires networks that enable an open dialogue about the public good. People have to make decisions, not just exchange thoughts or register interests.

If we are persuaded by this version of democracy, a further set of issues is raised. What type of collectivity is to do the deliberating? Who are the 'public'? The terms that define the community depend again, as with the choice between types of democracy, on political judgement. Do we want, for instance, to enshrine the notion of 'community' as the exclusive, rule-bound 'club' or as the more inclusive 'commonwealth' (Bellamy and Hollis, 1995)? These questions have to be settled both in terms of their political desirability and in terms of the conditions that make them possible. As we have already noted, the internet can, on the one hand, create different types of community (Friedland, 1996) and on the other, it can destroy community (S. Jones, 1995).

These questions require political debate and judgement, but they are not confined to the realm of political theory. They also engage with the ways in which forms of communication are organized. Political relationships depend upon the structures of communication that enable them to occur. This is not just a function of the political economy of communications, although this is clearly important; it is also dependent upon the forms of address which are allowed for. These questions cannot, therefore, be answered by political theorists alone. We need to integrate political theory, technical change and cultural practice. We have to see arguments about 'democracy', not as abstract ideas, but as contingent upon, and bound up with, the technology that helps constitute those ideas. Equally, the technology itself must be seen as part of the political and cultural realm, not as an instrument to be used or as an independent force to which we must be reconciled. It is not enough simply to identify a form of democracy as desirable, and to sketch out the role that the technology has to play in fulfilling it. The technology is itself the product and expression of competing and contradictory political interests.

Conclusion

If the debate about electronic democracy is to move beyond the crude dichotomy established by those who advocate it and those who decry it, and if we are to reflect cogently upon the experiments in such democracy which are emerging, we need to be explicit about what kind of democracy is being advocated. If deliberative democracy is the preferred option, it is important to state and defend this, but the argument cannot end there. It is not just a matter of applying the technology to this particular ideal. Rather we have to think through the implications of deliberative democracy for both the forms of address and the political economy of the means of communication. At the same time, the possibility of such a democracy cannot be attributed simply to acts of political will. That kind of control over the technology is not possible because technological change is not simply the product of political choice. So the idea of democracy to which we aspire must be understood as partly a product of the technology that surrounds it. Political ideas cannot be separated from the medium in which they are thought, and hence it makes little sense to talk of returning to ancient Greek democracy via new technology, or of simply 'improving' an existing democratic form. Technical change brings with it new ideas and possibilities, and new notions of democracy; at the same time, these possibilities have themselves to be subject to critical political analysis, informed by a particular notion of democracy. The politics of electronic democracy are also the politics of technology, and both are tied intimately to the fact that forms of communications are also systems of power.

11

Power and Mass Media

The media have power: they determine the fate of politicians and political causes, they influence governments and their electorates. They are, therefore, to be numbered with other political institutions – parliaments, executives, administrations and parties. As Paolo Mancini and David Swanson (1996: 11) write: 'No longer merely a means by which other subsystems, such as political parties, can spread their own messages, mass media emerge in modern poly-archies as an autonomous power center in reciprocal competition with other power centers.' Media power is now almost a common-place of modern commentary. Textbooks on the operation of the political system all include a chapter on the media. Twenty years ago, even ten years ago, this was not the case. Today mass media are taken as seriously as are parties and Parliament or Congress, sometimes more so. They receive this attention because, it is implicitly or explicitly assumed, television, radio, the press and the new media are 'powerful'.

The same assumption runs through this book. Media bias, the ownership and control of the media industry, the political uses of the media, all matter because they have some effect upon the way the political process works, and the interests that motivate the media also shape the outcomes of that process. But while this assumption is widely shared, there is considerable disagreement as to what exactly it means: where and how does this power manifest itself? This chapter tries to provide an answer.

Such questions as those above are central to mass media's relationship to democracy. To claim that some set of arrangements is 'democratic' is to make a claim about the distribution of power. Put simply, in a dictatorship power is held by an unaccountable elite who use their power to exploit the powerless; in a democracy power is 'legitimate' because those who exercise it are representative and accountable. This crude dichotomy reappears in accounts of the way the media operate. In a dictatorship, there is monopoly control of media, which are used to disseminate propaganda; in a democracy, control is dispersed and content is pluralistic. Of course, there is much to debate about the key terms, but the point is that 'power' – who controls the media and their content, about what effects they have – is the crucial one.

The study of power is driven by the desire to know who is responsible for the things that affect our lives: who is to blame for the current state of affairs, how can it be changed for the better (Morriss, 1987)? To answer such questions in relation to the media, it is important to acknowledge the different ways in which media may be implicated in the distribution and exercise of power. Media power does not, after all, take a single monolithic form. It appears in different guises and operates in different ways. We begin by looking at three forms of power: discursive power, access power and resource power. Each of these captures the ways in which media power is typically discussed, and each of them is linked to the debate about media and democracy, raising questions about how media content shapes political ideas and arguments and how media forms affect political access and participation.

Discursive Power

The familiar claim that 'knowledge is power' captures the most commonly cited connection between mass media and power. The idea that 'knowledge' is a source of power, and that mass media are central to this power, rests on some fairly straightforward, if not uncontroversial, claims. Power is taken here to refer to the capacity that A has to get B to do something they would not otherwise have done, and the suggestion is that the distribution of knowledge is a key technique for achieving this. Control of the flow of information about what the authorities are doing, keeping the people in ignorance, provides a way of preventing political protest. If people knew the government was systematically torturing dissidents, or if they knew that their rivers were being polluted or their food contaminated, there might be widespread public disruption and challenges to the legitimacy of the regime.

It is this sort of thinking that lies behind political censorship and repression. In May 2000, President Milosevic of Yugoslavia decided to try to stamp out opposition to his regime; to do this, 'masked police took over Studio B, Serbia's main opposition-controlled television station in the early hours of Wednesday morning and halted transmission in two prominent Belgrade radio stations' (*Financial Times*, 19 May 2000). The corollary of this kind of repression is the use of media to propagate false or distorted information. Here the media operate as part of a propaganda machine. Insofar as knowledge is power, then the media's role in providing or suppressing information implicates them in the exercise of power, although it might be contended that the important source of the power is not so much the medium itself as those who have access to it. This is a point to which we return.

Thinking of media power in terms of knowledge and information, though important, is rather limited and crude. It presumes a notion of truth and falsity, what is *really* happening versus what 'they' *pretend* is the case, that is hard to sustain. What if reality is itself an artifice? What if 'reality' is constructed, not reflected or revealed? What if our world is the product of the discourses we use to claim knowledge of it? Such questions are provoked by, among others, Michel Foucault (1984) and they have become influential in shaping understanding of media power. As Kate Nash explains: 'Knowledge as discourse is not knowledge of the "real" world as it exists prior to that knowledge. Although it presents itself as *representing* objective reality, in fact, discourses *construct* and make "real" the objects of knowledge they "represent"' (2000:21; original emphasis). From this perspective, media power operates through the way it privileges particular discourses and constructs particular forms of reality.

This is to see the media as exercising *discursive* power. The assumption is that the way people act is conditioned by what they think, and that what is thought is affected by the picture of the world conveyed by the mass media. This power may not be translated directly into particular behaviours. We do not have to assume that because newspapers support one party or ideology this will directly influence the way people vote, any more that we should assume that violent films will increase the level of violence in society. Some connection is supposed, but it is not a simple matter of cause and effect (see Chapter 4). Nonetheless, insofar as mass media are responsible for the circulation of particular ideas and images, and insofar as these shape thoughts and actions, the mass media are thought to wield discursive or ideological power. A further assumption is that the media operate on behalf of, or are shaped by, a distinct set of interests which benefit from the ideology being propagated. The implication of this approach to media power is that we need to analyse in detail the content of mass media texts, to reveal the particular account of the world encoded within them.

This emphasis on the way media may operate ideologically extends the notion of their power beyond 'information'. Media power is not confined to news and current affairs, the formal sources of 'information'; it includes soap operas and films which also create a 'common sense' for individual and collective action. In asking about media power, it is necessary to look at the full range of media output, to see how news and entertainment sustain particular versions of reality. It is also important to see the ways in which media help to construct people's identities and interests, and hence their relationship to 'reality'. People do not pick and choose freely, selecting identities and interests with the same apparent casualness as supermarket shoppers. Just as the design of super-markets, the organization of the shelves and aisles, is intended to increase the amount of money spent, and just as people's use of the stores is constrained by their resources, so encounters with the media are organized and affected by those supplying the images and by the resources (and skills) people have available in consuming them. But however the process is organized, what is at stake is the way people come to see, and think for, themselves. These identities have political consequences because they underpin the interests which animate peoples demands on, and expectations for, the political system.

Access Power

Implicit in the idea of the media's discursive role is the claim that there is a process which produces these discourses. One way to think of this is to ask whose voices, identities and interests populate our screens and newspapers. Insofar as the media provide a valuable resource for those who wish to promote or maintain their interests, there is the possibility that power may operate in decisions about who has access to this resource. This power of access refers to the way in which the operation of mass media controls the range of voices or interests able to use the various formats, either as viewers/ readers or as contributors. At one level, this can take the form of conglomerate control which narrows the variety of sources to which access is being gained. At another, it can refer to the range of interests or identities which find expression within the choice of media. (It was recently reported, for example, that the presenter of an Australian talk show, having spent months bemoaning the iniquities of the banking system, suddenly started taking a more supportive line. It transpired that his show had benefited from substantial donations from the Banking Federation.) Either of these forms of exclusion and inclusion have an impact on the status accorded to particular ways of life and interests: think of the way women are represented in the media: as victims of, or appendages to, men; think too of the way in which 'telegenicity' (or the idea of 'telegenicity') arbitrates over the fate of political careers. Those who do not meet the criteria of telegenicity, or those who are not deemed worthy of attention in their own right, are denied access to social and political power. Even if the decisions are being made by others (parties decide who is to be their leader), the criteria used in the selection are media-generated. In any case, the media are directly implicated in decisions about who to interview or what topic to address from what angle, thereby setting agendas that, at the very least, are only tangentially (if at all) linked to the concerns of viewers and readers.

These barriers to access may be shaped by a variety of factors. They may lie in the routine practices of journalists, whose news values identify certain incidents and witnesses as more or less important or relevant than others. They may exist in the ways in which commercial interests determine what kind of programmes are made or what coverage a newspaper provides. They may be found in the mechanisms for collecting and disseminating news, the way certain news sources are privileged over other ones. They may also be found in the ways in which divisions of labour operate within media institutions: how the conflict between the interests of editorial staff and marketing staff are resolved (a battle of the allocation of space in the paper or the schedule), or the conflict within editorial offices between foreign and domestic news, between sport and arts, and so on. The outcome of these turf wars finds expression in who and what is covered. The routines and cultures of media, their commercial and structural interests, all operate to determine the opportunities for access to the airwaves and newspaper columns. In other words, studying media power is like studying the operation of power in almost any institution; it is important to find out what happens, how and when – and who or what is responsible. This aspect of media power addresses the way in which media organizations control access to a key resource. It does not represent the end of the search for media power. Just as the power of the media may not refer only to their discursive effects, so it is not confined to its gatekeeping function.

Resource Power

A third form of media power is *resource* power. If discursive power refers to the way in which a popular common sense is created, and if access power refers to the way in which particular interests or identities are acknowledged or excluded, resource power refers to the way in which media conglomerates can affect the actions of governments and states. This form of power identifies the bargaining power that media conglomerates have in their dealings with national governments and other agencies. Governments need media conglomerates for the delivery of infrastructural services (the provision and circulation of information) and for the income and employment they generate. The need for such things makes governments vulnerable, limiting their capacity to regulate these valued media actors. Imposing barriers on cross-media ownership or enforcing particular regulations on media content can be costly for governments, either because of the antipathy they generate from the media conglomerates (expressed through their media outlets) or because these conglomerates may move elsewhere, to more 'liberal' regimes. The power relationship here is between the media industry and governments.

Theories of Media Power

These three possible forms of media power, discourse, access and resource, are not meant to constitute a definitive list. Rather they serve as an antidote to the temptation to see media purely in terms of ideological effects, measurable as 'bias' or 'influence'. Media power may be detected in many different ways and settings. These three aspects to media power are offered as illustrations of the ways in which mass media *might* be implicated in the exercise of power. This is partly an empirical matter (of seeing what is encoded in a text, of analysing the operation of media corporations), but it is also a conceptual matter, of clarifying how we identify and investigate power.

Steven Lukes (1974) famously introduced a three-dimensional account of power. In the first dimension, power is exercised when, in the public conflict between two contenders, one is seen to win and the other to lose. An example of this kind of power struggle can be found in the exercise of *resource power*, in the way media corporations have sought to resist (and succeeded in resisting) government attempts to regulate their activities.

But power struggles do not always take place in the open, and often one of the contenders finds himself at a disadvantage through the manoeuvring of the other. This is where Lukes introduces the second dimension of power. Power can be used to marginalize certain views, either by setting the agenda in a way that favours one side, or by creating the impression that one side in the dispute is less worthy or legitimate. The media are often accused (by the Glasgow University Media Group studies, for example) of exercising this kind of power in the way they report the news. Strikes are reported as alien to the 'normal' order, and as 'disruptions' to the lives of 'ordinary' people. Trade unionists are made to appear as undemocratic or uncooperative; they are made to look less 'respectable' when compared to management. Such representations legitimate the agenda and behaviour of management, and delegitimate those of trade unionists. These are examples of the exercise of access power.

Both these dimensions of power operate where there are identifiable contenders and issues: government versus media conglomerates; management versus workers. Lukes notes, however, that power can be exercised where no such conflict of interest appears to exist, where instead there is consensus and collaboration. Despite this, one party to this willing cooperation actually ends up being worse off, to the advantage of the other party. The third dimension of power creates a 'false consensus', in the sense that it would not command consent if people were aware of their 'real interests'. The point is that media power shapes people's political preferences in ways that are counter to what they would want were they free agents. Hence people come to identify with political values and organizations which actually work against their interests. This is a case of discursive power.

To draw attention to the fit between Lukes' categories and the different forms of media power is not, however, to prove anything, though it does indicate that discussion of media power must be rooted in an account of what power means. Not everyone subscribes to Lukes' account of power (see, for example, Dowding, 1996; Hindess, 1996; Morriss, 1987), but his three-dimensional approach does, at least, give an indication of the range of issues that need to be addressed in any theory of media power. What is evident is that the treatment these issues receive varies according to the approach of the analyst. In what follows we consider four variants which have tended to dominate discussion of media power: the liberal–pluralist, the New Right, the Marxist and the culturalist. Each provides a quite different account of the political importance and effect of mass media, and each provides a different perspective on the topics we have discussed in previous chapters (bias, packaging, political effects and so on).

Liberal Pluralism

This view has been described as the 'liberal orthodoxy' (Dunleavy and Husbands, 1985) and is one that attributes the least direct political influence to mass media. It has its origins in the reaction to 'mass society' theory, although the debate which it provokes can be traced back to the eighteenth century (Hall, 1982: 57). From the 1930s onwards, there was increasing talk of the emergence of a mass society, one in which individuality and difference were being eroded by a variety of processes, most obviously, mass production and mass consumption. Workers no longer made a complete product in small workshops, but instead repeated the same task endlessly as part of a production line. They seemed little more than automatons. Mass production was the corollary of mass consumption: the same product was available everywhere. Regional and individual differences were eroded. This process was fuelled by mass media. Radio attracted huge audiences, all of whom heard the same thing. These listeners, in losing their distinctive, rooted identities, became vulnerable to the power of the new medium. Advertisers were able to exploit the manipulative power of mass culture to fuel the drive towards mass consumption; they were able to play on the insecurities and anxieties of anomic individuals.

The power of the new forms of communication was given its most chilling representation in the propaganda machinery developed by Hitler and Stalin. The new mass media appeared to provide the power to enslave entire nations. This fear of the power of mass media could be detected in the reaction to popular culture in the 1950s, when politicians, priests and parents tried to control access to the sight of Elvis Presley's gyrating pelvis. It could also be detected in the restrictions imposed on the coverage of politics and in the use of classification of films and videos.

It was against this view of the media's power that the liberal–pluralist perspective was shaped. Research into audiences revealed that, in fact, the media had little or no impact, beyond reinforcing previously held views (Blumler and McQuail, 1968; Klapper, 1960). There was acknowledgement of the biases in the press, but because papers took up different political positions, voters were able to choose the papers that fitted their own views. Indeed the operation of market competition ensured that papers came to reflect the views of their readers. The press could not afford to ignore its readership if it wanted to maintain its market competitiveness. Besides, the opportunity to choose between ideologically different papers was combined with a regulated television system, which prided itself on the authoritative character of its political information.

Underlying this scepticism about the influence of the mass media is a view about the distribution of power generally and about the source of political preferences. The power of the mass media is counteracted by two important considerations. The first is that in any complex modern society there is no power elite: whatever power resided with the mass media, it was counterbalanced by other sources of power. Secondly, people's political interests derived from their social location and experiences, not from what they read in papers or saw on television. From the liberal–pluralist perspective, media conglomerates are neither disposed nor able to act in ways that threaten the interests of other groups within society.

Inside those conglomerates power tends to reside with managers, rather than with those who formally own the enterprise. The incentive structure to which such managers respond works to reflect the demands and preferences of readers and viewers. And, furthermore, any attempt to manage or manipulate the thoughts and actions of those readers is likely to prove ineffective. Such people respond selectively to what they see and read, using media messages to reinforce pre-existing dispositions. In summary, according to the liberal–pluralist, media power is minimal, tied as it is to transmitting pre-existing interests and to reflecting shifting concerns. Mass media act as a forum for political debates that begin and end elsewhere.

New Right

A rather less sanguine view of media power was taken by the New Right theorists whose ideas were so influential in governments of the 1980s. Its focus tended to be on one media form, that of broadcasting. The New Right devoted relatively little attention to the press, save to praise its populist instincts and market sensitivities. Broadcasting attracted their attention on a variety of counts. Firstly, there were those, like Neil Postman (1987) and Allan Bloom (1987), who bemoaned the way television (and many other popular cultural forms) was failing in its duty to educate and enlighten its audience. It was too populist. Secondly, there were others for whom television was not populist enough (Beesley, 1996). It was too elitist. These positions sometimes coexisted in the same polemics, but they have different policy implications: the former arguing for the need for regulation, the latter arguing for far greater deregulation. Both addressed the distribution of power in television, but they identified different incentives and interests to which the medium was subject. For those who worried about television's 'dumbing down', the problem was executives who had refused to exercise their own capacity to judge critically what they broadcast. For those concerned about the elitism, the problem was the dominance of unaccountable executives imposing their own interests and values on broadcasting.

For the most part, this tension was resolved in favour of the latter, the market liberals. The market was deemed to be the appropriate mechanism for determining media content, a solution made possible by technological advances that increased the choice of channels. It is only through the interplay of consumer choices in a competitive market that we discover what it is that people truly want. Put another way, bureaucratic systems, in which there is limited popular choice, are much less sensitive to the wishes of their people, and will tend to reflect the interests of the bureaucrats (rather than the wishes of the people). From this perspective, an unregulated press, in which there are few formal barriers to entry, will be forced to respond to the wishes of its readers. To ignore them is to risk going out of business. Editors and owners have to tailor their papers to the interests and concerns of their readers. Papers do not lead readers, they follow them. This does not create a case for complacency about the current system. Multimedia conglomerates can thwart competition, but such dangers are, according to the New Right, only real where there are 'substantial barriers to entry' (Beesley, 1996: 26).

The problem, for the New Right, occurs when media organizations are able to ignore their viewers and listeners. Then programme makers can set their own agendas, and pursue their own interests, secure in the knowledge that their audiences have nowhere else to go and no means of redressing the balance. This problem is compounded by the assumption that these programme makers belong to a particular social (left–liberal) elite with vested interests in maintaining the status quo. Newt Gingrich, for example, complained that National Public Radio was 'owned' by the liberals, and paid for by people's taxes, while the voice of the populist right – Rush Limbaugh – was paid for by advertising (Ledbetter, 1997: 1). NPR, like the BBC, was not constrained by the market, or by any other system of accountability. Under these circumstances, the New Right perspective sees the broadcast media as exercising a malign influence, by setting an agenda that favours political interests that are not those of the ordinary voter. Evidence for this is detected in the 'liberal consensus' that provides both entertainment and news/ current affairs coverage. It is this view which inspires attempts to deregulate broadcasting.

In summary, where broadcasting is isolated from the market, it is liable to distort the political agenda, skewing it in favour of powerful minorities rather than ordinary people. Newspapers, competing in an open market, are constrained to reflect their readers' views. They, therefore, represent a legitimate democratic voice, unlike television and radio. The New Right argue that, unless broadcasting is subject to some form of popular control, it will exercise access and discursive power to deny a place to alternative points of view and alternative providers of news and entertainment.

Marxism

There are many different Marxist readings of the power of mass media, of which the perspective outlined here is just one. A fundamental Marxist claim, however, common to all theories, is that ultimately political power derives from control over economic exchange. Where they differ is in the autonomy and role attributed to the political and cultural realms that coexist with the interests of capital. For some Marxists, politics forms part of the 'super-structure' which serves the 'base' forged by the ownership of capital. Politics and culture act only to legitimate or disguise economic reality, by providing distracting entertainment or by propagating democratic myths. But in other Marxist accounts, politics and culture are themselves producers of the relations and practices of capitalism, inscribing an ideology which suppresses the will to revolt against the injustices of capitalism. Instead of fostering the power to challenge capitalism, culture accommodates people to it.

In *The German Ideology*, Marx and Engels (1970: 64) write of the way the ruling class 'rule also as thinkers, as producers of ideas, and regulate the production and distribution of the ideas of their age: thus their ideas are the ruling ideas of the epoch'. Translating this to the modern era, instead of being aware of their own powers and capacities, the working class are encouraged to believe in the superhuman achievements of stars and celebrities, to believe in the false promises of the lottery rather than the emancipatory promise of the revolution. A key statement of this general argument can be found in an essay, written in the 1940s, by Theodor Adorno and Max Horkheimer (1979), in which they argue that mass culture generally creates the illusion of freedom and choice, while actually providing for a uniformity of thought and action. Mass culture provides a way of schooling and policing people, teaching them to accept (even embrace) the lessons which capitalism teaches.

From this perspective, the biases in the news and current affairs have to be understood as the expression of the dominant economic and political interests. Nightly news shows are not, however, just capitalists' newsletters to each other; they are also ways of distract-ing their class opponents from their oppression. Popular culture provides escapist fantasies which leave reality behind or 'realist' dramas which reinforce the moral codes of the status quo. News and entertainment are the product of state and corporate interests. Newspapers are commercial products which either make a profit in their own right or promote the other commercial ventures of the conglomerate to which they belong. Beyond this, they provide propaganda to sustain the general interests of capitalism. Owners appoint editors who share their political disposition, but who are aware of their obligation to satisfy the expectations of advertisers. The set of news values which define professional journalism also serves to maintain the existing order. Commercial broadcasting is subject to similar pressures, as is (less directly) state broadcasting. The interests of the state are inextricably tied to those of capitalism. Broadcasting is another method of policing the behaviour of their subjects in accordance with the demands of the economy.

In summary, the Marxist perspective treats the mass media as part of the capitalist's armoury. It imposes a particular view of the world on readers and viewers, thereby ensuring the maintenance of values and practices that serve the interests of capital and thwart the ambitions of those who seek to overthrow or reform the system. The Marxist perspective sees the media as operating through and on behalf of capitalism. The character of media discourse, the access granted to media outlets and the control of media resources have to be understood in terms of the interests of capital.

Culturalism

Just as the liberal–pluralist view emerges as a response to mass society theory, so the culturalist perspective derives from a rejection of what it sees as the economic reductionism of the Marxist approach. It is a view that is closely associated with the Birmingham University Centre for Contemporary Cultural Studies, and especially with the work of Stuart Hall. Like the Marxist, the culturalist sees the media as inextricably tied to the dominant interests in society. Media institutions, in Hall's words (1982: 86), 'produce consensus' in conditions of conflict and struggle (not just those generated by class, but also those created by gender and other social divisions). The values of the dominant group inform all media representations, not just those in the news, but in soap operas and situation comedies, in Hollywood films and pop records. But where the Marxist sees the audience for this culture as its passive recipient, the culturalist sees the audience as *interpreting* media representations, not just ingesting them. Where the Marxist perspective tends to assume these dominant images impose themselves upon audiences, the culturalist allows for the fact that the audience has to make sense of what it sees and reads. This process of interpretation is not 'free'; there are limits to the range of interpretations. Media texts constrain the possible readings, and each contains a 'preferred' version. The capacity to interpret against this preferred reading depends on the resources and experiences of the readers.

The power of mass media derives from the thought that there is no 'truth' against which media representations can be judged. All pictures are just that, portraits of the world giving a particular view of reality, an encoding that has to be decoded by the reader or viewer. Reality is a matter of representation, or as Hall (ibid.: 75) once put it: ' "True" means credible, or at least capable of winning credibility as a statement of fact.' We cannot in some way penetrate the array of images to reveal the truth, as the Marxist tends to suppose. 'The media,' writes Tony Bennett, 'are not *apart from* social reality, passively reflecting and giving back to the world its self-image; they are *a part* of social reality' (1982b: 288; original emphasis).

Where a Marxist tends to emphasise the resource base of media power, the culturalist focuses on its discursive power. One of the most vehement advocates of this position, John Fiske (1993: 15), gives this account of the culturalist perspective: 'Discourse represents the world by producing a knowledge of it and thus exercising power over it. There is a physical reality outside of discourse, but discourse is the only means we have of gaining access to it. It is going too far, though only by a smidgeon, to say that reality is the product of discourse; it is more productive to say that what is accepted as reality in any social formation is the product of discourse.' People's sense of themselves and their world is constituted through these discourses. Some understandings carry more weight, are more widely shared, than others. These are the expression of relations of power. Certain identities and sexualities, for example, are 'normalized' while others are represented as 'alien'. This state of affairs is not fixed, it is constantly being renegotiated and reinterpreted. No attempt to represent the world is a self-contained, consistent portrait. It always includes ambiguities and contradictions, sub-texts that pull against the official story – and it is these that make possible the alternative readings.

The culturalist approach locates power in media texts, in the possibilities they create and eliminate. Where the Marxist sees those texts as reproducing given interests, the culturalist points to the complexities of reading and interpreting any text. There is a logic within culturalism that sees culture as enclosing all reality, but there are culturalists who resist this move, arguing that culture acts on the material conditions that produce differences which are expressed ethnically, sexually and through class. According to this view, the media do not define completely the world for their readers or viewers. People engage with culture in particular institutional settings and with particular material and personal resources, and these settings and resources shape the way in which media are consumed and interpreted. To this extent, the media play a secondary role, putting a gloss on the primary definitions that derive from class, gender, ethnicity and the material conditions that constitute them.

Whichever strand is adopted, the culturalist perspective makes the media both more and less powerful: more powerful in the sense that it circulates images and ideas that constitute reality; less powerful in the sense that the meanings and interpretations to which these images are subject are not determined by their formal content.

Comparing Theories

To get a sense of the implications of these different perspectives on media power, we now consider how each deals with a number of issues that feature in the relationship between politics and mass media: bias, media influence, ownership and control, and the packaging of politics.

Bias

The liberal–pluralist acknowledges the bias in the press, but recognizes the possibility of impartiality (which is typically associated with the broadcast media). The New Right also acknowledges the biases in the press, but also detects an anti-right wing bias in the broadcast media. The Marxist detects bias in both the press and broadcasting, and sees both as biased against the left. The culturalist is uncomfortable with talk of bias, opting instead to identify the 'common sense' that the media convey, and seeing this as the partial sense of the dominant interests.

In taking up these positions on the biases they detect, they are also making claims about the relationship between media content and the representation of reality. Where the Marxist and New Right presuppose a truth which the media systematically distort, the culturalist (and, to a lesser extent, the liberal–pluralist) reject the idea of a truth against which the representations might be judged.

Political Effects

Each of the four perspectives encourages a different view on the effect of mass media on the political process. This is best illustrated by the positions they adopt on the electoral influence of mass media. The liberal–pluralist is generally sceptical of the view that mass media influence voter behaviour. The press reinforces existing prejudices, while impartial broadcasting tends to inform and educate, rather than influence. The New Right perspective takes a more critical stance, arguing that the agenda and judgements promoted by broadcasters fail to reflect those of the voter, thereby eroding the respect and support for New Right ideas and arguments. The Marxist sees a reverse effect. The media serve to distort popular perception of real interests and to maintain an unjustified legitimacy for ruling ideas. James Curran (1982: 15) suggests that the Marxist position is one in which the media act to sustain 'the myth of representative democracy, political equality and collective self-determination'. The culturalist is wary of the notion of 'effects', partly because of the plethora of cultural images and ideas (with their contradictions and their ambiguities) to which audiences are subject, but also because in the process of their consumption (their decoding) they are rewritten into the complex identities and conditions of people's lives. Which is not to say that the media do not create a common sense that helps to legitimate the existing order, only that it is mistaken to talk of a chain of cause and effect which necessarily results in a change in behaviour. The culturalist position is critical of liberal–pluralism because it adopts a very narrow view of politics and of political processes, in which power is seen only 'in terms of the direct influence of A on B's behaviour' and is assumed to lie with the ballot, and not with the 'social structure and economic relations' (Hall, 1982: 59).

Ownership and Control

Each of the perspectives is marked by the way it connects ownership and control in mass media. The pluralists reject the claim that owners control media in order to promote their commercial and political interests. Instead, they argue that the managerial structure provides a medium for responding to the popular preferences of its consumers. The New Right shares this view, seeing the market as a key mediating device. Marxists, by contrast, see corporate interests as dominating the daily practices of the media industry. While culturalists recognize the importance of media institutions, their arguments are more concerned with the theoretical connections which tie these corporations into the general production of ideology.

Packaging Politics

For the liberal–pluralist and advocates of the New Right, politics does not assume an absolute priority in human affairs and, to the extent that packaging reduces information costs and makes politics accessible, it is to be welcomed. From a Marxist perspective, however, packaging provides yet another symbol of the commercialization and commodification of politics and, with this, the weakening of popular control. The culturalists sits astride this divide, seeing on the one hand the attempt to reduce politics to the cash nexus and to isolated self-interested decision making; on the other hand, packaging draws attention to the different forms and forums in which political communication exists.

Recalling Lukes' three-dimensional model, we can see that each perspective finds a different location for media power. The liberal–pluralist places it outside the three dimensions, arguing that, for the most part, the media exercise very limited power, serving only to reflect existing predispositions. For the New Right, media power –

that is, the power of broadcasting – operates in the first and second dimension. It imposes views that do not reflect those of its audience and it creates a political agenda that is heavily skewed in favour of left–liberal issues, thereby marginalizing those issues and interests which the New Right sees as the true views of the people. The Marxist perspective, once again, reverses the New Right version, but also adds the third dimension. The first dimension is represented by the media's successful representation of (ruling class) causes. The second dimension is incorporated in the way in which the political agenda assumes the dominant, capitalist order, portraying strikes, for example, as disruptive problems, rather than as part of a struggle for autonomy and equality. The third dimension is to be found in the way in which the media promote the false consciousness of those who acquiesce in the system's operation, at considerable cost to their real interests. The culturalist also refers to all three dimensions, but is reluctant to talk in terms of a false consciousness, being unhappy with the idea of some fundamental real interest, against which consciousness can be judged. For the culturalist, no such foundation exists; ideology and consciousness are the product of the various discourses that are in play. The third dimension of power operates through the way in which a particular version of 'common sense' dominates culture.

As Hall (1982: 87) explains: 'One of the means by which the powerful can continue to rule with consent and legitimacy is . . . if the interests of a particular class or power bloc can be aligned with or made equivalent to the general interests of the majority.' 'Impartiality' becomes, in fact, partiality towards a manufactured consensus.

Conclusion

This chapter has tried to provide an even-handed summary of the different perspectives on the power of the mass media. It is important to stress, however, that much is at stake in the competing claims of the different perspectives. They each have implications for the reform of mass media. This is dealt with more fully in the next chapter; here we need only observe that, while the liberal–pluralist may be able to reconcile the location of power and the demands of democracy, the other perspectives imply some measure of reform to realize this reconciliation. Such reforms extend from the introduction of the market into bureaucratic monopolies to the introduction of the state into the market. But such initiatives become appropriate only once the actual location of power (and its (il)legitimacy) has been established. There are two elements to this. The first involves the empirical analysis of the political economy of media industries, of the content of media messages and the ways in which they exercise influence over political thought and action. The other involves debate over the need for and character of media reform. It is important to stress that no empirical investigation of power (whatever its form) will yield definitive results. As Morriss (1987: 124) observes: 'we cannot hope to *prove* power ascriptions; nor can powers be directly observed. A claim about power, like one about any dispositions, will go beyond the evidence on which it is based.' Power is like many 'essentially contested' concepts (Connolly, 1974; Gallie, 1955–6) in that its definition and character rest on assumptions and values which admit of no final resolution. They trade on accounts, say, of what constitutes a 'free act' which are ultimately dependent on moral claims about human capacities and character. Nonetheless, this should not preclude a detailed study of the ways in which media conglomerates affect government policy, or media campaigns result in shifts in public opinion, or production practices deny opportunities for participation of certain groups or interests.

In focusing on these questions, this chapter has concentrated on traditional accounts of power, accounts which define the subject matter of politics: who gets what, when and how. It has, however, deviated from the conventional picture to the extent that it has appealed to a broader notion of the 'political' to capture the way in which entertainment, as well as news and current affairs, engages with political values, identities and interests. It has also appealed to accounts of power which are not confined to the open conflict of rival contenders for scarce resources, but describe the ways in which the identity and interests of those contenders are themselves a product of the operation of media power. Whatever position is taken in the analysis of media power, however, one point remains true: theories of media power feed directly into ones about media and democracy.

12

A Free Press: Democracy and Mass Media

The constitutions of almost all modern states include some reference to the role of the media. They do not agree, however, as to what exactly that role should be. So it is that the US Constitution's First Amendment insists that 'Congress shall make no law . . . abridging the freedom of speech, or of the press' while, by contrast, Saudi Arabia's Fundamental Law (Article 39) requires that 'The media and publishing houses, as well as other forms of expression, must respect the words and laws of the State . . . Publication of anything that might lead to internal rifts or struggle, or that might harm state security or foreign relations, is forbidden in accordance with the law.' In each case, the assumption is that, in establishing the political order, the place and function of mass media has to be clearly demarcated. For one state, this means protecting press freedom; for another, it means restricting press freedom.

Of course, it is nowhere near this simple. No state, whatever its constitution, tolerates complete freedom of expression. All states operate codes which provide for restrictions on the content of videos, films and television programmes. What freedom means, and what limits should apply to it, form part of an endlessly evolving political debate. It is a debate that has echoed throughout this book, and especially the last chapters, where we have looked at the ways in which new forms of political communication ('packaging') and new technologies of communication (the internet) are raising questions about the relationship between democracy and mass media. In this chapter, we focus on the issues that underlie this relationship. What principles are supposed to apply to the organization and character of mass media in a democracy? The need to answer such questions stems, first, from the fact that democracy places considerable weight upon communication (for accountability, for deliberation, for representation) and the system of communication, therefore, must meet these requirements. The second reason for addressing this topic is that, typically, democratic theorists have paid relatively little attention to the question of what principles and practices should guide the operation of mass media in a democracy (for notable exceptions, see Keane, 1991, 1992; Lichtenberg, 1990).

It might be objected, of course, that there is no real need to reflect upon the way to manage mass media in a democracy because, by design or default, a satisfactory solution has emerged. Think of the way elections are covered across the globe. Election coverage tends to be very earnest, almost obsessive. Every nuance of style and speech is pored over; every fluctuation in the opinion polls recorded; every advertisement and broadcast subjected to semiotic scrutiny. Candidates are trailed everywhere they go, photographed in a variety of guises and predicaments. And all of this is done in the name of democracy. The media treat elections as the lifeblood of the democratic process, and their coverage of them provides citizens with a wealth of information on which to base their vote. There does not seem to be any need for further philosophical reflection.

In any case, most states go further, establishing rules and regulations which enshrine the requirements for responsible election coverage. In the USA, there are rules about political advertising; in France, rules about the use of particular images. In Italy, these rules apply to the relationship between media outlets and political partisanship; in Britain, the law is employed to control the way in which broadcast journalists (if not their newspaper colleagues) report the election. In other words, a combination of rules and common practices has created a working relationship between mass media and democracy.

But while states have indeed evolved systems for regulating mass media in a democracy, they have all produced *different* systems. The fact that the relationship does not take one single form suggests that there are important questions of value and judgement entailed. We can see what is involved by imagining what might happen if the regulations were changed. What if, as some have suggested, the rules governing reporting of elections were relaxed? Would the democratic roof fall in? What if the media were to ignore the election campaigns, or to treat them as a joke? (Some might say that they do so already. During the 1997 British election, one tabloid newspaper sent a man dressed as a 'headless chicken' to harass John

Major. This was a response to the Conservative Party's decision to send a man dressed as a chicken to pursue Tony Blair, to create the impression that Blair was 'chicken', that is, frightened of Major.) What exactly is the proper role of mass media in a democracy and what is the best means of ensuring that this role is enacted? Answers to such questions usually begin with a qualification: 'It depends what you mean by "democracy"'.

There are, of course, as many definitions of democracy as there are democratic theorists. They include liberal, direct and deliberative democracy. Each generates very different positions on the question of the media's role in a democracy. Liberal democracy argues for some notion of a free, but responsible, press; direct democracy for more tightly regulated media, in which there is some form of popular control; and deliberative democracy requires, according to John Thompson (1995), 'regulated pluralism' to enable citizens to reach informed, collective views of the public good. This chapter looks at all these versions of democracy, and at the role of media within them, but it concentrates mostly upon the liberal democratic version, the model that fits most closely with actually existing systems in the West.

Liberal Democracy and the Free Press

The liberal democratic model goes under a variety of guises. Variants extend from those, like the democratic elitists (Joseph Schumpeter, for example), who place the emphasis on the election of relatively autonomous representatives, to those, like the pluralist Robert Dahl (at least in his earlier writings), who model democracy on the interaction of interest groups. What they have in common is a view of democracy in which individual preferences take precedence and in which the state's role is constrained out of respect for individual freedom. Indeed, priority is given to freedom, characterized negatively, in Isaiah Berlin's (1969) famous distinction, as the absence of impediment.

The rationale for this is, among other things, the thought that there is no single answer to the question of how we ought to live. There are many alternative versions of the 'good life', and there is no way of determining a priori which is the better (Dworkin, 1978; Rawls, 1971). It is a matter of choice. So it is that the important political questions should be settled by voting (the formal equality of one person, one vote) and that the government be enjoined to respect the aggregate choices made by its citizens. It is not intended that citizens vote on all public issues; matters of detailed policy are left to their representatives. One of the reasons for this system being favoured is that it allows citizens to be spared the business of directly running their political affairs. This is deemed to be both practical and desirable – practical because of the constraints of time and competence, desirable because of the dangers of populism (Dahl, 1956; Schumpeter, 1943). The task of government is best left to those with the skills and aptitude for such pursuits.

Within such a democratic order, the media perform a particular political function. First, they are not bound to provide an endless diet of politics. The liberal assumption is that people are not political animals, and that politics is to be viewed instrumentally, as a means to an end. Where the media are to provide a political forum, their aim should be, firstly, to enable people to choose between those who wish to stand for office and to judge those who currently are in office and, secondly, to provide a platform for interest groups to publicize their concerns and claims. This means informing citizens about their (prospective) representatives' plans and achievements; it also means reflecting the range of ideas and views which circulate within society, subjecting those who act in the name of the people to scrutiny, to make them accountable. These conditions allow citizens to make informed choices.

The realization of this ideal is captured in the notion of a 'free press' (an idea that refers not just to newspapers but to television as well). The free press is defined as a medium which allows for a diversity of ideas and opinion; it is not an agent of a single view or of state propaganda. The media are 'free' precisely in the sense that they are not subject to centralized control. Any control of content represents a loss of freedom. This notion of a free press, notes James Curran (2000: 121), has become attached to that of a free market: 'Only by anchoring the media to the free market, in this view, is it possible to ensure the media's complete independence from government.' Two moves are being made here: firstly, 'freedom' is being defined as the absence of interference; secondly, the achievement of this ideal is dependent on market competition between media outlets. Before looking more closely at the conditions which make a free press possible, we need to consider in more detail why freedom of expression, the right to speak out, is valued.

The liberal notion of the free press emerged over time, and through the application of a number of different arguments. John Keane (1991: 10–20) picks out several separate strands which have gone into establishing the case for a free press. They first emerged in the seventeenth and eighteenth centuries. The first argument for a free press derives, according to Keane, from the writings of the poet John Milton, who was greatly concerned about the tyrannous effects of religious orthodoxy. Milton was a vehement critic of religious censorship and an advocate of religious tolerance. People had to be free to follow their conscience and able to test their convictions against rival claims, thereby strengthening their faith. Any attempt to impose a particular view would be counterproductive. Milton's seventeenth-century rationale for non-interference is echoed in the nineteenth century by John Stuart Mill. For Mill, knowledge of the world depended upon constant cross-examination of conventional wisdom. Dogmas could not be allowed to stand unexplored; they had to be subject to rigorous scrutiny. Only with the public demonstration of diversity and difference could ideas flourish and people cultivate their individual character. Mill (1972: 119) writes in *On Liberty* of the way people live 'under the eye of a hostile and dreaded censorship'. He is here referring to the controlling powers of conformity, the pressure to do what is expected of one. The consequence of this is that 'the mind itself is bowed to the yoke' (ibid.). To break this yoke, it is important that different ideas be circulated and subjected to public scrutiny. Eccentricity or heresy are to be welcomed, not suppressed. A free press is a necessary corollary of this.

Running parallel to the arguments for a free press based on freedom of conscience and thought, there are those based on individual rights. Deriving from the claims of writers like John Locke, Thomas Paine and Mary Wollstonecraft, the liberal asserts that individuals have rights which have to be respected by a legitimate government. Rule has to be by consent, and this entails the right to dissent: the opportunity to hold and express dissident views. A state press or state censorship would be an infringement of these rights.

These justifications for the free press continue to circulate within current discussion of the issue, and in their different ways they contribute to the ideological rationale for a free press today. They echo through arguments about censorship or through celebrations of the apparent freedom afforded by the internet. Stephen Holmes (1990), for example, cites Milton, among others, in his defence of the notion of a free press and the means it provides for limiting, and rendering accountable, political power. They are enshrined in the US Constitution and in the European Convention on Human Rights, but these principles, important though they are, form only one dimension of the modern liberal notion of a free press. The fact that these ideas took hold, that they commanded support, is indicative of the way they fitted the material circumstances to which they were applied. In other conditions, at other times, they might not have won the argument. It is necessary, therefore, to put the notion of the free press in its context.

Firstly, it is evident that commercial and economic change have helped to promote the idea of a 'free press'. In the late nineteenth and early twentieth centuries, newspaper publishing ceased to be a matter of personal political indulgence, and became instead a viable commercial venture. The key to this was the emergence of advertising as a major source of revenue (Curran and Seaton, 1997). The notion of a free press was, in this context, an extension of the idea of a free market, one in which the press responded to the commercial incentives and opportunities created by advertising. Globalization, the liberalization of tariffs and border controls, is a modern equivalent of these earlier industrial pressures for a free press.

Secondly, the commercial pressure that helped establish the case for a free press was itself dependent on the technology that made mass production possible. The move from the hand-operated press to the production-line system allowed for a greatly increased circulation, and with this the possibility of a mass readership, 'popular' press (Winston, 1998). Technical change has continued to be instrumental in the evolution of the idea of a free press.

The story of broadcasting is, in part, a story of emerging technologies. Initially, the technologies of transmission and reception were associated with the need to restrict and regulate access to the airwaves, partly because their use was linked to military and security interests, but partly because the resource on which they depended was limited. There were only so many radio frequencies available; broadcasters using the same or proximate frequencies would interfere with each other. Systems of regulation and licensing were needed to distribute and control this access. Freedom, in this context, was defined through the principles which organized this access and the conditions imposed on licence holders.

The new possibilities of digital broadcasting have essentially ended the problems of scarcity, and hence have changed the terms in which broadcasting freedom is conceived. Regulation is no longer required to manage scarcity. This shift is paralleled by the trend towards globalization in communications. The modern technologies make state borders ever more permeable, and therefore make regulation increasingly difficult. The image of a global, largely unregulated internet has become a symbol of the modern ideal of the 'free press'.

What should be apparent, though, from both the technology-driven and commerce-driven account of press freedom, is that both are linked to political change. The third factor creating the context for the emergence of the 'free press' is politics. The linking of the market to freedom is as much a matter of ideology and interest as it is of fact. The industrialization of the press, just as with the industrialization of other areas of society, severed the connection with the traditional, feudal order. State control was gradually eroded. In the nineteenth century, capitalist governments ceded their power to control the press, just as in the twentieth century they deregulated broadcasting. These policy changes occurred within a political framework in which states, in the name of freedom, also controlled access to the airwaves and oversaw the content of mass media (via laws of libel, secrecy, obscenity, copyright, rights of ownership and so on). The same basic technologies have, after all, been regulated differently in different states and systems, and have as a consequence engendered different notions of press freedom. What is understood as the 'free press' depends on the combination of a particular set of ideas and material circumstances. It is neither simply the product of rational reflection nor the pragmatic consequence of commercial and technical change. Different ideas, different circumstances, would produce a different rationale and institutional formation. The question remains, however, whether the form of press freedom instituted in the West does, in fact, serve the interests of democracy. Does it, via the institutions and ideas that animate it, provide the opportunity for a diverse set of views to be expressed, interests to be represented and power holders to be scrutinized?

We can only really begin to answer these questions if we first ask what it means, in a democracy, to provide a 'diverse' set of views or to represent people's interests. There are no easy answers and, to reveal their complexities, we concentrate on two issues: content and access.

Content

Should the media in a liberal democracy provide 'unbiased' coverage? Bias can have two obvious adverse effects upon democracy: it can misrepresent the people or it can misinform them. Just as an elected assembly should represent the nation, so a media should represent the views, values and tastes of its viewers. More than this, 'representation' is not just taken to mean giving space to the range of formally articulated political and moral views, it also has to include the representation of *cultural difference*, the way people live as well as the way they think. Biases which marginalize or misrepresent individuals or groups effectively deny influence and status to those people. They cease to be full participants or citizens.

The other adverse effect which results from bias is misinformation. If people use the mass media to inform themselves about their society and about the performance of their politicians, and if they use this information to direct their political choices and participation, then inadequate or inaccurate information is liable to result in misconceived political acts.

For reasons of both representation and information, therefore, it seems that a democratic society requires unbiased media. But this raises two sets of very difficult questions. The first concerns the possibility of removing 'bias'. It may be reasonable to expect the media to provide factual information – they can get the details right: what a peace agreement says, or who the signatories were, for example. But such criteria do not take us far. There are an infinite number of details to any story; the problem is identifying the salient detail. Relevance can be defined by the way a particular detail fits into an explanation of an event (an irrelevant detail – 'the president is a Taurean' – contributes nothing to our understanding) or determined by the interests of the audience (such as the priority given to national news over international news). Either way, there will be no settled view as to what constitutes relevant information (whether or not it is accurate). The problem does not necessarily disappear if the media simply seek to elicit different opinions. At least, not if it is assumed that beneath these competing views lies a 'right' answer or a consensus. Certainly such an approach is sometimes implied by the idea of balance, because it assumes a fulcrum, a central position around which to balance the 'extremes'; but this position can be seen as an arbitrarily selected point, or one that serves certain political interests. It does not represent any objective truth.

Once again, therefore, it seems that bias is inevitable, and cannot provide a criterion in itself for a democratic media. But the logic of this argument does not lead to an uncritical relativism. Standards of accuracy and truthfulness still have some validity in the assessment of media coverage. To this extent then, a liberal democratic media should aspire to represent events accurately, but beyond this there is a political debate to be had about the *way* the facts or events are represented. As we saw in discussion of the frames that are imposed in the reporting of politics, quite different perspectives and understandings can be introduced through the way the story is told. Political actions can be interpreted cynically or as the product of principle; events can be seen as episodic or the result of long-run processes. The appropriate frame is a matter of analysis and argument, but there is clearly scope for discriminating between them in terms of the values and principles of democracy. What is left unresolved by addressing these issues is how such standards might be achieved. This is a matter to which we will return. In the meantime we need to consider the second criterion by which to assess the democratic character of media: how adequately are interests in society represented?

The problem with making 'representativeness' a criterion of a democratic medium is that the term itself is complex and confusing. To represent the people may mean to provide a mirror image of them, one in which the mix of men and women, young and old, sexualities and ethnic backgrounds, are those of the population at large. The problem here is to determine which characteristics need to be recognized and which ignored, given that there are limits to the time and space available in the media. There is also the question of how these characteristics should be portrayed: how should nationalities or sexualities be represented? But even if these issues can be resolved, there remains the question as to whether social representativeness is what is needed.

An alternative criterion is political representativeness; that is, the media should give due weight to the range of opinions and attitudes which people have. This would produce a different picture, since there is no necessary correlation between social characteristics and political views, and the one cannot be assumed from the other. In trying to represent the full range of political views, the question is then how these should be discerned. If through opinion polls or through the existence of interest groups, such methods raise further problems of their own, on the grounds that they too may distort the actual distribution of interests. To counter these problems some might argue for 'enlightened representation', where others speak on behalf of the rest. It was this kind of representation that Edmund Burke (1975) famously claimed for himself in his address to the electors of Bristol in 1774, but it is also present in public service broadcasting commitments to 'education'. This version of representation involves *anticipating* people's interests. This, too, poses difficulties because of the problems of making such a system work within the media. In politics, there is the election mechanism. Is it possible to provide the same form of accountability in the media?

One final problem is the danger of eliding 'the people' and the 'audience' or the 'readership.' In thinking about representativeness, should the media reflect those who watch and read it, or should they refer to a nation or region (including those who do not buy the paper or watch that channel)? This is not to argue against all attempts at representativeness, only to draw attention to the difficulties – both practical and theoretical – in making it work. Any answer will be open to criticism, but the liberal democratic notion of a free press requires some judgement to be made about media content. The problem is finding the right criteria and the right process for implementing them.

Access

The problems posed by identifying the appropriate content for democratic media can lead to the adoption of a different approach. Instead of focusing on the content of the media, we can look at access to it. Who should have access to the means of communication and how should this access be used? Participation may, for example, help to improve the standards of accuracy which are important to democratic media. The more voices, the wider the range of experiences that participate in the production of media texts, the closer we will come to achieving an accurate account of what is happening and the easier it is to correct inaccurate reporting. Put another way, relying on a single source risks the possibility of both inaccurate reporting and a lack of accountability. The guiding thought is that, in a liberal democracy, the media should in some sense be 'open', making it possible for these diverse views and experiences to appear, and facilitating redress and correction where standards of accuracy lapse. As with representativeness, there are various ways in which openness can be measured. Here we sketch two different forms of access, which can be labelled indirect and direct.

Indirect access involves the opportunity for people to express their views about what is written or broadcast, but does not guarantee them control over the product. Letter columns (and increasingly, e-mail), 'right to reply' programmes and readers/ viewers polls are examples of this kind of access. This media-based access is supplemented by institutions whose job is to monitor codes of media conduct and to rule on abuses of it. These forms of access allow people with an interest or view to respond to news stories and other kinds of coverage. There are limits, however, to this monitoring because it is by definition retrospective and because it does not guarantee any change in media behaviour. Another form of indirect participation is the political interview. The connection with the public is made explicitly or implicitly by the interviewer who claims to speak on behalf of the voters. But while the interviewer appears to speak on behalf of his or her audience, this is more a matter of rhetoric than reality. Interviewers do not have any formal links, and very few informal ones, with those they represent.

Direct participation, by contrast, shifts the balance of power from television producers and journalists, towards audiences. The phone-in (or other such events) allow members of the public to interrogate politicians. Because the ordinary citizen is unschooled in interview techniques, or the codes that constrain professional interviewer–interviewee relations, they can speak from personal experience, they can persist (where the professional might move on to another subject) and they can unsettle politicians who cannot easily resort to typical answer-avoidance techniques. On the other hand, such participation is closely mediated, and the amateur's opportunity to probe is limited by the professional presenter. The politician has, furthermore, the resources of status and experience with which to 'handle' awkward questions and questioners. There is, in short, likely to be an uneven (and undemocratic) distribution of cultural capital in this relationship (Bourdieu, 1986).

Another form of direct access is provided by community and alternative programming, where people either make their own programmes to be shown on the main networks or they evolve alternative networks around independent news sources. One example of the latter is Small World Media, an independent news organization that produced a series of videotapes called *Undercurrents*. These worked to a completely different news agenda and adopted a quite different perspective from those of the traditional media. The rationale of Small World Media is to provide another view. As one of the film makers said: 'If what you see on TV were fair, there'd be no need for *Undercurrents*' (quoted in *New Statesman*, 24 March 1995: 24).

People can air their grievances or promote their cause. But these opportunities are constrained by the limited resources and space available for such ventures. Those who want their work to appear on the main networks have to compete for limited airspace and accept editorial control, while those who work within alternative networks are left to address a small, self-selecting audience.

So far we have been considering some of the criteria that might be used to judge the democratic character of media. The media reforms we have considered have not questioned the principle of limited state involvement and market provision of media goods and services, nor have they questioned the priority given to individual preference satisfaction. But there are those who would argue that delimiting the focus in this way imposes impossible constraints on the realization of a democratic media.

Does a Free Press Require a Free Market?

In the film *The Insider* (directed by Michael Mann, 1999), the story is told of a whistleblower who wants to expose tobacco industry malpractice. His claims are about to be aired on CBS's *60 Minutes* when the plug is pulled. The television executives feared that the tobacco company would engage in expensive litigation, and that this in turn would jeopardize an imminent bid to take over CBS. Corporate interests clashed with news values, and appeared to win, until a last minute initiative by the show's producer. Such an incident, and the film is based on a true story, illustrates what critics of the 'free press' see as an irreconcilable tension between a free press and a free market.

Curran (2000) provides a neat summary of these concerns. He notes that, though much is made of the media's function as a scrutineer of power, remarkably little time and space are given over to this function. The media are much less vigilant than might be expected, given the rhetoric, and the reason for this, Curran suggests (ibid.: 123–4), is that market incentives work against such vigilance. Firstly, the media are themselves big businesses with close links to other state and corporate interests, and as such wary of investigating their own kind. Secondly, the profit motive works against investigative work because of its costs and its relative weakness in attracting advertising revenue. Equally, the media's ability to provide a range of different views is compromised by the cost of gaining access to media space. The free market, argues Curran (ibid.: 128), restricts 'the freedom to publish', 'the circulation of public information' and 'participation in public debate'. Readers and audiences do not have the ability, via the market, to influence media content. The concentration of ownership and the high entry costs marginalize consumers (ibid.: 131).

If the free market fails to provide for a free press, what is the alternative? Torbjorn Tannsjo (1985) argues that, for liberal democrats to realize their ambitions for a democratic mass media, they cannot be indifferent to the issue of the ownership and control of media conglomerates. If a democratic order is one which seeks to enhance the growth of knowledge, cultural pluralism and access, it cannot afford to allow an unfettered right to private ownership of media. The threat to democracy, by this account, comes not from the state but from the mass media industries themselves. Private ownership necessarily limits access, and in pursuit of its interests it will seek to control and limit the supply of knowledge and information; it will create an undemocratic media. Tannsjo's argument is that there is a tension between the ideal of 'free expression', which entitles people to say what they like, and 'sound mass communications', which is about guaranteeing a plurality of views, growth of knowledge and equality of access (ibid.: 553). 'Freedom of expression', he argues, 'is neither necessary nor sufficient for sound mass communications' (ibid.: 554). The reason for this is that 'freedom of expression', the right to say what you want, justifies the private ownership of media outlets. This has two consequences which work against sound mass communications. The first is that private ownership leads to the creation of media monopolies; the second is that these monopolies come to treat news as a commodity, whose value is determined by the operation of the market. These two consequences work directly against the growth of knowledge (news is not valued for its contribution to knowledge and understanding, but for its commercial value: its ability to deliver audiences to advertisers). They also work against the principles of pluralism and open access because monopoly control by its nature restricts access.

Tannsjo is not alone in drawing these conclusions about the problems for democracy of private ownership. John Keane, for example, argues that 'information' needs to remain a public not a private commodity in a democracy. He writes, 'friends of the "liberty of the press" must recognise that *communications markets restrict freedom of communication* by generating barriers to entry, monopoly and restrictions upon choice, and by shifting the prevailing definition of information from that of a public good to that of a privately appropriable commodity. In short, it must be concluded that there is a structural contradiction between freedom of communication and unlimited freedom of the market' (1991: 89; original emphasis). The effects of the market are felt not just on news and current affairs, but on entertainment too. Philip Green (1998: 57) ends his lament for the decline of American popular culture with this claim: 'the free market can never produce anything but unfree culture'. The quality of culture, it is assumed, is as important to democracy as the quality and accuracy of news. Keane, Tannsjo and Green all conclude that regulation of ownership is necessary for media to fulfil their democratic role. This is not a matter of state ownership and control, but rather a matter, according to Tannsjo (1985: 553, 558), of putting all media 'under political, democratic control'. We return to the implications of these recommendations later, but first it is necessary to consider in more detail the ends to which such control might be put.

Does a Free Press Mean an End to Censorship?

One of the defining characteristics of 'democracy', it is commonly assumed, is the absence of censorship. This would suggest that democratic media are media which provide the conditions for free speech and are not subject to content control. But this is a false conclusion. As Simon Lee (1990: 11) once observed, 'In our everyday lives, censors are all around us. We censor one another through withering looks, subtle threats of sticks or promises of carrots.' And just as we practise censorship on a routine, daily basis, so too do democratic societies. This is not to say that all states censor equally or that all censorship is acceptable, but the point is to adopt a rather more sensitive account of censorship.

This is what Jim McGuigan (1996: 155–61) proposes when he maps out the distinction between *regulative* and *constitutive* censorship. The former is composed of the formal institutional mechanisms for controlling the content of mass media; the latter refers to the internalized constraints – often contained in social convention and habits of thought – that regulate discourse in order to enable society – any society – to function. Censorship can be both a necessary component of social cohesion and a restraint on free political thought. To acknowledge this is to create a new set of considerations for what count as democratic media. It does this, in part, by questioning the liberal democratic account of the individual agent (and the place of communication within that account).

By way of illustration, consider the arguments of Onora O'Neill (1990). Like Tannsjo, she argues that a liberal democratic medium must set the right to speak freely against other rights which might be compromised by free speech. Her argument focuses, not on problems derived from the political economy of private ownership, but on the kind of exchange that 'free expression' defends or encourages. The problem with freedom of expression, suggests O'Neill, is that it protects an individual's right to say whatever they like, but it pays no heed to those on the receiving end. If mass media are in the business of *communication* rather than expression, the rights of receivers have to be protected too, and this means curbing freedom of expression. Communication involves the interaction of two or more people. Expression requires only one person. Different conditions apply in each case. For O'Neill, communication requires protection of the rights of both parties. She writes,

'Toleration of *expression* may need only noninterference; toleration of *communication* must also sustain conditions of communication' (ibid.: 167, original emphasis). In other words, O'Neill, like Tannsjo and Keane, argues for regulation in the name of democracy. The case for such restriction derives from a critique of the liberal account of the lone individual subject (the source of the 'free expression'). Michael Sandel (1998) has characterized the dominant liberal perspective as one in which the 'unencumbered self' engages with a 'procedural republic'. What he means by this is that individuals, according to the established liberal tradition, are to be regarded as free agents, making relatively autonomous choices. Given this perspective on the individual, the responsibility of government then becomes that of respecting the differences between individuals. Its processes and actions must be judged in terms of their 'fairness', the even-handed way they deal with differences. When applied to free speech and the regulation of the media, the logic of this position, at least as it is interpreted by the US courts, means that the fact that the views are abhorrent is not in itself a reason for banning them. The content is 'bracketed' by the judges, and treated as irrelevant. In 'bracketing' the content and the competing claims made for it, the courts deal only with the question of whether there is any other legitimate basis (threats to public order, for instance) for banning the source of offence (for example, pornography or neo-Nazi propaganda). The rationale for this bracketing of the images and ideas themselves stems from liberal wariness about pronouncing on the competing conceptions of the good life that are assumed to find expression in media content.

Sandel is critical of this version of liberalism. He argues that, first, people must be understood as 'situated selves', as having identities that are constituted by the groups to which they belong and the self-understandings that derive from dialogue with others. This version of the self makes speech an integral part of the constitution of identity. The views we hold and the images we encounter are co-extensive with our identity; they are not things we *choose* to see or utter, they *are* us. Thus insofar as speech is more than 'opinion', more than mere utterances, it has the potential to make or damage identities (ibid.: 1998: 89). The liberal demand for respect for persons, argues Sandel, cannot allow the 'bracketing' of morally repugnant expressions. Certain speech acts should be condemned because of the way they compromise the integrity of an individual's or a group's identity. Democracy, by this account, requires censorship. What O'Neill and Sandel represent is a liberal democratic argument for the regulation of media content, based on a different account of the liberal ideal. Their position derives from a particular set of assumptions about the nature of the self and the place of speech in the constitution of that self. Other accounts of both will, of course, produce other conclusions. But if, for the moment, we accept their reformulated liberalism, we are still left with the need to determine how such ideas and assumptions should be enacted. In the final section of this chapter, we consider the kind of political structures that would give substance to these alternative liberal principles.

Alternative Models of a Democratic Media: Direct and Deliberative

The challenge to the dominant liberal orthodoxy's view of the self and free speech has important consequences for related conceptions of democracy. The protective state of liberal democracy, in which individual preferences are given priority, is seen as failing to recognize the processes by which identity and the 'preferences' entailed by that identity are constituted. The importance of speech and dialogue in the formation of that identity means that democracy becomes less a matter of *reflecting* preformed choices and more a matter of providing a means for *creating* choices. In the classical account of democratic theory, this marks a turning away from representative democracy to direct or participatory democracy.

Where liberal democracy aspires to aggregate individual preferences, direct democracy aspires to the collective realization of a common good. Rather than asking the question 'what do I want?', the direct democrat asks 'what do *we* want?' The good of the collectivity is the prime goal. And in order to understand who 'we' are and what 'we' want, it is necessary for individuals to participate in the administration of their society. Only then can people come to understand their fellow citizens' aspirations and experiences. Participation results in education, in developing our sensitivity and understanding (Barber, 1984; Pateman, 1970). Such an approach means an element of self-denial, at least to the extent that individual preferences are suppressed or silenced in recognition of the collective good. This model of democracy owes much to Jean-Jacques

Rousseau (1762/1968), whose notion of the General Will represents the collective deliberations of the citizens about what is best for all, given that aggregating individual preferences will only result in collective irrationality. In order to achieve the General Will, citizens have to set aside what suits them best individually (the 'will of all') in preference to what can be achieved collectively, taking into account everyone else's wishes. For this solution to work, people have to be discouraged from acting selfishly, from free-riding on other people's willingness to cooperate.

This version of democracy has obvious implications for mass media. One consequence is that the media's function is defined by the need to create a sense of collective identity and the need to guard against dissent which may subvert collectively agreed aims. Media become involved in creating a sense of community through dialogue and providing a disciplining mechanism to guard against free-riding. There is evidently a tension between these two roles: the first requires open discussion, the other requires propaganda. And there are plentiful examples, the Soviet Union being the most familiar, where the principles of direct democracy have resulted in the dominance of propaganda and the silencing of dialogue. Rather than some open discussion about the 'people's will', the state claims authoritative knowledge of this and imposes it through its media. State media become the weapons of tyrants who use them to suppress dissent.

To avoid these consequences, direct democracy has to emphasize the media's discursive role, with the state being expected to enable, via subsidy and a regulatory framework, the emergence of relatively autonomous media. This revised version of direct democracy, which draws on early twentieth-century ideas of Guild Socialism, has been labelled 'associative democracy' because of its emphasis on devolving power to autonomous associations. In this reconfiguration of democracy, the key term ceases to be power (and propaganda) and becomes information (and communication) (Hirst, 1994). Democracy, according to Paul Hirst (ibid.: 34–40), is to be defined in terms of communication; it is this that allows associations to coordinate their actions and register their demands. The state's responsibility is primarily to enable this communication to occur. Apart from the constraints imposed by laws of libel, racial incitement and the like, there would be no pressure on these media outlets to present themselves as impartial or authoritative, but rather they would be expected to make explicit their own political perspective in order to advance the debate about shared goals and purposes. This is the line adopted by Nicholas Garnham (1986: 50) who writes: 'the debate function needs to be more highly politicized, with political parties and other major organized social movements having access to the screen on their own terms'. In a similar vein, Curran (1997) once proposed that the governors of the BBC should be appointed by an independent, non-state, body.

These arguments represent a shift from the monolithic model of direct democracy to a more pluralist one. The idea is not that 'bias' can be replaced by 'truth', but that bias is to be acknowledged as a necessary and desirable part of political discourse. The logic of this is that we need a plurality of points of view and perspective, but the overarching purpose remains that of finding some agreed notion of the good life and some method for resolving the conflicting claims it generates. The emphasis shifts from direct democracy's old concern with power to a version of democracy more concerned with deliberation and dialogue.

The collapse of the traditional institutional form of direct democracy, and the move away from state-centred systems, have led to the rise of an argument for deliberative democracy (Miller, 1992). As a consequence, emphasis is placed on the conditions which allow people to reflect collectively on questions of public policy. Again the intention is not to make decisions based on the aggregation of individual preferences, but rather to allow for deliberation about common purposes. The implications for mass media lie not in state control, but in the state enabling or facilitating independent media enterprises. Keane (1992: 120) writes of the need for 'the establishment of media enterprise boards to fund alter- native ownership of divested media. . . Freedom of communication undoubtedly requires the establishment of publicly owned printing and broadcasting enterprises.'

A similar logic animates John Thompson's (1995) arguments for mass media's role in a deliberative democracy. He too is sceptical about the possibility and desirability of the two models that have tended to dominate discussion: the traditional liberal and direct versions. The reason for his scepticism stems from his understand- ing of the emerging world order. Both of the old models, he argues, appeal to a world of discrete nation states and a managed (or manageable) media corporate structure. The reality is one of globalized political economy, in which the powers of nation states are attenuated and the powers of media corporations extended. Thompson argues that mass media now operate within a framework that makes the previous models of democracy irrelevant. The traditional notion of the free press depended upon competition between relatively small corporations. The new conglomerates represent major power blocs. Furthermore, the state, one possible source of regulation, is now dwarfed by these conglomerates and is in a dependency relationship with them. These developments compromise the capacity of the system to provide a forum within which deliberation about political concerns and interests can take place. In these circumstances, Thompson argues, we need a new sense of 'publicness' and a new kind of infrastructure.

Thompson favours what he calls 'regulated pluralism'. Regulated pluralism entails the decentralization of resources and the separation of the state from media institutions. Regulated pluralism, as he explains (ibid.: 240–41), 'is the establishment of an institutional framework which would both accommodate and secure the existence of a plurality of independent media organizations. It is a principle which takes seriously the traditional liberal emphasis on the freedom of expression and on the importance of sustaining media institutions which are independent of state power. But it is a principle which also recognizes that the market left to itself will not necessarily secure the conditions of freedom of expression and promote diversity and pluralism in the sphere of communication.' The market, he concludes, has to be managed. This means limiting the concentration of media corporations and encouraging the development of new ones. But such intervention must itself operate independently of the state.

Thompson himself further distances the state by requiring it to play an 'enabling' function, along the lines proposed by Garnham. But where Thompson's argument differs from those of Garnham is in his emphasis on deliberative democracy (rather than on direct democracy). His view is that regulated pluralism does not make for direct involvement or dialogue, but for a more distant relationship. This is what he means by a new version of 'publicness', which (unlike the dialogic publicness of Rousseau's General Will) is a mediated one that is not confined to a particular locale and is not dialogical. Instead it is open-ended and provides the citizen with a new 'space of the visible' which politicizes the everyday, and allows citizens to form their own judgements through their interactions with the media. The media provide the resources through which citizens come to construct their identities and to deliberate about the realization of their interests. This is not a matter of controlling the media in the name of particular interests; it is about a process of discovery and construction. Democratic media are not, therefore, marked just by the systems of control which organize them, but also by the way in which their content, and the accessibility of this content, allows for people to know and comprehend each other.

One critic of public broadcasting in the USA pointed to the way it was organized 'for' the people, not by them, and this was evident in the Olympian attitude whereby audiences were offered education from on high. 'Rational thinking' was preferred over 'emotionally and bodily invested political participation, such as women's consciousness raising groups, boisterous union meetings and bar-room debates' (Ouellette, 1999: 76). Curran (2000: 148) echoes this argument when he writes that a democratic media system 'should empower people by enabling them to explore where their interests lie'. He goes further (ibid.: 142ff) by offering a 'working model' for democratic media, where he argues for the creation of different media sectors, each of which provides space for particular skills and expertise. These include a 'civic media sector' for parties, social movements and interest groups, and a 'professional media sector' for journalists and others to produce work that is committed to 'truth telling', whether in fiction or in news. Curran's model is an attempt to combine elements of public service media and private sector media, and to combine principles of advocacy and impartiality.

Both Thompson and Curran may be accused of being idealistic in their proposals, but they do at least force us to focus on the central issues that should concern anyone intent upon creating a democratic media system.

In ending here, it is important to recall that the arguments in the latter part of the chapter have been rooted in a break from traditional liberal theories of press freedom and of democracy itself. This has been done for two reasons. The first was to acknowledge the logic of this revisionist liberalism, and to explore its implications for the role of mass media in a democracy. If we do adopt the notion of a 'situated self', if we do embrace a form of 'deliberative democracy', there are important implications for the operation and organization of mass media. The second reason is that, even if this alternative liberalism is unattractive and unpersuasive, the fact of its existence does at least draw attention to the *politics* that underpins the discussion of mass media's place in a democracy. We are not just dealing with competing notions of media power but also with contested concepts of the person and of politics itself.

Conclusion

In thinking about the ways in which the media might be changed in order better to serve democracy, there is a danger that we will overlook other aspects of the problem. However democratic the media, they cannot fulfil their allotted function if, for example, they confront a wall of official secrecy. Freedom of information is a fundamental feature of a democratic society. Equally, the conditions under which politics is conducted affect the media's capacity to fulfil a useful role. Ronald Dworkin (1996: 19) argues, for instance, that restrictions on campaign spending are a necessary corollary of media effectiveness: 'If politicians had much less to spend on aggressive, simple-minded television spots . . . political campaigns would have to rely more on reporters and on events directed by non-partisan groups, like television debates, and political argument might become less negative and more constructive.' Dworkin's faith in media coverage may be misplaced, but his argument does recognize the link between political life and its media representation. The other side to this general argument is that restrictions on the media are not in themselves restrictions on democracy. It would be perfectly possible to defend, for example, stricter privacy laws in the name of democracy. The German media are prevented (albeit not always effectively) from publishing photos that 'violate the dignity' of an individual, a policy that is entirely in keeping with Sandel's notion of civic republicanism. Democratic media do not, in and of themselves, create democracy. Democratic media need a democratic polity, and vice versa.

What this chapter has tried to illustrate is some of the issues that need to be addressed in deciding what kind of contribution the mass media can make to democracy. It does not follow that democratic media are dull. There is no reason why coverage of politics needs to be treated with the solemnity and earnestness of a funeral. It could as well be treated like a branch of showbusiness, and subjected to the same pressures and demands that we apply to that. Democratic media must, after all, serve to keep our rulers in their place, and as Andrew Marr (1996: 299) notes: 'Laughter is the secret weapon of democrats.'

The thought that satire has a valid place in a democracy, and that the formal boundaries that mark the divide between politics and entertainment are permeable, returns us to an earlier discussion in this book. The point is that reflections on the relationship between democracy and mass media cannot be divorced from the character and content of the programmes and papers themselves. The debates about bias, about the way politics is represented, are crucial to the question of what constitutes democratic media, as are arguments about ownership and control, and about state regulation. If there is one theme that underpins much that has gone before, it is that we cannot draw neat dividing lines between news and entertainment, between politics and popular culture. What we understand by 'politics' is not defined by the formal prescriptions of constitutions; equally, our view of the world and of ourselves does not exist independently of communications media. In the end, it is not a matter of politics *and* mass media, of two separate entities, but of one set of complex relations: mass media politics.

Conclusion

This book began with the observation that, these days, a politician's taste in music can assume as much political importance as do their policies or their values. That this happens is, for many commentators, a cause of some regret. It seems to suggest that politicians are no longer valued as *leaders*; they have become 'one of us'. Writing in the *Financial Times* (12 September 1998), Gerard Baker remarks: 'In the television era, presidents have ceased to be inaccessible figures placed on pedestals for public admiration. They have invited themselves into the nation's sitting rooms, and have openly discussed their personal lives as a way of furthering their popularity in increasingly non-ideological times.' If this seemed to be the case in 1998, how much truer it may appear today. As I was writing this, Prime Minister Tony Blair became a father for the fourth time and the media were filled with stories about his new baby. One newspaper devoted seven pages to the story; the birth of Leo Blair led the television news broadcasts; later in the week pictures of the prime minister and his son were sold for £500, the proceeds going to a children's charity. And, most extraordinary of all, the birth improved Blair's standing in the polls: his popularity rose by several points with Leo's arrival. Politics, it seems, had been truly 'personalized', and politicians had become part of a nation's soap opera, just as had happened with Bill Clinton and the endless saga of his relationship with Monica Lewinsky. To leave it here, however, would be to miss a parallel move. Just at the moment when politicians are becoming 'ordinary people', so ordinary people are becoming celebrities and stars.

The welter of docusoaps and the popularity of shows like *Jerry Springer* are creating a world in which people's everyday lives are assuming a new public form. The very 'ordinariness' to which politicians appear to aspire is being transformed. The media make the ordinary 'extraordinary': the everyday sacrifices of parents become acts of heroism, the most banal of misfortunes become 'tragedies'. The most common of events become 'unique' – politicians become parents. And in the making of the ordinary extraordinary, notions of 'normality' lose their grip. In the USA a business tycoon selects his bride-to-be with the help of a television game show. People's deaths are now recorded for the benefit of the watching millions. In such a world, it is no surprise that the pop tastes of politicians count as important details.

This transformation of political life and ordinary life, and the blurring of the two, has led some writers to perceive a bleak future, one in which politics becomes demeaned (literally, de-meaned, deprived of meaning). Politics has become just another game show, another docusoap. 'The real electors,' writes Danilo Zolo (1992: 163–4), 'see themselves replaced by their own demoscopic and televisual projection, which anticipates them and leaves them the passive observers of themselves. Individual citizens, despite being the true holders of the right to vote, find themselves subjected to the pressure of public predictions which tend circularly to be self-fulfilling by edging them out of the electoral event.' In the same way, Michael Sandel (1998: 350) worries that 'the narrative resources' that are essential to a functioning civic republic are being 'strained' by the prevalence of 'the soundbites, factoids and disconnected images of our media-saturated culture'. The proliferation of channels, the generation of interactive systems, the sheer explosion of information, have created a world in which the media are the only reality, and in which the demands of sponsors and advertisers create pressure for ever more spectacular or humiliating shows. The world is constantly being made and remade, as facts and fictions become entwined. News and politics are reduced to slogans and sound bites, mimicking the aesthetic of the pop video and of MTV. It is a world in which newscasters are celebrities, and celebrities become politicians.

Others, though, offer a less bleak picture of the future, seeing, in the blending of the cultural and the political, a new politics emerging. The author Naomi Klein reported how, during a demonstration, the policeman standing next to her said into his walkie-talkie: 'This is not a protest. . . . It is some kind of artistic expression' (*Select*, April 2000: 75). For Klein, there is a new cultural politics emerging out of the personalized politics of the everyday; it is a world of heterogeneous and fluid social movements, not hierarchical parties. A powerful political force is being born at the interface between art and politics, consumption and conscience.

It would be a rash author who predicted the future of the relationship between politics and mass media, but it is clear that a number of different scenarios are competing for attention. The first of these focuses on the new communications technologies: digital broadcasting, the internet and the new forms of access to it via mobile phones and television sets. The promise here, at least in terms of the way these technologies are marketed, is of greater choice and control for consumers. We will create our own viewing schedules from an ever-expanding range of alternatives; we will use the channels available to shop, vote, play video games, book holidays and so on. The days of mass consumption and mass viewing will give way to individuals choice and niche markets, to many private worlds. The balance of power will have shifted from states, conglomerates and parties to the world of the voraciously consuming individual.

It is just this prospect that prompts a second scenario to appear over the horizon. This is a world of isolated individuals, disconnected from communities and groups, vulnerable and manipulable. The new technologies do not represent choice and devolved power; they represent surveillance and centralized suppression. The emerging systems of communication provide conglomerates and state authorities with the ability to monitor movement and thought in ways that were never possible previously. Every cash transaction, every electronic communication, provides data on the desires and actions of citizens. Political parties now no longer lead, they merely follow the swerves and switches of populist opinion. As they acquire more and more data on their constituents, so their policies become ever shallower responses to the twitch of public opinion.

Yet these same technologies form part of a third scenario, one in which the powers of states, parties and conglomerates are threatened by electronically coordinated social movements that spring up with apparent spontaneity. E-mail networks of networks create a covert system of dissidents who owe no allegiance to the powers that pretend to control them. Using digital camcorders and new communications technologies, these social movements can get their message out without depending on the mediating powers of mainstream television or without state-designated regulations.

In the end, of course, all of these scenarios will prove to be wrong – and right. Elements of each are already with us, and will probably become much more pronounced, but there will be consequences that are beyond our best imaginings. What can be certain is that, just as the relationship between politics and mass media has changed dramatically in the last decades, so it will in the future. It is important, though, to think critically about these changes. We will no doubt see political parties devise ever more sophisticated ways of exploiting the opportunities offered by the media. We will see politicians increasingly taking on the guise of popular culture's celebrities. The point, however, is not to move automatically to the conclusion that we are seeing the 'dumbing down' of politics. We need to assess what is happening in terms that are sensitive to the processes involved. Rather than dismiss such a state of affairs as a sign of cultural and political terminal decline, we should understand it first as part of a wider set of factors and changes. This is not to foreclose any judgement we may subsequently make, but rather to set such judgements within a realistic appraisal of the process being judged. After all, to dismiss modern political campaigning as mere artifice and show is simply to connect it to many other cultural forms which are also artifice and show. We need to discriminate between artifices, not to imagine that we can go beyond them to some authentic reality. The culture of politics, as with all forms of culture, is a product of a complicated set of interests, regulations and institutions, which organize, reproduce and police that culture.

We need also to be aware of the profoundly important stakes that are being played out in the way media are organized and used. While it has been fashionable to make fun of 'media studies' and dismiss its concerns as the pseudo-scientific pursuit of trivia, our mass media are a vital element in the way we live our lives and come to know ourselves and our world. They contain our memories and our histories; their resources provide for the stories people tell each other. As Sandel (1998: 350) argues: 'Political community depends on the narratives by which people make sense of their condition and interpret the common life they share; at its best political deliberation is not only about competing policies but also about competing interpretations of the character of the community, of its purpose and ends.' This is why we should both value and criticize the forms taken by media culture. We should value it because of the role it has in constructing those narratives; we should criticize it for its failure to enrich them. Sandel makes a direct connection between the quality of political and cultural discourse and the well-being of the democratic order.

It may be that political life is being damaged by a media obsessed with ratings and politicians desperate for votes; it may be that the commercial interests of multimedia corporations are putting a price on everything (and selling it cheap), but to complain is not enough. We have to understand the causes of the phenomenon and not focus only on its symptoms. Equally, we should not be too quick to condemn. Maybe we do not need to know the details of Bill Clinton's love affairs or of Tony Blair's family life, but these episodes did prompt a public political debate – about relations between the sexes, about public and private morality, about child care and men's domestic role. It may be that the traditional forms of political communication are being replaced, and that politicians are becoming performers in popular culture's circus, but this does not mean that politics has stopped. It has just moved on, and our job is to follow it, arguing as we go.

Bibliography

Abramson, J. B., F. C. Arterton and G. R. Orren (1988) *The Electronic Commonwealth: The Impact of New Media Technologies on Democratic Politics*, New York: Basic Books.

Adonis, A. and G. Mulgan (1994) 'Back to Greece: The scope for direct democracy', *Demos Quarterly*, 3, 2–9.

Adorno, T. and M. Horkheimer (1979) 'The Culture Industry: Enlightenment as Mass Deception', in *Dialectic of Enlightenment*, London: Verso, pp. 120–67

Anderson, P. and A. Weymouth (1999) *Insulting the Public? The British Press and the European Union*, London: Longman.

Ang, I. (1996) *Living Room Wars: Rethinking Media Audiences for a Postmodern World*, London: Routledge.

Arblaster, A. (1987) *Democracy*, Milton Keynes: Open University Press.

Arterton, C. (1987) *Teledemocracy*, London: Sage.

Asp, K. and P. Esaiasson (1996) 'The Modernization of Swedish Campaigns: Individualization, Professionalization, and Medialization', in D. Swanson and P. Mancini (eds), *Politics, Media, and Modern Democracy*, New York: Praeger, pp. 73–90.

Atkinson, M. (1988) *Our Masters' Voices: The Language and Body Langauage of Politics*, London: Routledge.

Bailey, D. (1999) 'Politics on the Internet', *American Voices*, September.

Barber, B. (1984) *Strong Democracy: Participatory Politics for a New Age*, San Francisco: University of California Press.

Barber, B. (1997) *Jihad vs McWorld: How Globalism and Tribalism are Reshaping the World*, New York: Ballantine Books.

Barker, M. and J. Petley (1997) *Ill Effects: The Media/Violence Debate*, London: Routledge.

Barnett, S. (1993) 'Sliding Down the Market Slope' *British Journalism Review*, 4(1), 67–9.

Barthes, R. (1967) *Elements of Semiology*, London: Jonathan Cape.

Becker, T. and C. D. Staton (1981) 'Hawaii Televote', *Political Science*, 33(1), 52–6.

Beesley, M (ed.) (1996) *Markets and the Media*, London: Institute of Economic Affairs.

Belfield, R., C. Hird and S. Kelly (1991) *Murdoch: The Decline of an Empire*, London: Macdonald.

Bellamy, R. and M. Hollis (1995) 'Liberal Justice: Political and Metaphysical', *The Philosophy Quarterly*, 45(178), 1–19.

Bennett, T. (1982a) 'Media, "Reality", Signification', in M. Gurevitch, T. Bennett, J. Curran and J. Woollacott (eds), *Culture, Society and the Media*, London: Routledge, pp. 287–308.

Bennett, T. (1982b) 'Theories of the Media, Theories of Society', in M. Gurevitch, T. Bennett, J. Curran and J. Woollacott (eds), *Culture, Society and the Media*, London: Routledge, pp. 30–55.

Bennett, W. and D. Paletz (eds) (1994) *Taken by Storm: The Media, Public Opinion and US Foreign Politcy in the Gulf War*, Chicago: University of Chicago Press.

Benton, S. (1997) 'Political News', *Soundings*, 5, Spring, 137–48.

Berlin, I. (1969) *Four Essays on Liberty*, Oxford: Oxford University Press.

Billig, M., D. Deacon, P. Golding and S. Middleton (1993) 'In the Hands of the Spin-doctors: Televison Politics, and the 1992 General Election', in N. Miller and R. Allen (eds), *It's Live – But Is It Real?*, London: John Libbey, pp. 111–21.

Bin, Z. (1998) 'Popular Family Television and Party Ideology: The Spring Festival Eve Happy Gathering', *Media, Culture and Society*, 20, 43–58.

Blain, N., R. Boyle and H. O'Donnell (1993) *Sport and National Identity in the European Media*, Leicester: Leicester University Press.

Bloom, A. (1987) *The Closing of the American Mind*, New York: Simon & Schuster.

Blumler, J. and M. Gurevitch (1995) *The Crisis of Public Communication*, London: Routledge.

Blumler, J. and D. McQuail (1968) *Television in Politics: Its Uses and Influences*, London: Faber & Faber.

Bourdieu, P. (1986) *Distinction: A Social Critique of the Judgement of Taste*, London: Routledge.

Bourdieu, P. (1991) *Language and Symbolic Power*, Cambridge: Polity.

Bower, T. (1988) *Maxwell: The Outsider*, London: Aurum.

Bowes, M. (1990) 'Only When I Laugh', in A. Goodwin and G. Whannel, *Understanding Television*, London: Routledge, pp. 128–40.

Boyd-Barrett, O. and T. Rantanen (1998) 'The Globalization of News', in O. Boyd-Barrett and T. Rantanen (eds), *The Globalization of News*, London: Sage, pp. 1–14.

Brants, K., M. Huizenga and R. van Meerten (1996) 'The New Canals of Amsterdam: An Exercise in Local Electronic Democracy', *Media, Culture and Society*, 18(2), 185–212.

Bryan, C., R. Tsagarousianou and D. Tambini (1998) 'Electronic Democracy and the Civic Networking Movement in Context', in R. Tsagarousianou, D. Tambini and C. Bryan (eds), *Cyberdemocracy: Technology, Cities and Civic Networks*, London: Routledge, pp. 1–17.

Budge, I. (1996) *The New Challenge of Direct Democracy*, Cambridge: Polity.

Budge, I. *et al.* (1998) *The Politics of the New Europe*, London: Longman.

Burke, E. (1975) 'Speech to the Electors of Bristol', in B. Hill (ed.), *Edmund Burke on Government, Politics and Society*, London: Fontana, pp. 156–8.

Butler, D. and D. Kavanagh (1997) *The British Election of 1997*, London: Macmillan – now Palgrave.

Buxton, D. (1990) *From The Avengers to Miami Vice: Form and Ideology in Television Series*, Manchester: Manchester University Press.

Calabrese, A. and M. Borchert (1996) 'Prospects for Electronic Democracy in the United States: Rethinking Communication and Social Policy, *Media, Culture and Society*, 18(2), 249–68.

Campbell, D. and S. Connor (1986) *On the Record*, London: Michael Joseph.

Cappella, J. and K. Jamieson (1997) *Spiral of Cynicism*, New York: Oxford University Press.

Carey, J. (1989) *Communication As Culture*, London: Unwin Hyman.

Carpenter, H. (2000) *That Was Satire That Was: The Satire Boom of the 1960s*, London: Victor Gollancz.

Carruthers, S. (1998) '"The Manchurian Candidate" (1962) and the Cold War Brainwashing Scare', *Historical Journal of Film, Radio and Television*, 18(1), 75–94.

Carruthers, S. (2000) *The Media at War*, Basingstoke: Macmillan – now Palgrave.

Castells, M. (1996) *The Rise of the Network Society*, Oxford: Blackwell.

Chalaby, J. (1998) 'A Charismatic Leader's Use of the Media: De Gaulle and Television', *Harvard International Journal of Press/Politics*, 3(4), 44–61.

Christensen, T. (1987) *Reel Politics: American Political Movies from Birth of a Nation to Platoon*, Oxford: Basil Blackwell.

Clark, C. (1997) 'In Favour of Civic Journalism', *Harvard International Journal of Press/Politics*, 2(3), 118–24.

Clark, T. N. and V. Hoffman-Marinot (eds) (1998) *The New Political Culture*, Boulder, Col.: Westview.

Clark, T. N. and Inglehart, R. (1998) 'The New Political Culture: Changing Dynamics of Support for the Welfare State and Other Policies in Postindustrial Societies', in T. N. Clark and V. Hoffman-Marinot (eds) (1998) *The New Political Culture*, Boulder, Col.: Westview, pp. 9–72.

Cloonan, M. (1996) *Banned! Censorship of Popular Music in Britain*, Aldershot: Arena.

Cockerell, M. (1988), *Live From Number 10*, London: Faber & Faber.

Cockerell, M, P. Hennessy and D. Walker (1985) *Sources Close to the Prime Minister*, London: Papermac.

Coleman, S. (1998) 'Interactive Media and the 1997 UK General Election', *Media, Culture and Society*, 20, 687–94.

Connolly, W. E. (1974) *The Terms of Political Discourse*, Lexington, Mass.: D. C. Heath.

Corner, J. (1995) *Television Form and Public Address*, London: Edward Arnold.

Corner, J. (2000) 'Mediated Persona and Political Culture: Dimensions of Structure and Process', *European Journal of Cultural Studies*, 3(3), 389–405.

Crewe, I. and M. Harrop (eds) (1986), *Political Communications: The General Election of 1983*, Cambridge: Cambridge University Press.

Crewe, I. and M. Harrop (eds) (1989) *Political Communications: The General Election of 1987*, Cambridge: Cambridge University Press.

Crewe, I. and B. Sarlvik (1983) *The Decade of Dealignment*, Cambridge: Cambridge University Press.

Crissell, A. (1991) 'Filth, Sedition and Blasphemy: The Rise and Fall of Satire', in J. Corner (ed.), *Popular Television in Britain*, London: BFI Publishing, pp. 145–58.

Cumberbatch, G (1998) 'Media Effects: The Continuing Controversy', in A. Briggs and P. Cobley (eds), *The Media: An Introduction*, London: Longman, pp. 262–74.

Curran, J. (1982) 'Communications, Power and Social Order', in M. Gurevitch, T. Bennett, J. Curran and J. Woollacott (eds), *Culture, Society and the Media*, London: Routledge, pp. 202–35.

Curran, J. (1986) 'The Impact of Advertising on the British Mass Media', in R. Collins, J. Curran, N. Garnham, P. Scannell, P. Schlesinger and C. Sparks (eds), *Media, Culture and Society: A Critical Reader*, London: Sage, pp. 309–35.

Curran, J. (1991) 'Mass Media and Democracy: A Reappraisal', in J. Curran and M. Gurevitch (eds), *Mass Media and Society*, London: Edward Arnold, pp. 82–117.

Curran, J. (1997) 'Media Soundings', *Soundings*, 5, Spring, pp. 127–36.

Curran, J. (2000) 'Rethinking Media and Democracy', in J. Curran and M. Gurevitch (eds), *Mass Media and Society*, 3rd edn, London: Arnold, pp. 120–54.

Curran, J. and J. Seaton (1997) *Power without Responsibility*, 5th edn, London: Routledge.

Curran, J. and C. Sparks (1991) 'Press and Popular Culture,' *Media, Culture and Society*, 13(2), pp. 215–37.

Curtice, J. and H. Semetko (1994) 'Does it Matter What the Papers Say?', in A. Heath *et al*, *Labour's last Chance? The 1992 Election and Beyond*, London: Dartmouth, pp. 43–63.

Curtis, L. and M. Jempson (1993) *Interference on the Airwaves*, London: Campaign for Press and Broadcasting Freedom.

Dahl, R. (1956) *A Preface to Democratic Theory*, Chicago: University of Chicago Press.

Datta-Ray, S. (1996) 'Does a Free Press Hinder Progress?', *British Journalism Review*, 7(3), 30–5.

Day, R. (1991) 'Interviewing Politicians', in I. Crewe and M. Harrop (eds), *Political Communications: The General Election Campaign of 1987*, Cambridge: Cambridge University Press, pp. 126–36.

Deacon, D., P. Golding and M. Billig (1998) 'Between Fear and Loathing: National Press Coverage of the 1997 British General Election', in D. Denver, J. Fisher, P. Cowley and C. Pattie (eds), *British Elections and Parties Review*, 8, London: Frank Cass, pp. 135–49.

De Launey, G. (1995) 'Not-so-big in Japan: Western Pop Music in the Japanese Market', *Popular Music*, 14(2), 203–26.

Dennett, D. (1986) 'Information, Technology, and the Virtues of Ignorance', *Daedalus*, 115(3), 135–53.

de Sola Pool (1990) *Technologies without Boundaries*, Cambridge, Mass.: Harvard University Press

282   *Bibliography*

Doig, A. (1997) 'The Decline of Investigative Journalism', in M. Bromley and T. O'Melley (eds), *A Journalism Reader*, London: Routledge, pp. 189–213.

Dooley, P. and P. Grosswiler (1997) ' "Turf Wars": Journalists, New Media and the Struggle for Control of Political News', *Harvard International Journal of Press/Politics*, 2(3), 31–51.

Dowding, K. (1994) 'The Compatibility of Behaviouralism, Rational Choice and "New Institutionalism" ', *Journal of Theoretical Politics*, 6(1), 105–17.

Dowding, K. (1996) *Power*, Milton Keynes: Open University Press.

Downs, A. (1957), *An Economic Theory of Democracy*, New York: Harper & Row.

Dunleavy, P, and C. Husbands (1985) *Democracy at the Crossroads*, London: Allen & Unwin.

Dunleavy, P. and B. O'Leary (1987) *Theories of the State: the Politics of Liberal Democracy*, London: Macmillan – now Palgrave.

Dworkin, R. (1978) 'Liberalism', in S. Hampshire (ed.), *Public and Private Morality*, Cambridge: Cambridge University Press, pp. 114–43.

Dworkin, R. (1996) 'The Curse of American Politics', *New York Review of Books*, 17 October, pp. 19–24.

ECN (Eastern Counties Newspapers) (n.d.) *Editorial Policy*, Norwich: ECN.

Eldridge, J. (1993) 'News, Truth and Power', in Glasgow University Media Group (ed.), *Getting the Message: News, Truth and Power*, London: Routledge, pp. 3–33.

Ellul, J. (1964) *The Technological Society*, New York: Vintage.

Elshtain, J. B. (1982) 'Democracy and the QUBE Tube', *The Nation*, 7–14 August: pp. 108–9.

Entman, R. (1993) 'Framing: Toward Clarification of a Fractured Paradigm', *Journal of Communications*, 43(4), 51–8.

Entman, R. M. (1996) 'Reporting Environmental Policy Debate: The Real Media Biases', *Harvard International Journal of Press/Politics* 1(3), 77–92.

Entman, R. M. (1997) 'Manufacturing Discord: Media in the Affirmative Action Debate', *Harvard International Journal of Press/Politics*, 2(4), 32–51.

Ess, C. (ed.) (1996) *Philosophical Perspectives on Computer-Mediated Communication*, Albany, NY: State University of New York Press.

Esser, F., C. Reinemann and D. Fau (2000) 'Spin Doctoring in British and German Election Campaigns', *European Journal of Communication*, 15(2), 209–39.

Euromedia Research Group (1986) *New Media Politics*, London: Sage.

Eyerman, R. and A. Jamison (1998) *Music and Social Movements*, Cambridge: Cambridge University Press.

Fenchurch, R. (1994) 'Network Wonderland', *Demos Quarterly*, 4: 11.

Fishkin, J. (1991) *Democracy and Deliberation*, New Haven: Yale University Press.

Fiske, J. (1993) *Power Plays, Power Works*, London: Verso.
Flyvberg, B. (1998) *Rationality and Power: Democracy in Practice*, Chicago: University of Chicago Press.
Foucault, M. (1984) *The Foucault Reader*, ed. P. Rabinow, New York: Pantheon.
Franklin, B. (ed.) (1992) *Televising Democracies*, London: Arnold.
Franklin, B. (1994) *Packaging Politics: Political Communications in Britain's Media Democracy*, London: Edward Arnold.
Franklin, B. (1998) *Newszak and News Media*, London: Arnold.
Friedland, L. (1996) 'Electronic Democracy and the New Citizenship,' *Media, Culture and Society*, 18(2), 185–212.
Frith, S. (1988) 'The Pleasures of the Hearth: The Making of BBC Light Entertainiment', in S. Frith, *Music for Pleasure*, Cambridge: Polity, pp. 24–44.
Frith, S. and J. Street (1992) 'Rock Against Racism and Red Wedge: From Music to Politics, from Politics to Music', in R. Garofalo (ed.), *Rockin' the Boat: Mass Music and Mass Movements*, Boston: South End Press, pp. 67–80.
Gallagher, R. (1989) 'American Television: Fact and Fantasy', in C. Veljanovski (ed.), *Freedom in Broadcasting*, London: Institute of Economic Affairs, pp. 178–207.
Gallie, W. B. (1955–6) 'Essentially Contested Concepts', *Proceedings of the Aristotelian Society*, 56, 167–98.
Gamson, W. A. and A. Modigliani (1989) 'Media Discourse and Public Opinion on Nuclear Power: A Constructionist Approach', *American Journal of Sociology*, 95(1), 1–37.
Garnham, N. (1986) 'The media and the public sphere', in P. Golding, G. Murdock and P. Schlesinger (eds), *Communicating Politics*, Leicester: Leicester University Press, pp. 55–67.
Garnham, N. (2000) *Emancipation, the Media, and Modernity*, Oxford: Oxford University Press.
Genovese, E. (1976) *Roll, Jordan, Roll: The World the Slaves Made*, New York: Vintage Books.
George, N. (1999) *Hip Hop America*, London: Penguin.
Geraghty, C. (1992) 'British Soaps in the 1980s', in D. Strinati and S. Wagg (eds), *Come On Down? Popular Media Culture in Postwar Britain*, London: Routledge, pp. 133–49.
Giddens, A. (1979) *Central Problems in Social Theory*, London: Macmillan – now Palgrave.
Gilliam, F., S. Iyengar, A. Simon and O. Wright (1996) 'Crime in Black and White: The Violent, Scary World of Local News', *Harvard International Journal of Press/Politics*, 1(3), 6–25.
Gitlin, T. (1991), 'Bites and Blips: Chunk News, Savvy Talk and the Bifurcation of American Politics', in P. Dahlgren and C. Sparks (eds), *Communication and Citizenship: Journalism and the Public Sphere*, London: Routledge, pp. 119–36.
Glencross, D. (1993) 'Convergence at Aspen', *Spectrum*, Autumn, 3.

Golding, P and G. Murdock (2000) 'Culture Communication and Political Economy', in J. Curran and M. Gurevitch (eds), *Mass Media and Society*, London: Arnold, pp. 70–92.

Goodwin, A. (1990) 'TV News: Striking the Right Balance?', *Understanding Television*, London: Routledge,pp. 42–59.

Gray, H. (1995) *Watching Race: Television and the Struggle for 'Blackness'*, Minneapolis: University of Minnesota Press.

Green, P. (1998) 'American Television and Consumer Democracy', *Dissent*, Spring, 49–57.

Griffin, D. (1994) *Satire: A Critical Reintroduction*, Lexington, Kentucky: University Press of Kentucky.

Grimes, C. (1997) 'Whither the Civic Journalism Bandwagon?', *Harvard International Journal of Press/Politics*, 2(3), 125–30.

GUMG (Glasgow University Media Group) (1976) *Bad News*, London: Routledge.

GUMG (1980) *More Bad News*, London: Routledge.

GUMG (1985) *War and Peace News*, Milton Keynes: Open University Press.

Habermas, J. (1971) *Towards a Rational Society*, London: Heinemann.

Habermas, J. (1989) *The Structural Transformation of the Public Sphere*, Cambridge: Polity.

Habermas, J. (1996) *Between Facts and Norms*, Cambridge: Polity.

Hall, S. (1980) 'Encoding/Decoding', in S. Hall, D. Hobson, A. Lowe and P. Willis (eds), *Culture, Media, Language*, London: Hutchinson, pp. 128–38.

Hall, S. (1982) 'The Rediscovery of "Ideology": Return of the Repressed in Media Studies', in M. Gurevitch, T. Bennett, J. Curran and J. Woollacott (eds), *Culture, Society and the Media*, London: Routledge, pp. 56–90.

Hallin, D. (2000) 'Commercialism and Professionalism in the American News Media', in J. Curran and M. Gurevitch (eds), *Mass Media and Society*, London: Arnold, pp. 218–37.

Harris, R. (1983) *Gotcha! The Media, The Government and the Falklands Crisis*, London: Faber & Faber.

Harris, R. (1990) *Good and Faithful Servant*, London: Faber & Faber.

Harris, S. (1991) 'Evasive Action: How Politicians Respond to Questions in Political Interviews', in P. Scannel (ed.), *Broadcast Talk*, London: Sage.

Harrison, M. (1985) *TV News: Whose Bias?*, London: Policy Journals.

Harrison, M. (1994) 'Exploring the Information Superhighway: Political Science and the Internet', Keele Research paper, no. 6.

Harrop, M. (1986) 'The Press and Post-war Elections', in I. Crewe and M. Harrop (eds), *Political Communications: The General Election Campaign of 1983*, Cambridge: Cambridge University Press, pp. 137–49.

Harrop, M. (1987) 'Voters', in J. Seaton and B. Pimlott (eds), *The Media in British Politics*, Aldershot: Gower, pp. 45–63.

Hart, P. (1999) 'Social Capital in Britain', *British Journal of Political Science*, 29, 417–61.

Hart, R. (1999) *Seducing America: How Television Charms the Modern Voter*, New York: Oxford University Press.

Hay, C. (1997) 'Divided by a Common Language: Political Theory and the Concept of Power', *Politics*, 17(1), 45–52.

Heath, A., J. Curtice, R. Jowell, G. Evans, J. Field and S. Witherspoon (1991) *Understanding Political Change*, Oxford: Pergamon.

Hebdige, D. (1979) *Subculture: The Meaning of Style*, London: Methuen.

Held, D., A. McGrew, D. Goldblatt and J. Perraton (1999) *Global Transformations*, Cambridge: Polity.

Hennessy, P. (1990) *Whitehall*, London: Fontana.

Henningham, J. (1998) 'Ideological Differences between Australian Journalists and Their Public', *Harvard International Journal of Press/Politics*, 3(1), 92–101.

Herman, E. and N. Chomsky (1988) *Manufacturing Consent: The Political Economy of the Mass Media*, New York: Pantheon.

Herman, E. and R. McChesney (1997) *The Global Media: The New Missionaries of Corporate Capitalism*, London: Cassell.

Herman, E. and R. McChesney (1999) 'The Global Media in the Late 1990s', in H. Mackay and T. O'Sullivan (eds), *The Media Reader: Continuity and Transformation*, London: Sage, pp. 178–210.

Herzog, H. (1998) 'More than a Looking Glass: Women in Israeli Local Politics and the Media', *Harvard International Journal of Press/Politics*, 3(1), 26–47.

Hewison, R. (1988) *Too Much: Art and Society in the Sixties*, London: Methuen.

Hindess, B. (1996) *Discourses of Power*, Oxford: Blackwell.

Hirst, P. (1994) *Associative Democracy: New Forms of Economic and Social Governance*, Cambridge: Polity.

Hollis, M. and S. Smith (1991a) *Explaining and Understanding International Relations*, Oxford: Clarendon Press.

Hollis, M. and S. Smith (1991b) 'Beware of Gurus: Structure and Action in International Relations', *Review of International Studies*, 17, 393–410.

Holmes, S. (1990) 'Liberal Constraints on Private Power?: Reflections on the Origins and Rationale of Access Regulation', in J. Lichtenberg (ed.), *Democracy and the Mass Media*, Cambridge: Cambridge University Press, pp. 21–65.

Hong, L. (1998) 'Profit or Ideology? The Chinese Press between Party and Market', *Media, Culture and Society*, 20, 31–41.

Hughes, T. (1983) *Networks of Power*, Baltimore: Johns Hopkins Press.

Humphreys, P. (1988) 'New Media Policy Dilemmas in West Germany', in K. Dyson and P. Humphreys (eds), *Broadcasting and New Media Policies in Western Europe*, London: Routledge, pp. 185–222.

Illich, I. (1975) *Tools for Conviviality*, London: Fontana.

Index on Censorship (2000) *Manufacturing Monsters*, 5, London: Index on Censorship.

Iyengar, S. (1991) *Is Anyone Responsible? How Television Frames Political Issues*, Chicago: University of Chicago Press.

Jackson, W. (1997) 'Save Democracy from Civic Journalism: North Carolina's Odd Experiment', *Harvard International Journal of Press/ Politics*, 2(3), pp. 102–17.

Jakubovicz, K. (1996) 'Television and Elections in Post-1989 Poland: How Powerful is the Medium?', in D. Swanson and P. Mancini (eds), *Politics, Media and Modern Democracy*, New York: Praeger, pp. 129–54.

Jamieson, K. (1984) *Packaging the Presidency*, Oxford: Oxford University Press.

Jamieson, K. H. (1992) *Dirty Politics: Deception, Distraction, and Democracy*, Oxford: Oxford University Press.

Jones, N. (1995) *Soundbites and Spin Doctors*, London: Cassell.

Jones, S. (ed.) (1995) *Cybersociety*, London: Sage.

Kavanagh, D. (1995) *Election Campaigning: The New Marketing of Politics*, Oxford: Basil Blackwell.

Keane, J. (1991) *The Media and Democracy*, Cambridge: Polity.

Keane, J. (1992) 'Democracy and the Media – Without Foundations', *Political Studies*, XL, Special Issue, 116–29.

Kellner, D. (1995) *Media Culture*, London: Routledge.

Khazen, J. (1999) 'Censorship and State Control of the press in the Arab World', *Harvard International Journal of Press/Politics*, 4(3), 87–92.

Klapper, J. (1960) *The Effects of Mass Communication*, New York: Free Press.

Klein, N. (2000) *No Logo*, London: Flamingo.

Kohut, A. and R. Toth (1998) 'The Central Conundrum: How Can the People Like What They Distrust?', *Harvard International Journal of Press/Politics*, 3(1), 110–17.

Kurtz, H. (1998) *Spin Cycle: Inside the Clinton Propaganda Machine*, London: Pan.

Labour Party (1995) *The Net Effect*, London: Labour Party.

Ledbetter, J. (1997) *Made Possible By . . . The Death of Public Broadcasting in the United States*, London: Verso.

Lee, C.-C. (1998) 'Press Self-Censorship and the Political Transition in Hong Kong', *Harvard International Journal of Press/Politics*, 3(2), 55–73.

Lee, S. (1990) *The Cost of Free Speech*, London: Faber & Faber.

Leigh, D. (1979) *The Frontiers of Secrecy*, London: Junction Books.

Lewis, P. and J. Booth (1989) *The Invisible Medium: Public, Commercial and Community Radio*, Basingstoke: Macmillan – now Palgrave.

Lichtenberg, J. (ed.) (1990) *Democracy and the Mass Media*, Cambridge: Cambridge University Press.

Lichter, R. and T. Smith (1996) 'Why Elections are Bad News: Media and Candidate Discourse in the 1996 Presidential Primaries', *Harvard International Journal of Press/Politics*, 1(4), 15–35.

Littlewood, J. and M. Pickering (1998) 'Heard the One about the White Middle-class Heterosexual Father-in-law? Gender, Ethnicity and Political Correctness in Comedy', in S. Wagg (ed.), *Because I Tell a Joke or Two: Comedy, Politics and Social Difference*, London: Routledge, pp. 291–312.

Lively, J. (1975) *Democracy*, Oxford: Basil Blackwell.

Lloyd, A. (1983) 'Europe Examines Electronic Democracy', *New Scientist*, 2 June, p. 634.

Loader, B. (ed.) (1997) *The Governance of Cyberspace*, London: Routledge.

Lukes, S. (1974) *Power: A Radical View*, London: Macmillan.

Lyon, D. (1986) *The Electronic Eye*, Cambridge: Polity.

Malm, K. and R. Wallis (1993) *Media Policy and Music Activity*, London: Routledge.

Mancini, P. and D. Swanson (1996) 'Politics, Media, and Modern Democracy: Introduction', in D. Swanson, and P. Mancini (eds), *Politics, Media, and Modern Democracy*, New York: Praeger, pp. 1–26.

Marnham, P. (1982) *The Private Eye Story: The First 21 Years*, London: André Deutsch.

Marqusee, M. (1994) *Anyone But England: Cricket and the National Malaise*, London: Verso.

Marr, A. (1996) *Ruling Britannia*, London: Penguin.

Marshall, D. (1997) *Celebrity and Power: Fame in Contemporary Culture*, Minneapolis: University of Minnesota Press.

Marx, K. and F. Engels (1970) *The German Ideology*, London: Lawrence & Wishart.

Masters, R., S. Frey and G. Bente (1991) 'Dominance & Attention: Images of Leaders in German, French & American TV News', *Polity*, 23(3), 373–94.

Mathews, T. D. (1994) *Censored!* London: Chatto & Windus.

McEnteer, J. (1996) 'Guns, Goons, Gold, and Glitz: Philippine Press Coverage of the 1995 National Elections', *Harvard International Journal of Press/Politics*, 1(1), 113–20.

McGinniss, J. (1969) *The Selling of a President*, New York: Trident Press.

McGuigan, J. (1996) *Culture and the Public Sphere*, London: Routledge.

McKibbin, R. (1998) *Classes and Culture: England 1918–1951*, Oxford: Oxford University Press.

McLean, I. (1989) *Democracy and the New Technology*, Cambridge: Polity.

McLuhan, M. (1994) *Understand the Media: The Extensions of Man*, London: Routledge.

McNair, B. (1995) *An Introduction to Political Communication*, London: Routledge.

McQuail, D. (1992) *Media Performance*, London: Sage.

McQuail, D. (1994) *Mass Communication Theory*, 3rd edn, London: Sage.

Merelman, R. (1991) *Partial Visions: Culture and Politics in Britain, Canada and the United States*, Madison: University of Wisconsin Press.

Meyrowitz, J. (1985) *No Sense of Place: The Effect of Electronic Media on Social Behavior*, New York: Oxford University Press.

Mickiewicz, E. and A. Richter (1996) 'Television, Campaigning, and Elections in the Soviet Union and Post-Soviet Russia', in D. Swanson and P. Mancini (eds), *Politics, Media, and Modern Democracy*, London: Praeger, pp. 107–28.

Mill, J. S. (1972) *On Liberty*, London: J. M. Dent.

Miller, D. (1992) 'Deliberative Democracy and Social Choice', *Political Studies*, Vol. XL, Special Issue, 54–67.

Miller, D. (1993) 'The Northern Ireland Information Service and the Media: Aims, Strategy, Tactics', in GUMG (ed. J. Eldridge), *Getting the Message: News, Truth and Power*, London: Routledge, pp. 73–103.

Miller, W. (1991) *Media and Voters*, Oxford: Oxford University Press.

Miller, W., N. Sonntag and D. Broughton (1989) 'Television in the 1987 British Election Campaign: Its Content and Influence', *Political Studies*, 37(4), 626–51.

Mills, C. W. (1956) *The Power Elite*, New York: Oxford University Press.

Modleski, T. (1987) 'The Search for Tomorrow in Today's Soap Operas', in D. Lazere (ed.), *American Media and Mass Culture*, Berkeley: University of California Press, pp. 266–79.

Morley, D. (1986) *Family Television: Cultural Power and Domestic Leisure*, London: Routledge.

Morley, D. (1992) *Television, Audiences and Cultural Studies*, London: Routledge.

Morrison, D. and H. Tumber (1988) *Journalists at War: the Dynamic of News Reporting During the Falklands Conflict*, London: Sage.

Morriss, P. (1987) *Power: A Philosophical Analysis*, Manchester: Manchester University Press.

Murdock, G. (1982) 'Large Corporations and the Control of Communications Industries', in M. Gurevitch, T. Bennett, J. Curran and J. Woollacott (eds), *Culture, Society and the Media*, London: Routledge, pp. 118–50.

Nash, K. (2000) *Contemporary Political Sociology: Globalization, Politics and Power*, Oxford: Blackwell.

Neale, S. (1980) *Genre*, London: British Film Institute.

Negrine, R. (1994) *Politics and the Mass Media in Britain*, 2nd edn, London: Routledge.

Negrine, R. (1996) *The Communication of Politics*, London: Sage.

Negus, K. (1999) *Music Genres and Corporate Cultures*, London: Routledge.

Neil, A. (1997) *Full Disclosure*, London: Pan Books.

Neve, B. (2000) 'Frames of Presidential and Candidate Politics in American Films of the 1990s', *The Public/Javnost*, 7(2), 19–32.

Newton, K. (1989) 'Media Bias', in R. Goodin and A. Reeve (eds), *Liberal Neutrality*, London: Routledge, pp. 130–55.

Nicholson, J. (2000) 'The Rise of the "E-Precinct" ', *Harvard International Journal of Press/Politics*, 5(1), 78–81.

Nimmo, D. (1996) 'Politics, Media, and Modern Democracy: The United States', in D. Swanson and P. Mancini (eds), *Politics, Media, and Modern Democracy*, New York: Praeger, pp. 29–48

Nimmo, D. and Combs, J. (1990), *Mediated Political Realities*, 2nd edn, London: Longmans.

Norris, P. (1996) *Electoral Change Since 1945*, Oxford: Blackwell.

Norris, P. (ed.) (1997a) *Women, Media, and Politics*, New York and Oxford: Oxford University Press.

Norris, P. (1997b) 'Women Leaders Worldwide: A Splash of Color in the Photo Op,' in P. Norris (ed.), *Women, Media, and Politics*, New York and Oxford: Oxford University Press, pp. 149–65.

Norris, P., J. Curtice, D. Sanders, M. Scammell and H. Semetko (1999) *On Message: Communicating the Campaign*, London: Sage.

O'Donnell, H. (1999) *Good Times, Bad Times: Soap Operas and Society in Western Europe*, London: Leicester University Press.

Olson, M. (1971) *The Logic of Collective Action: Public Goods and the Theory of Groups*, 2nd edn, Cambridge, Mass.: Harvard University Press.

O'Neil, O. (1990) 'Practice of Toleration', in J. Lichtenberg (ed.), *Democracy and the Mass Media*, Cambridge: Cambridge University Press, pp. 155–85.

Ouellette, L. (1999) 'TV Viewing as Good Citizenship? Political Rationality, Enlightened Democracy and PBS', *Cultural Studies*, 13(1), 62–90.

Pateman, C. (1970) *Participation and Democratic Theory*, Cambridge: Cambridge University Press.

Paterson, C. (1998) 'Global Battlefields', in O. Boyd-Barrett and T. Rantanen (eds), *The Globalization of News*, London: Sage.

Phillips, M., I. Gaber, A. Rose and S. Barnett (1993) 'Pressures on Broadcast News: Political, Financial, Institutional Issues', in N. Miller and R. Allen (eds), *It's Live – But Is It Real?*, London: John Libbey, pp. 34–51.

Philo, G. (1990) *Seeing and Believing: The Influence of Television*, London: Routledge.

Pickerill, J (2000) 'Environmentalists and the Net: Pressure Groups, New Social Movements and New ICTs', in S. Ward (ed.), *Reinvigorating Government? British Politics and the Internet*, Aldershot: Ashgate.

Ponting, C. (1985) *The Right to Know: The Inside Story of the Belgrano Affair*, London: Sphere.

Ponting, C. (1986) *Whitehall: Tragedy and Farce*, London: Hamish Hamilton.

Postman, N. (1987) *Amusing Ourselves to Death*, London: Methuen.

Putnam, R. (1995) 'Tuning In, Tuning Out: The Strange Disappearance of Social Capital in America', *PS: Political Science and Politics*, December, 664–83.

Putnam, R. (2000) *Bowling Alone: The Collapse and Revival of American Community*, New York: Simon & Schuster.

Radway, J. (1991) *Reading the Romance: Women, Patriarchy and Popular Literature*, London: University of North Carolina Press.

Rawls, R. (1971) *A Theory of Justice*, Oxford: Oxford University Press.

Read, D. (1992) *The Power of News: The History of Reuters 1849–1989*, Oxford: Oxford University Press.

Regan, S. (1976) *Rupert Murdoch: A Business Biography*, London: Angus and Robertson.

Reporters Sans Frontières (1993) *1993 Report: Freedom of the Press Throughout the World*, London: John Libbey.

Rheingold, H. (1992) *Virtual Community*, London: Mandarin.

Robertson, R. (1995) 'Glocalization: Time–Space and Homogeneity–Heterogeneity', in M. Featherstone, S. Lash and R. Robertson (eds), *Global Modernities*, London: Sage, pp. 25–44.

Rogin, M. (1987) *Ronald Reagan, the Movie and Other Episodes in Political Demonology*, Berkeley: University of California Press.

Romer, R. (2000) 'An "Interactive" Opportunity', *Harvard International Journal of Press/Politics*, 5(1), 82–5.
Rose, T. (1994) *Black Noise: Rap Music and Black Culture in Contemporary America*, London: Wesleyan University Press.
Rosenbaum, M. (1997) *From Soapbox to Soundbite*, London: Macmillan–now Palgrave.
Rospir, J. (1996) 'Political Communication and Electoral Campaigns in the Young Spanish Democracy', in D. Swanson and P. Mancini (eds), *Politics, Media, and Modern Democracy*, London: Praeger, pp. 155–69.
Rousseau, J.-J. (1762/1968) *The Social Contract*, London: Everyman.
Said, E. (2000) 'Apocalypse Now', *Index on Censorship*, 5, London: Index on Censorship, pp. 49–53.
Sandel, M. (1998) *Democracy's Discontent: America in Search of a Public Philosophy*, Cambridge, Mass.: Belknap Press/Harvard University Press.
Sanders, D. (1996) 'Economic Performance, Management Competence and the Outcome of the Next General Election, *Political Studies*, 44(2), 203–31.
Sartori, C. (1996) 'The Media in Italy', in T. Weymouth and B. Lamizet (eds), *Markets and Myths: Forces for Change in the European Media*, London: Longman, pp. 134–70.
Sartori, G. (1989) 'Video Power', *Government and Opposition*, 24(1), 39–53.
Sassatelli, R. (1998) 'Justice, Television and Delegitimation', *Modern Italy*, 3(1), 108–15.
Scammell, M. (1995) *Designer Politics: How Elections are Won*, London: Macmillan – now Palgrave.
Scammell, M. (1999) 'Political Marketing: Lesson for Political Science', *Political Studies*, XLVII, 718–39.
Scannell, P. (1991) 'Introduction: The Relevance of Talk', in P. Scannell (ed.), *Broadcast Talk*, London: Sage.
Schickler, E. (1994) 'Democratizing Technology: Hierarchy and Innovation in Public Life', *Polity*, 27(2), 175–99.
Schlesinger, P. (1987) *Putting 'Reality' Together*, London: Methuen.
Schlesinger, P., G. Murdock and P. Elliott (1983) *Televising 'Terrorism': Political Violence in Popular Culture*, London: Comedia.
Schoenbach, K. (1996) 'The "Americanization" of German Election Campaigns: Any Impact on the Voters?', in D. Swanson and P. Mancini (eds), *Politics, Media, and Modern Democracy*, New York: Praeger, pp. 91–104.
Schudson, M. (2000) 'The Sociology of News Production Revisited (Again)', in J. Curran and M. Gurevitch (eds), *Mass Media and Society*, London: Arnold, pp. 175–200.
Schultz, J. (1998) *Reviving the Fourth Estate: Democracy, Accountability and the Media*, Cambridge: Cambridge University Press.
Schumpeter, J. (1943) *Capitalism, Socialism and Democracy*, London: Allen & Unwin.
Scott, A. (1997) 'Introduction – Globalization: Social Process or Political Rhetoric?', in A. Scott (ed.), *The Limits of Globalization*, London: Routledge, pp. 1–24.

Scott, A. (1999): 'War and the Public Intellectual: Cosmopolitanism and Anti-cosmopolitanism in the Kosovo Debate in Germany', SOCIO-LOGICAL RESEARCH ONLINE; 4(2): *http//www.socresonline.org.uk/4/2/scott.html.*

Scott, J. (1990) *Domination and the Arts of Resistance,* New Haven: Yale University Press

Seisselberg, J. (1996) 'Conditions of Success and Political Problems of "Media-Mediated Personality-Party"': The Case of Forza Italia', *West European Politics*, 19(4), 715–43.

Semetko, H. (1996) 'Political Balance on Television: Campaigns in the United States, Britain, and Germany', *Harvard International Journal of Press/Politics*, 1(1), 51–71.

Semetko, H., J. Blumler, M. Gurevitch and D. Weaver (1991) *The Formation of Campaign Agendas: A Comparative Analysis of Party and Media Roles in Recent American and British Elections,* Hillsdale, NJ: Lawrence Erlbaum.

Semetko, H., M. Scammell and T. Nossiter (eds),(1994) 'The Media's Coverage of the Campaign', in A. Heath, R. Jowell and J. Curtice (eds), *Labour's Last Chance: The 1992 Election and Beyond,* Aldershot: Dartmouth pp. 25–41.

Seymour-Ure, C. (1974) *The Political Impact of Mass Media,* London: Constable.

Shawcross, W. (1992) *Rupert Murdoch,* London: Chatto & Windus.

Silverstone, R. (1994) *Television and Everyday Life,* London: Routledge.

Slaatta, T. (1998) 'Media and Democracy in the Global Order', *Media, Culture and Society,* 20, 335–44.

Snoddy, R. (1992) *The Good, the Bad and the Unacceptable,* London: Faber & Faber.

Sparks, C. (1998) *Communism, Capitalism and the Mass Media,* London: Sage.

Sparks, C. (2000) 'From Dead Trees to Live Wires: The Internet's Challenge to the Traditional Newspaper', in J. Curran and M. Gurevitch (eds), *Mass Media and Society,* London: Arnold, pp. 268–92.

Sreberny, A. (2000) 'The Global and the Local in International Communications', in J. Curran and M. Gurevitch (eds), *Mass Media and Society,* London: Arnold, pp. 93–119.

Sreberny-Mohammadi, A. (1990) 'US Media Covers the World', in J. Downing, A. Mohammadi and A. Sreberny-Mohammadi (eds), *Questioning the Media: A Critical Introduction,* London: Sage, pp. 296–307.

Starr, S. F. (1983) *Red & Hot: The Fate of Jazz in the Soviet Union,* Oxford: Oxford University Press.

Statham, P. (1996) 'Berlusconi, the Media and the New Right in Italy', *Harvard International Journal Press/Politics,* 1(1), 87–106.

Staton, C. D. (1994) 'Democracy's Quantum Leap', *Demos Quarterly,* 3, 31–2.

Stonor Saunders, F. (2000) *Who Paid the Piper? The CIA and the Cultural Cold War,* London: Granta.

Straw, J. (1993) 'Democracy on the Spike', British Journalism Review, 4(4), 45–54.

Street, J. (1986) Rebel Rock: The Politics of Popular Music, Oxford: Blackwell.

Street, J. (1992) Politics and Technology, London: Macmillan – now Palgrave.

Street, J. (1997) Politics and Popular Culture, Cambridge: Polity.

Sussman, G. (1997) Communication, Technology, and Politics in the Information Age, London: Sage.

Swanson, D. and P. Mancini (eds) (1996) Politics, Media, and Modern Democracy, New York: Praeger.

Tannsjo, T. (1985) 'Against Freedom of Expression', Political Studies, 33(4), 547–59.

Taylor, L. and B. Mullan (1986) Uninvited Guests: The Intimate Secrets of Television and Radio, London: Coronet.

Thompson, D. (1998, 'Privacy, Politics and the Press', Harvard International Journal of Press/Politics, 3(4), 103–13.

Thompson, E. (1968) The Making of the English Working Class, Harmondsworth: Penguin.

Thompson, H. S. (1973) Fear and Loathing on the Campaign Trail '72, New York: Popular Library.

Thompson, J. (1988) 'Mass Communication and Modern Culture: Contribution to a Critical Theory of Ideology', Sociology, 22(3), 359–83.

Thompson, J. (1995) The Media and Modernity: A Social Theory of the Media, Cambridge: Polity.

Thompson, J. (1997) 'Scandal and Social Theory', in J. Lull and S. Hinerman (eds), Media Scandals, Cambridge: Polity, pp. 34–64.

Tiffen, R. (1989) News and Power, Sydney: Allen & Unwin.

Tolson, A. (1991) 'Televised Chat and the Synthetic Personality', in P. Scannell (ed.), Broadcast Talk, London: Sage, pp. 178–201.

Tomlinson, J. (1999) 'Cultural Globalisation: Placing and Displacing the West', in H. MacKay and T. O'Sullivan (eds), The Media Reader: Continuity and Transformation, London: Sage, pp. 165–77.

Tracey, M. (1985) 'The Poisoned Chalice? International Television and the Idea of Dominance', Daedalus, 114(4), 17–56.

Tsagarousianou, R., D. Tambini and C. Bryan (1998) Cyberdemocracy: Technology, Cities and Civic Networks, London: Routledge.

Tunstall, J. (1996) Newspaper Power: The New National Press in Britain, Oxford: Oxford University Press.

Tunstall, J. and M. Palmer (1991) Media Moguls, London: Routledge.

Tutt, B. (1992) 'Televising the Commons: A Full, Balanced and Fair Account of the Work of the House', in B. Franklin (ed.), Televising Democracies, London: Routledge, pp. 129–48.

Van de Donk, W., I. Snellen and P. Tops (1995) Orwell in Athens, Amsterdam: IOS Press.

Van Zoonen, L. (1998a) ' "Finally, I Have My Mother Back": Politicians and Their Families in Popular Culture', Harvard International Journal of Press/Politics, 3(1), 48–64.

Van Zoonen, L. (1998b) 'A Day at the Zoo: Political Communication, Pigs and Popular Culture', *Media, Culture and Society*, 20(2), 183–200.

Vickers, G. (1965) *The Art of Judgment*, London: Chapman & Hall.

Vilches, L. (1996) 'The Media in Spain', in T. Weymouth and B. Lamizet (eds), *Markets and Myths: Forces for Change in the European Media*, London: Longman, pp. 173–201.

Wagg, S. (1992) ' "You've Never Had It So Silly": The Politics of British Satirical Comedy from *Beyond the Fringe* to *Spitting Image*', in D. Strinati and S. Wagg (eds), *Come On Down? Popular Media Culture in Postwar Britain*, London: Routledge, pp. 254–84.

Wagg, S. (1998) ' "They've Already Got a Comedian for Governor": Comedians and politics in the United States and Great Britain', in S. Wagg (ed.), *Because I Tell a Joke or Two: Comedy, Politics and Social Difference*, London: Routledge, pp. 244–72.

Wajcman, J. (1991) *Feminism Confronts Technology*, Cambridge: Polity.

Wallis, R. and S. Baran (1990) *The Known World of Broadcast News*, London: Routledge.

Walzer, M. (1985) *Spheres of Justice*, Oxford: Basil Blackwell.

Washbourne, N. (1999) 'New Forms of Organizing? Translocalism, Networks and Organizing in FoE', paper to 'A New Politics?' conference, University of Birmingham.

Weizenbaum, J. (1984) *Computer Power and Human Reason*, London: Penguin.

Whannel, G. (1992) 'The Price is Right but the Moments are Sticky: Television, Quiz and Game Shows, and Popular Culture', in D. Strinati and S. Wagg (eds), *Come On Down? Popular Media Culture in Postwar Britain*, London: Routledge, pp. 179–201.

Wiener, J. (1984) *Come Together: John Lennon in His Time*, New York: Random House.

Williams, R. (1981) *Culture*, London: Fontana.

Winder, R. (1999) *Hell for Leather: A Modern Cricket Journey*, London: Indigo.

Winner, L. (1986) *The Whale and the Reactor*, Chicago: University of Chicago Press.

Winner, L. (1994) 'Three Paradoxes of the Information Age', in G. Bender and T. Druckrey (eds), *Culture on the Brink: Ideologies of Technology*, Seattle: Bay Press, pp. 191–7.

Winston, B. (1998) *Media Technology and Society*, London: Routledge.

Wober, M., M. Svennevig, and B. Gunter (1986) 'The Television Audience and the 1983 General Election', in I. Crewe and M. Harrop (eds), *Political Communications: The General Election Campaign of 1983*, Cambridge: Cambridge University Press, pp. 95–103.

Zhao, B. and G. Murdock (1996) Young Pioneers: Children and the Making of Chinese Communism', *Cultural Studies*, 10(2), pp. 201–17.

Zhao, X. and G. Bleske (1998) 'Horse-Race Polls and Audience Issue Learning', *Harvard International Journal of Press/Politics*, 3(4), 13–34.

Zolo, D. (1992) *Democracy and Complexity*, Cambridge: Polity.

Index